T0258777

DATA GOVERNANCE

Creating Value from
Information Assets

DATA GOVERNANCE

Creating Value from Information Assets

Edited by Neera Bhansali

CRC Press
Taylor & Francis Group
Boca Raton London New York

CRC Press is an imprint of the
Taylor & Francis Group, an **informa** business
AN AUERBACH BOOK

CRC Press
Taylor & Francis Group
6000 Broken Sound Parkway NW, Suite 300
Boca Raton, FL 33487-2742

© 2014 by Taylor & Francis Group, LLC
CRC Press is an imprint of Taylor & Francis Group, an Informa business

---

Library of Congress Cataloging-in-Publication Data

Data governance : creating value from information assets / [edited by] Neera Bhansali.
   pages cm
   Includes bibliographical references and index.
   ISBN 978-1-4398-7913-9
   1. Database management. 2. Management information systems. 3. Information resources management. 4. Information technology--Management. I. Bhansali, Neera.

QA76.9.D3D1559135 2013
005.74--dc23   2013005398

Visit the Taylor & Francis Web site at
http://www.taylorandfrancis.com

and the CRC Press Web site at
http://www.crcpress.com

Contents

Preface

As a rule, he or she who has the most information will have the greatest success in life.

Benjamin Disraeli

In recent years, there has been enormous growth of data in organizations. This data has become the basis of competition, productivity, growth, and innovation. The rise in volume of data through the Internet, social media, and multimedia is adding new challenges and opportunities for harnessing the power of information. There is much discussion today on using organizational data to derive value. As organizations respond to strategic and operational challenges that demand high-quality data, data governance is emerging as an important area in enterprise information management.

As organizations deploy business intelligence and analytic systems to harness information and business value from their data assets, programs for the governance of data are gaining prominence. Data management issues have traditionally been assigned to and addressed by IT departments in organizations. However, organizational issues critical to successful data management require the implementation of enterprise-wide accountabilities and responsibilities. Data governance encompasses both the decision domains and the accountability for decision making. Effective data management requires a data governance structure and framework that emphasizes collaboration between business and IT to support organizational goals. It brings together diverse expectations and expertise from across the enterprise to achieve an agreed upon, consistent, and transparent set of processes that enable data-informed decision making. This book looks at the needs and processes for data governance to manage data effectively. It addresses the complete life cycle of effective data governance from metadata management to privacy and compliance. These also are highlighted through case studies.

The goal of this book is to assist others who are on the journey to derive value from informational assets using data governance. The book is a summation of experiences of experts and addresses an area that is of growing interest to the information systems and management community. Book chapters present how ideas have been adapted as techniques and policies for practice in organizations in their journey to successful data governance. Case studies from healthcare and financial sectors, two industries that have successfully leveraged the potential of data-driven strategies, provide further insights into real-time practice.

> A popular government without popular information or the means of acquiring it is but a Prologue to Farce, or a Tragedy, or perhaps both. Knowledge will forever govern ignorance and a people who mean to be their own Governors, must arm themselves with the power which knowledge gives.
>
> **James Madison**

Acknowledgments

My happiest task is to thank my co-authors who have come together from around the globe to share their experiences and contribute to the book. Thanks Charlyn, Dasaratha, Michael, Christopher, Osamu, Julia, Gladys, and Fernando. Without you this book would not have been possible.

My thanks to Shekhar, Divya, and Shrenik for their unwavering support and patience during the writing of this book.

Contributors

Neera Bhansali
Executive Director, Biomedical
    Informatics
Herbert Wertheim College of
    Medicine
and
Faculty Director, MS HI&MS
Department of Decision Sciences
    and Information Systems
Florida International University
Miami, Florida

Fernando A. Faria
Analyst
Banco Central do Brasil
Brasilia, Brazil

K. Hasida
Social Intelligence Technology
    Research Laboratory
National Institute of Advance
    Industrial Science and
    Technology
Tokyo, Japan

Charlyn A. Hilliman
Chief Technology Officer
The Learningateway
New York, New York

N. Izumi
Social Intelligence Technology
    Research Laboratory
National Institute of Advance
    Industrial Science and
    Technology
Tokyo, Japan

K. Murata
School of Medicine
Kitasato University Hospital
Sagamihara, Japan

Dasaratha Rama
Professor
Department of Decision Sciences
    and Information Systems
Florida International University
Miami, Florida

Michael Schrader
Vice President, Data Architecture
Fidelity Investments
Evergreen, Colorado

Gladys E. Simpson
Visiting Faculty
Department of Decision Sciences
    and Information Systems
Florida International University
Miami, Florida

Christopher B. Sullivan
President and CEO
Image Research LLC
Miami, Florida

Osamu Takaki
School of Knowledge Science
Japan Advanced Institute of
    Science and Technology
Ishikawa, Japan

Julia Zhang
Associate Director, Project
    Management Strategy, Standard
    and Architecture
R&D IS
Sanofi
Cambridge, Massachusetts

The Editor

Neera Bhansali, PhD, has more than 20 years of experience in information technology with an emphasis on strategic data warehousing. She is executive director of Biomedical Informatics at Herbert Wertheim College of Medicine (Florida International University (FIU), Miami). In Dr. Bhansali's previous roles, she was head of informatics at CTNeT, the Statewide Clinical Trials Network of Texas, and held leadership positions, including director of Data Quality and Standards at the H. Lee Moffitt Cancer Center and Research Institute, Tampa, Florida.

Dr. Bhansali is the author of *Strategic Data Warehousing: Alignment to Business* (CRC Press, 2009).

She earned a doctorate in business and a master's in business (information technology), both from the Royal Melbourne Institute of Technology, Melbourne, Australia.

1

The Role of Data Governance in an Organization

Neera Bhansali

CONTENTS

INTRODUCTION

In today's fast-paced global economy, changes in the environment result in new opportunities for wealth creation that decision makers use in strategy formulation and implementation. Organizations have grown global by not only expanding businesses and setting up branches overseas, but they have grown global in a different kind of way—leveraging on knowledge tapped globally rather than merely growing outward from a domestic base. In organizations, information from various departments and functions, as well as formal and informal sources of information, are bought together to detect and interpret problem areas, identify opportunities, and implement strategic objectives. Strategies define the purpose of organizations, the competitive domain of firms, and the resource commitment these organizations make to achieve and sustain competitive advantage. Hence, developing an appropriate data strategy that fits the marketplace is one necessary ingredient for business success. Effective data governance reduces uncertainty and helps improve an organization's performance. An organization's ability to collect pertinent information and act on signals that others miss provides it a strategic advantage.

THE NEED FOR DATA GOVERNANCE

In the twenty-first century, organizational business is supported by data and information in many ways and forms. A large part of data generated today is in the form of electronic or digital data. For example, high-volume transaction processing systems (financial or accounting systems) generate reports, statements, and electronic checks; analytical systems produce documents, spreadsheets, forecasting models, visual images; marketing and planning systems generate emails, Web pages, XML from the Web or corporate intranet, and so forth. Data resides in databases, files, and other media. All this data needs data management to identify, categorize, preserve, and retrieve data when required for business purposes or regulatory needs. A rule of thumb often used is that corporate data volumes double every 18 months. However, mobile and online data are growing at an even faster rate. From cost containment, regulatory compliance, strategic initiatives, and beyond, the need for businesses to manage proliferating data is becoming even more urgent.

Maintaining an ever-increasing volume of data, processing it, and deriving information from it to meet the competitive needs of the market requires not only good data management practices, but a data governance process as well. Effective data governance improves data safety and security, improves data quality, and ensures compliance with data-focused regulations as well as helps an organization manage and use its data effectively. It increases data consistency, increases accountability for the organization's data, and improves decision making. Data governance must be a business-driven program that uses a data-governance maturity model to build a strategic road map.

Organizations in the public and private sectors continue their efforts to manage this enormous data and information inventory, regardless of medium. While there are many challenges associated with this effort, in today's highly complex business environment, one challenge that stands out is retaining and leveraging all knowledge assets. As we emerge slowly from the economic downturn of the past few years, growth continues against a backdrop of cost cutting. Data governance programs can help by delivering a unified view of the world. Organizations realize that to remain competitive, they must take advantage of what they know and what they are learning. A nonproactive approach to managing data leads to many pitfalls. Data governance process supports business strategies of operational excellence, cost reduction, and cost-effective regulatory and legal compliance while meeting the strategic objectives of the organization.

PLACE FOR DATA GOVERNANCE IN ORGANIZATIONAL STRATEGY

According to Porter (1980), successful strategy formulation involves the identification and exploitation of a firm's competitive advantage. There are five forces that affect a firm and its competitors in any given industry: threat of new entrants, threat of substitute products, jockeying for position among competitors, power of buyers, and power of suppliers. In Porter's framework, a firm's performance in the industry is a function of the environment and the firm's positioning in the market based upon the five forces that help establish competitive advantage over its rivals. Distinctive competencies and organizational effectiveness determine how a business performs. In today's data- and information-intensive age, good data governance strategies provide organizations with a distinctive competency in data and information management that enhances the effectiveness of business strategies.

In today's digital world, technology makes it easy to create, transmit, store, access, and use information that is becoming the basis for business operations, customer service, and government relations. However, technology itself is so ubiquitous that by itself it no longer provides a distinguishing competitive advantage in business. It is rather people's creative use of information that counts rather than the technology. A distinguishing feature of sound strategic management is its flexibility, responsiveness to change, and ability to respond to new challenges. Information and data governance supports an organization's strategic approach involving planning, choosing, and sometimes improvising or shifting approaches dynamically based on the competitive environment. Data governance supports the systematic management and use of information to achieve objectives that are clearly aligned with and contribute to the organization's objectives.

To compete in the global arena, organizations adopt two broad strategies types: either Adaptive/Defender or Proactive/Prospector strategies. Organizations pursuing the Defender strategy type respond to competitive forces with better management of costs and reliance on internal strengths for their positioning in the marketplace. Organizations pursuing Prospector strategy type utilize marketing strengths in response to competitive pressures. In both the cases, data and information are utilized to assess, evaluate, and formulate these business strategies. Data and information internal to the organizations are used in Defender strategies to lower operating costs and achieve efficiencies to better position the organization in the competitive marketplace. Similarly, data and information of external environment and marketplace play a strong role in the formulation of proactive strategies. Organizations with Prospector strategy are å and marketing-oriented, focusing on identifying and satisfying the needs of customers with value, quality, and product offerings based upon their knowledge of customer and industry trends. Good data governance policies and procedures are invaluable in the management of data and information in organizations of both types of strategies, and contribute to building distinctive competencies for the organization.

DATA GOVERNANCE ACROSS INTRAFIRM NETWORKS

"Intrafirm networks" are a set of formal and/or informal relationships among business units of the same legal entity (Achrol and Kotler, 1999). Each business unit has a sufficient degree of freedom to make its own resource allocation and data governance decisions while still working in close cooperation with its affiliated business units. Business units obtain and utilize data and information from within their formal boundaries and from other business units. In order to acquire this data, business units within the organization must follow some procedures and policies.

Data governance across the business units in an organization facilitates easy and timely access to each other's data and to data from businesses outside the organization. Data governance also helps the business units to be better prepared for information sharing with the other units within the organization. Data governance structures promote the development of intrafirm networks within the organization in order for data and other resources to be transferred or exchanged and distributed efficiently throughout the organization to gain competitive advantage. Strong intrafirm networks enhance reciprocity, cohesiveness, and connectivity among business units (Rindfleisch and Moorman, 2001).

Globalization of the economy, dealing with trusting business partners at great distances and ensuring that information is properly used and has agreed-upon qualities and limits, emphasizes the need of a data governance structure. These needs are met by data governance policies that oversee the flow of information and design information products to meet new values criteria. Managements have to make data governance decisions as to what information should be shared, what quality controls should be in place to assure others of its validity, who should have access to data and information, in what forms, and at what levels of access,

DATA GOVERNANCE CHARACTERISTICS OF ORGANIZATIONS THROUGH THEIR LIFE CYCLE

Organizations face many challenges in this era of high growth and competition. It encompasses the numerous demands of new product innovation, increasing market shares, and customer satisfaction. To address time and resource constraints, companies formulate and disseminate an elaborate, structured policy of data governance based on the guidelines of accountability, responsibility, internal controls, and audit procedures. A well-developed system of corporate governance, along with data governance, adds to the needed synergy for growth. Data governance encompasses features such as ethics policy, reporting transparency, and corporate citizenship. It is a mechanism to maximize data and information value.

Good governance systems lead to better access to data and information, higher quality data, and reduction of risk due to inaccurate data. However, implementing effective governance systems also comes at a cost. Resource constraints, lack of business understanding of the system, and the cost of implementing and communicating data governance policies throughout the organization are crucial barriers that many organizations face. Once a successful working environment is established, a well-oiled system of data governance will be highly rewarding. However, in the beginning, the tendency of management will be to focus resources on revenue increase and the value chain that links data and customers through the organization.

Organizations move through various stages in their life cycle from start-up phase, growth phase to maturity phase, renewal, and, finally, decline phases. Different stages in an organization's life necessitate different roles for data governance. In the early phases of the life cycle, data governance is a regulatory requirement and not a competitive tool. It consists of policies, control procedures, guidelines, and mechanisms to ensure accountability. A data governance structure specifies the distribution of rights and responsibilities amount different participants in the data governance process. It spells out the rules and procedures for making decisions on data affairs so that the organization's data and information needs and objectives are met.

In the early stages of an organizations growth, the management hierarchy usually remains flat rather than layered. Management executives of such organizations are still trying to find an internal organizational structure that works well and, therefore, will not have the time or the opportunity to set up a well-defined data governance system. An effective system of data governance has many features that involve board structure, planning and monitoring, risk management, audit committees, internal control, ethics, and transparency. An organization in its early stages of growth may not have the resources to develop every facet of an effective data governance policy.

The growth of an organization usually implies constant changes to products, processes, and organizational and managerial practices. This also requires continuous adaptation to the changing business environment, and developing sustainable data governance processes. A structure of rules and regulations to effectively govern data and information is established to encourage the efficient use of resources and to require accountability of those resources.

Mature organizations would not have "flat" management systems, but well-developed hierarchical structures that require a good system of data governance for effectiveness and transparency. In later stages of an organization's life cycle, a good system of data governance enhances returns, provides for better risk management, improves customer satisfaction, and increases the organization's reputation. Costs involved are generally increased managerial and supervisory time.

DATA GOVERNANCE PROGRAM

A data governance program provides an opportunity of taking an enterprise-wide view rather than focusing on a particular department, involving business heads in planning, devising budgets that meet the needs of the enterprise, and being aware of the powerful effect data and information have on organizational competitiveness. Increasing awareness at the executive level of the importance of managing data and information strategically is an integral part of increasing the recognized value of the data governance program.

To begin a successful data governance program in an organization, aligning the program with the business strategy is important. A multi-year-phased data governance program should focus on critical business scenarios rather than invest into the technology fostered by vendors selling compliance wares. From an assessment of the business use cases and scenarios, a business case should be developed that draws a distinction between strategic business and operational needs. The governance plan should present an end-to-end view of both strategic business and operational needs and requirements with established priorities.

A data governance program requires significant investment from the organization in terms of time and resources. However, these costs are offset by the business value it delivers. The data governance solution should be enterprise-wide and the enabling components should fit and function within the strategic direction of the organization. With a defined business case, clearly defined business drivers, and executive sponsorship, an enterprise-wide data governance program can be successfully launched to provide significant returns.

An enterprise data governance program impacts and touches upon the organization, its processes, people, and enabling technologies comprised of hardware and software. An assessment of the business use cases and scenarios presents not only an understanding of the issues, but of the current business context, the processes followed, the technologies employed, and the interactions among people, groups, and departments. It presents an understanding of the organizational practices, challenges and issues, and priorities and opportunities for data governance. Business use cases and scenarios present a description of current processes and practices, help identify improvement opportunities, and help identify the business and technology operation's roles required. It helps define a common vocabulary in managing both structured and unstructured data.

Understanding an organization's current processes and issues is not enough to build an effective data governance program. To gather business, functional, and technical requirements, understanding the future vision of the business or organization is important. This is followed with the development of a visual prototype or logical model, independent of products or technology, to demonstrate the data governance process. This business-driven model results in a definition of enterprise-wide data governance based on key standards and processes. These processes are independent of the applications and of the tools and technologies required to implement them. The business and functional requirements, the discovery of business processes, along with the prototype or model, provide an impetus to address the "hard" issues in the data governance process.

Building an effective enterprise-wide data governance program, aligned with the strategic direction, maintains a business focus rather than a product or technology focus. A business architecture should be developed identifying the domains of data, its owners, users and custodians, and their roles and responsibilities. To establish a common vocabulary, standards should be adopted for naming, metadata, and records management definitions. The data governance process should include structured data and unstructured data, data extraction, data retention, data sharing, legacy data, and data archiving processes.

The need for a comprehensive strategy cannot be underestimated. An organization is constantly undergoing change. Although a data governance program could be on track and progressing, constant justification and rejustification have to be provided to the sponsors of the program. Toward this end, education, meetings, governance functions, and presentations become significant aspects of the program. Establishing a data governance committee early in the process provides the necessary direction and momentum. A diverse set of skills are required to bring data governance into practice, including application developers, subject matter experts, process control leaders, and business users. Data governance committees usually include a broad spectrum of stakeholders: users, sponsors, business department leaders, IT staff, and consultants.

Key to good data governance is co-ordination and communication. Through constant communication, all members and stakeholders are involved in the process and informed of what is being developed and implemented. Through this practice, the contrarians surface early and resistance to change is addressed. Communication also fosters a sense of ownership and contribution. Feedback and an iterative process help manage change and maintain the momentum for an effort that takes time to show tangible results. Recruiting ambassadors throughout the organization at various levels of the organization further strengthens the data governance process.

Actively engaging executive sponsors is vital for a successful governance program. Continuous involvement and contribution of key executive sponsors maintains the focus of the program. Business leader support helps maintain resources needed for the program. Consistency among the leaders involved, a sound business proposition, and a value-focused enterprise approach provides the best strategic direction for data governance programs.

One of the challenges in this information age is the superabundance of information. It overwhelms an organization's ability to sift through, organize, and act on it. Information has varying degrees of timeliness, pertinence, and importance. Governance structures provide opportunities to share or withhold information. Informal or formal meetings where individuals from different departments meet and have the opportunity to informally share information face-to-face is still one of the most effective means of sharing relevant and current information.

Data governance is the systematic management of information to achieve objectives that are clearly aligned with and contribute to the organization's objectives. There is a growing recognition that it is the information rather than the information technology that really counts. An enterprise-wide data governance program should be flexible, responsiveness to change, and have the ability to respond to new challenges. As discussed above, a strategic approach to data governance involves planning, choosing, trading off, improvising, and shifting approaches to meet the changing needs of the organization.

BENEFITS FROM DATA GOVERNANCE

One of the main benefits of data governance is recognizing the value inherent in data and treating data as a valuable and manageable organizational asset. Information governance strategy and process establishes the necessary framework to turn data into business value. An effective data governance framework can help organizations manage data more efficiently. It provides consistent definition, establishes enterprise data management, and measures and tracks the quality of transactional and analytical data used across the organization. It also improves coordination between different functions of business and provides broader insights into data across the products and business units. The data steward groups, part of the data governance framework, help create, implement, and establish measures of the standards across the enterprise.

An effective data governance framework leads to a lowering of information costs. With the reduction of duplicative data stores throughout the organization, iterative data cleansing costs can be reduced via better quality source data. Through the application of standard processes across the business, substantial information cost reduction is achieved as well. It also leads to a higher data quality, greater trust in the data leading to greater insight and better decision making aligned to business goals. With proper data governance over their lifetime, organizations are better equipped to deliver competitive offerings to the market faster and support business goals with less risk.

Effective data governance helps improve compliance and control efforts. Today, organizations are information-aggressive. To conduct business, they routinely collect, analyze, and use information in key areas relating to customers, products, changes in the business environment, and other areas. Unexpected and unintended disclosure of data and information negatively impacts the business and reinforces the need for data governance. Many businesses lose sensitive information because of a lack of proper data governance policies and a lack of understanding and appropriate use of data.

With effective data governance, data standards facilitate high-quality data. Data standards applying uniformly across business functions and lines of business create a uniform transactional and analytical environment for compliance monitoring. Also, with effective data governance, data stewardship is an organization-wide effort, which reduces risk of noncompliance with regulatory and statutory requirements.

DATA QUALITY AND DATA GOVERNANCE PROCESS

Research by Information Difference (Waddington, 2010) suggests that the top six main drivers for implementation of data governance are to support business intelligence and data warehousing initiatives, to support master data management initiatives, to facilitate the migration of legacy data, to meet compliance and legislative requirements, and to improve corporate flexibility and business agility.

Data governance includes establishing who in the organization holds decision rights and is accountable for an organization's decision making about its data assets. Khatri and Brown's (2010) framework for data governance includes five interrelated decision domains: data principles, data quality, metadata, data access, and data life cycle. An organization's data principles set the boundary requirements for the intended uses of data and establishes the extent to which data is an enterprise-wide asset. It specifies appropriate data policies, standards and guidelines, and principles for sharing and reusing data. Data principles also consider the regulatory environment that influences the business uses of data.

Business users play an important role in managing data quality as well as its life cycle, interpretability, and access. As poor data quality can impact an enterprise at both operational and strategic levels, data governance helps set the organization's standards for data quality. The quality of data refers to its ability to satisfy its user requirements. Data quality dimensions, such as accuracy, timeliness, completeness, and trustworthiness, are defined in the context of the end use of data. This, in turn, is the basis of how data is interpreted through metadata and accessed by users. Metadata describes the data and provides a mechanism for a concise and consistent description of the representation of data. The definition of the production, retention, and retirement of data, which constitutes the data life cycle, plays a key role in operationalizing the data principles into IT (information technology) infrastructure.

After enterprise resource planning and data warehousing, the focus of organizations is now toward data governance, especially to aid in improving reporting and business intelligence. There is a growing awareness of the costs of inconsistent, inaccurate, and unreliable data. A growing number of organizations have either already implemented data governance in a limited way or enterprise-wide or are planning to implement it in the coming years. Estimating the cost to the business of poor data is key to building a business case for implementation of data governance and ensuring that the program receives ongoing support and funding.

Data governance is the process of establishing and maintaining common standards between functions/departments within an organization to establish how common business data and metrics are created, defined, propagated, owned, and enforced throughout the organization. Data governance helps to improve and maintain the quality of data in the organization. Data quality is continuously measured and monitored and the results fed back to the data governance process. Effective data governance leads to formal, standardized data quality processes and clearly defined quality metrics in place throughout the organization. These processes govern the performance of daily activities, such as data entry, change management, improvement, and migration activities. Metrics provide quality checks to identify any potential problems before they proliferate through the organization's systems.

Data quality is a prerequisite for master data management (MDM), which is the management of data that is shared between computerized systems. Both MDM and data quality are key components of a data governance initiative. Data governance helps in ensuring the use of timely and reliable information, improving the quality of business decision making, and ensuring the consistent use of information.

Poor data quality results in increased costs due to wasted resources. It is not always easy or tangible to measure the full cost of poor-quality data. It involves resources spent on correcting errors, lost revenue due to customer dissatisfaction, and the costs of poor decision making based on the flawed data. To ensure data quality, data governance processes need to be developed. It ensures that data can be trusted and that there is accountability for any business impact of poor data quality. Data validation and utilizing data standards are some ways to improve data quality. Using data standards can increase process efficiency and effectiveness, saving resources as well as improving compliance. Data validation improves data quality and ensuring that data provided meets all specified requirements. Data validation provides data quality checks based on implemented standards. It helps in correct data collection, transmission, and data derivation processes, and can identify data outliers and data errors. As part of a data governance process, a quality control process for assessing, improving, monitoring, maintaining, and protecting organizational information is required, along with metrics to gauge data quality

It is a commonly known fact that "garbage in" leads to "garbage out" in computerized systems. Sound data collection techniques lay the foundation to data quality efforts. It starts with an inventory of data in existing systems. An inventory of data fields, their data type, and data format ensures that the analyses are based on meaningful data fields. Adopting the practice of naming identical data with identical field names from one analysis to another and naming dissimilar data with different names promotes transparency and consistency in analyses both individually and as a whole. Knowing the audience, context, and purpose of data collection leads to good data stewardship. By implementing standards and data governance processes, organizations are able to reduce potential risk of accepting and analyzing poor quality data, and the costs of rework and duplicate data.

DATA GOVERNANCE AND MASTER DATA MANAGEMENT

Organizations need governance for many reasons. Data governance function permeates major areas of an organization by providing the structure for the creation, deletion, approval, and distribution rights of corporate information. It provides the decision rights to determine the direction of data management efforts, the subject areas, sources of data, targets of data, and business rules involved. It is involved in deciding the accountabilities and responsibilities in the organization for creating, approving, enforcing, and monitoring data. Data governance determines the workflow of data and these are implemented through the master data management workflow by data stewards. Often MDM is the means of effective implementation of data governance in a data warehouse or business intelligence project. Without data governance, MDM is reduced to a data integration project.

MDM is critical to achieving effective information governance. Automating currently existing practices does not result in adequate data governance. Translating poor practices to business rules would not create the real benefits of a data governance program. Executive involvement in analyzing and refining current practices and processes with participation from all stakeholders, both current business users and users from yet to be scoped business areas, would lead to improved processes and MDM workflow.

MANAGING RISK WITH DATA GOVERNANCE

The transformation of data into electronic format, the rising value of data to businesses, and the industry's heightened concern about privacy have created the need for enterprises to develop formal data governance strategies and programs. In the financial sector, compliance, data security, brand and trust protection, and the need for quality data are all elements critically important to the sector. Technological advances have provided wider access to data that has been accompanied by widening data security problems. This dynamic nature of security threats makes a strong corporate data governance program essential. Data governance is an ongoing process of monitoring, evaluating, and assessing data, its users, and database activity to better understand and control data risk; and to ensure that data is being used for the maximum benefit of all stakeholders.

Data governance provides a system of checks and balances. Data governance comprises the people, processes, and technology necessary for an entity to properly use and manage data. It uses technology tools and solutions to protect the integrity and security of the data and monitoring and reporting processes to ensure the data governance policies of the organization are adhered to.

There are major data risk categories across a variety of data sources. Data sources could be Web data, such as email, Internet; mobile data, such as laptops, USB; or core data stored in databases and file servers. Data risks could comprise confidentiality, integrity, and availability risks for data. The data governance program puts into practice risk management across these data sources to meet governance goals at the business level. The data governance program prioritizes risks and data sources and outlines appropriate measures to contain the risks. These measures are based on the sensitivity of the business data (person-identifiable data, such as Social Security numbers, private health information), the security of the stored data (encrypted or unencrypted), the controls around accessing the data (type of users, data flow, application access), and processes toward reduction of risks caused by data access (risk mitigation policies enforced, user access control, firewalls).

INFORMATION GOVERNANCE AND CLOUD COMPUTING

Reduced transaction costs, increased computational power, and new communication technologies are shifting many interactions from the physical realm to the virtual. Cloud computing is a movement that allows organizations to lease shared hardware/software facilities over a network. It allows an organization to reduce costs and changes the way IT resources are used. However, cloud computing also creates new risks and challenges for data governance. Cloud computing can offer software, data storage, or development and hosting of customized applications in the cloud over either a public or private network. However, it is found that cloud architectures often lack formal standards on how data is manipulated in the cloud environment.

Common risks and governance issues associated with cloud computing (Blair, 2010) include :

- Availability of information: This relates to challenges to access the organization's information and an understanding of the disaster recovery plan and resiliency of the provider's infrastructure.
- Electronic-discovery requirements: This relates to how easy it is to search within an individual or multiple cloud computing environment for information. Complex search protocols may create performance issues and increase costs.
- Retention requirements: This relates to how information retention and disposition periods are enforced through either the cloud-based application or data storage.
- Privacy requirements: This relates to how personally identifiable information is secured and protected.
- Portability of information: This relates to the ease with which information can be transferred from one cloud provider to another. Lack of adherence to common standards increases risk here.

These issues can be mitigated to some extent by explicitly addressing them in the contract with the cloud computing vendor.

CONCLUSION

The digital world has led to an exponential growth in both the volume and detail of information that can be captured. The McKinsey Global Institute estimates that data volume is growing 40% per year, and will grow 44-fold between 2009 and 2020. Big data, which is information gleaned from nontraditional sources such as blogs, social media, email, sensors, photographs, and video footage, provides organizations with a multidimensional view and deeper insight into their customers and business. Analyzing large data sets (big data) is now becoming the cornerstone of competition, productivity, and innovation in all industries. Big data is now seen as a transformational opportunity and will become a key basis of competition and growth for organizations capturing value from traditional and real-time information. While numerous advances have been made in mining the data, the success of big data will eventually depend on the quality and integration of data. To capture the full potential of big data, the importance of data governance cannot be emphasized enough.

REFERENCES

Achrol, R., and P. Kotler. 1999. Marketing in the network economy. *Journal of Marketing* 63: 146–163.

Blair, B. T. 2010. Governance for protecting information in the cloud. *Information Management* 44 (5): HT1–HT4

Khatri, V. and C. V. Brown. 2010. Designing data governance. *Communications of the ACM* January 53 (1): 148–152.

Porter, M. E. 1980. *Competitive Strategy: Technique for analyzing industries and competitors.* New York: The Free Press.

Rindfleisch, A., and C. Moorman. 2001. The acquisition and utilization of information in new product alliances: Strength of ties perspective. *Journal of Marketing* 65 (2): 1–18.

Waddington, B. 2010. Data governance, MDM, and data quality. *Information Management* (Sept./Oct.) 10: 14–16.

FURTHER READINGS

Craine, K. 2007. Managing the cycle of change: Resisting change is normal, but it is problematic for organizations looking to make changes or implement new technologies. *Information Management* 41 (5) September-October: 44.

Dearstyne, B. 2004. Strategic information management: Continuing need, continuing opportunities. *Information Management* 38 (2) March-April: 28.

Griffin, J. 2010. Four critical principles of data governance success: Appreciation for the true value of business data is key. *Information Management* 20 (1) Feb 1: 28.

Lam, L. T., and S. Kirby. 2002. Is EQ an advantage? An exploration of the impact of emotional and general intelligence on individual performance. *Journal of Social Psychology* 142: 133–143.

Marvel, M. R., and M. Afzalur Rahim. 2011. The role of emotional intelligence in environmental scanning behavior: A cross-cultural study. *Academy of Strategic Management Journal* 10 (2) July: 83.

Oracle White Paper. 2012. Big data for the enterprise. Available online at: http://www.oracle.com/us/products/database/big-data-for-enterprise-519135.pdf

Salovey, P., and J. D. Mayer. 1990. EQ. *Journal of Imagination, Cognition, and Personality* 9 (3): 85–211.

Sparrow, P. R. 2000. Strategic management in a world turned upside down: The role of cognition, intuition and emotional intelligence. In *Managing strategy implementation*, eds. P. Flood, T. Dromgoole, S. Carroll, and L. Gorman, pp. 15–30. Oxford, U.K.: Blackwell.

Vednere, G. 2010. Harnessing the winds of change. *Information Management* 44 (6) November-December: 28.

2

Navigating the Organization to Ensure Data Governance

Neera Bhansali

CONTENTS

INTRODUCTION

In today's increasingly digital environment, organizations are information-aggressive. They routinely collect, analyze, and use information in key areas relating to customers, products, changes in the business environment, and other areas. Information is recognized and understood to be an important strategic resource and asset in advancing organizational goals. Organizations recognize that for surviving and growing in this highly competitive and digital environment, controlling all aspects of data and information is essential. Organizations are increasingly realizing the inherent value of their data as they exploit the services offered by cloud computing. Data governance facilitates an organization in taking control of its data resources. The need for data governance has risen as the necessity to coordinate, control, and manage all aspects of data in an enterprise has grown. Data governance is a convergence of several areas concerned with data, such as data management, data security, data administration, and data quality.

Data governance initiatives are funded in diverse manners within different organizations, such as out of operational budgets. In some cases, it is a one-off executive decision. Sometimes the costs are buried in different departments within the organization, e.g., information technology (to buy software tools to support data quality), sales, or planning. Data governance is not a one-time project, but an ongoing exercise of continuous improvement and, therefore, requires continued support in the organization.

Understanding the readiness of the organization for data governance is the first step in the implementation of data governance in an organization. Certain parts of the organization are more ready than others. Data governance must be a business-driven program that uses a data governance maturity model to build a strategic road map. Apart from strong executive sponsorship (working across the dimensions of people), process, technology, and information are critical to the success of the data governance program.

DATA GOVERNANCE MATURITY MODELS

Data governance is usually a part of the enterprise-wide governance program. A lack of proper data governance can lead to costs for the organizations. It could result in conflicting data based on redundant sources, which, in turn, could translate into inaccurate information and ineffective decision making. Organizations routinely spend considerable time researching the various sources of data to determine which is the accurate or most appropriate source for information.

Accurate and timely data leads to effective decision making. With good data governance in place, an information system gains credibility with its users based on accurate and consistent data. Effective data governance enhances the quality, availability, and integrity of an organization's data and directly impacts in increasing revenue, lowering costs, reducing risks, and increasing data confidence by fostering cross-organizational collaboration and structured policy making (IBM, 2007). Data governance adds rigor to the process of managing organizational information.

Data governance maturity assessment is undertaken to establish the current state of data management and control. Organizations can be at different levels of maturity of data governance. They may be about to embark on a data governance initiative and is in fact-finding mode, or it may have very limited data governance, usually with no clear responsibility for data ownership. Or there may be awareness of the need for data governance, but not enterprise-wide. In organizations building data warehouses and other data solutions, they may have a data governance program alongside master data management (MDM) and data quality initiatives.

To achieve good data governance, organizations must develop strategies and commit to managing their information and knowledge assets. Governing and effectively managing the information and knowledge assets of an organization take sustained effort and commitment from the organization. Data governance involves defining the custodians of the data assets in an organization and the assigning of responsibilities and accountabilities for making decisions regarding data. Maturity models assist in preparing for this journey and managing the impacts of transformations through change management. It describes the journey from the "as is" state of managing data, information, and knowledge assets to the "should be" state.

Several maturity models for data governance have been proposed (NASCIO, 2009). They include: DataFlux (Cary, NC), EWSolutions (Chicago), Gartner (Stamford, CT), IBM (Armonk, Town of North Castle, NY), MDM Institute (Burlingame, CA), and ARMA International (Overland Park, KS), and are summarized below.

The **DataFlux** data governance maturity model takes an enterprise perspective, which moves through four phases of maturity: undisciplined (think locally, act locally), reactive (think globally, act locally), proactive (think globally, act collectively), and, finally, governed (think globally, act globally). The DataFlux maturity model describes each phase along the dimensions of people, policies, technology, and risk. As the organization moves along the phases of data governance maturity, the value derives from the information and knowledge assets increasing and the risks associated with bad data decreasing.

EWSolutions presents five phases of data governance maturity, progressing from informal processes (reactive), emerging processes (initial approaches to data stewardship and governance), engineered processes (with standard processes), controlled processes (with established measurable process goals) to optimized processes (with qualitative and qualitative understanding used for continuous process improvement).

Gartner's EIM (enterprise information management) maturity model views managing information as a strategic asset. The maturity model moves through five levels and action items are provided for each level of maturity. The levels of maturity include: Unaware (where strategic decisions are made without adequate information), Aware (where there is development in understanding of the value of information), Reactive (where business understands the value of information), Proactive (where information is viewed as necessary for improving performance), Managed (where the enterprise understands information is critical) to, finally, Effective (where information value is harvested throughout the information supply chain). Gartner's EIM discipline has five major goals: (1) data integration across the IT portfolio, (2) unified content, (3) integrated master data domains, (4) seamless information flows, and (5) metadata management and semantic reconciliation.

IBM presents a five-level path in its Data Governance Council's maturity model that offers a steady, measurable progression to the final state of fully mature processes. At maturity level 1 (initial), processes are unpredictable, poorly controlled, and reactive. At maturity level 2 (managed), processes are characterized for projects and are manageable. At maturity level 3 (defined), processes are characterized for the organization and are proactive. At maturity level 4 (quantitatively managed), processes are quantitatively measured and controlled. At maturity level 5 (optimizing), focus is on continuous process improvement. The Data Governance

Council maturity model measures data governance competencies over 11 domains. These include:

1. Organizational structures and awareness
2. Stewardship
3. Policy
4. Value creation
5. Data risk management and compliance
6. Information security and privacy
7. Data architecture
8. Data quality management
9. Classification and metadata
10. Information life cycle management
11. Audit information, logging, and reporting

The maturity model acts as a framework and as a tool to assess an organization's current state of data governance effectiveness and gain insight on how to establish the governance plan.

The **MDM Institute** defines data governance as "the formal orchestration of people, processes, and technology to enable an organization to leverage data as an enterprise asset." The MDM Institute presents a data governance maturity model that consists of four levels of maturity: Basic (anarchy), Foundational (IT monarchy), Advanced (business monarchy), and Distinctive (federalist).

ARMA International's information governance maturity model recognizes that information is one of the most vital, strategic assets organizations possess. Organizations depend on information to develop products and services, make critical strategic decisions, protect property rights, propel marketing, manage projects, process transactions, service customers, and generate revenues. The maturity model is useful to organizational leaders to identify the gaps between the organization's current practices and the desirable level of maturity, assess the risks to the organization, based on the gaps, help in determining whether additional information and analysis is necessary, and help in developing priorities and assigning accountability for further development of the program.

The information governance maturity model is based on the eight GARP® (generally accepted recordkeeping principles): accountability, transparency, integrity, protection, compliance, availability, retention, and disposition. For each of these, the GARP consists of the following five levels:

- Substandard: Where data concerns are addressed in an ad hoc manner.
- In Development: The organization is beginning to recognize the impact of data governance.
- Essential: The organization is addressing the essential or minimum requirements to meet its legal and regulatory requirements.
- Proactive: Information governance considerations are integrated into the organization's business decisions on a routine basis.
- Transformational: Information governance is integrated into the overall corporate infrastructure and business processes to such an extent that compliance with program requirements is routine.

The maturity models above illustrate the complexities of achieving data governance. It takes sustained efforts to move from a reactive state to a predictive state of a data governance. The elements of a data governance program in an organization would depend on where they are on the maturity model, what the enterprise strategic goals are, and how information assets can enable achieving those goals. Regardless of the maturity level within an organization, effective data governance requires commitment at all levels of the organization and must embrace people, processes, software, and executive buy-in and support.

DATA GOVERNANCE STRUCTURE

Data governance involves determining the distribution of decision-making responsibilities and defining the roles that various organizational members and committees have for data. Creating the right structure and securing effective leadership for the data governance organization is an important step. A three-level model is commonly adopted by most organizations, but what is most important is an organizational structure that is appropriate for the particular organization's operations.

At the top of the structure is the data governance council or steering committee (Figure 2.1). It is the decision-making body for data governance. This is a cross-functional, executive-level group that makes policy decisions, including senior representation from all business and technical

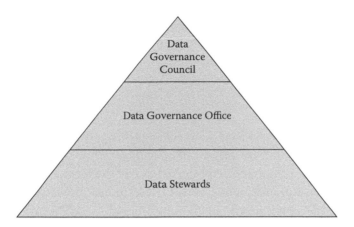

FIGURE 2.1
Data governance structure.

stakeholders. Depending on the size of the organization, multiple governance organizations may roll up in a hierarchical manner. Existing management groups that have tangential function to data governance may need to be included as well as leveraging existing council, committee, or steering groups for data governance.

Business ownership of corporate data encompasses the overarching definition of data governance, the business-driven policymaking, and oversight of corporate information. Data is owned by the business, which circumscribes its definitions, rules, access, and usage policies.

The next level is the data governance office, which coordinates data governance (strategic) and stewardship (tactical) activities. This layer typically manages communications from the steering council to data stakeholders. This is the most critical part of the data governance organization translating the phenomenon of meaningless, unavailable, duplicated, siloed data into an information-cleansing, integration, and deployment strategy that serves the organization. This layer provides oversight, manages risks, and assesses compliance on data assets. It helps in acknowledging the business problem, scoping the project, and leading to definable measures that can prove the value of data governance.

At the lowest level are data stewardship teams in each functional area, which provide guidance to individual data stewards. This is often a federated function, while the two higher levels are usually more centralized. However, there are constant interactions between these three levels of the data governance structure as people at one level represent their team to the next level, as in the case when a data stewardship team escalates issues to the data governance office for resolution. The leader of the data governance program usually displays a strong leadership style and holds delegated authority from the CEO.

Data Stewardship

Data stewards include business stewards (who are responsible for the data) and IT stewards (who are responsible for the technology). Data governance is an organizational discipline, driven by the business, but enabled by IT. The data stewards, along with IT, create new processes that span enterprise-wide applications, to handle anomalies in the master data, to correct error conditions across multiple databases, and to create data governance policies and processes that are enforced automatically. The data governance organization, while being business-driven, utilizes technology to attain its goals. The tactical execution of data governance policies and decisions is through data management. Just as data governance is business-driven, data management is often IT driven. This includes tools for master data management (MDM), data integration, data quality and data profiling, metadata management, business process management, business rules management, data policy management, collaboration tools, and data security management.

Data stewardship is handling data in a responsible, consistent, and trustworthy way. Many data-intensive industries have recognized the need for employees whose role is to monitor and enforce good data practices. The data stewards enable the management of data as an enterprise asset. The data stewards from the business areas are each responsible for a set of data. That responsibility includes providing definitions, establishing quality expectations, and ensuring compliance. It also includes establishing business rules for acquisitions, maintenance, and use of data. A data stewardship program helps perform these business functions in a systematic manner. To effectively perform these roles, the data steward needs to have appropriate technical, interpersonal, and positional skills.

Because data stewards are responsible for making the decisions in their areas, it is essential that they have a solid understanding of the business area they represent, the data used within that area, and the business processes that impact that data and its use. The data stewards have data quality responsibilities as well. It requires their comprehensive understanding of quality improvement concepts, including data profiling, to understand the data's current state and determine data quality issues, root cause analysis to identify the reasons for data quality issues, and continuous quality improvement to identify preventive and corrective actions. Data stewards ensure that the data definitions, data standards, and the associated business rules are defined and documented within their domain for organizational use and that the data is profiled. They also track data deficiencies and help in formalizing and improving data management processes. An overall knowledge of data modeling and database design also is required as they interact with IT to determine the way data is stored and recorded in physical databases. Apart from technical skills, possessing interpersonal skills for a data steward is very important. Excellent people and negotiating skills allow them to be diplomatic, be a team player where necessary, and mandate changes where appropriate.

Organizations have begun to recognize the need to define terminology and business rules around data that is increasingly shared across business processes and organizations. Business leaders are recognizing the costs incurred in the enormous and often-replicated efforts involved in finding, gathering, annotating, consolidating, and deploying data to support growing projects. Clear policies for the definition, access, and use of corporate information raise the probability of data being leveraged to streamline business processes, generate new revenue, and drive innovation.

As data governance involves people and processes in addition to data, business process management or process automation is often the way to effectively solve some governance problem costs. As data governance evolves, it encompasses new roles, new processes, and specialized skills to support it. It cultivates an awareness of specialized skills, processes, and tools needed to define, maintain, and provision data across the enterprise.

ORGANIZATIONAL RESPONSIBILITIES FOR DATA GOVERNANCE

Data governance incorporates five major components:

1. Data governance principles: High-level statements about how data is used
2. Data architecture: Set of data choices to guide the organization
3. Data infrastructure strategies: Technical infrastructure needed to deliver reliable, secure, and efficient data

4. Business applications: Process of identifying needed applications for collecting, maintaining, and distributing data
5. Data prioritization: Mechanism for making decisions about project approvals relating to improving data collection, quality, or security

For successful data governance, the organization bears certain responsibilities as a whole. These include:

- Developing and managing the data governance plan
- Developing data standards
- Defining procedures to assess sourcing options
- Managing the portfolio of applications, infrastructure, and services
- Establishing communication mechanisms
- Maintaining relationships with stakeholders

Though all these responsibilities are important, maintaining excellent stakeholder relationships has shown to be the most relevant in data governance success. It is discussed in more detail in the following section.

Stakeholder Relationships

Stakeholder relationships are important in data governance and data management. The relevance of stakeholder relationships is even greater given governance failures involving data warehouses. This section discusses the importance and determinants of stakeholder relationship and the role it plays in determining whether data governance will be effective. An organization's ability to develop and maintain strong relationships with their salient stakeholder groups improves the chance that data governance will continue.

Superior stakeholder satisfaction is critical for successful data governance in a hypercompetitive environment. The success or failure of data governance is dependent on both the characteristics of the organization as well as the specific stakeholder groups and the nature of the interaction between them. Porter (1980) recognized the importance of the stakeholder groups when he formulated his "Five Forces" model of competition, which includes the bargaining power of customers and the bargaining power of suppliers. The nature of stakeholder relationships can be very dynamic. Data managers should promote stakeholder relationship strategies as effective managerial tools for their organizations. Stakeholders are those without whose continuing participation, the data governance cannot survive as an ongoing goal. Data managers' relationships with stakeholders are one of mutual interdependence. The stakeholders are comprised of the producers of data, the custodians of data, and the users of data. The "web of life" view of data and information is a complex set of relationships between and among these groups with different needs, goals, rights, accountabilities, expectations, and responsibilities. By entering into good relationships, organizations gain stakeholder satisfaction and loyalty while stakeholders look for quality. Participation-based governance infrastructures help adapt to the scale of problems and reduce artificial conflict.

Stakeholder relationships in a data warehouse environment can be complex. Some stakeholders in data governance may forego better exchange of data and information because of their commitment and loyalty to a particular department in the organization. They may not be willing to share metadata or data, because it may be perceived as giving up the benefits associated with the ownership of the data, even though it would lead to better governance. Also, if one of the stakeholders represents a major portion of the other's business, there may be a risk of overdependence and there would be reluctance to data sharing. Since relationships between the IT department and key stakeholder groups evolve over time, it is important to understand the development of these relationships. One way to ensure strong stakeholder relationship is to determine what is important in the relationship from the stakeholder's perspective, explore issues that are important to the stakeholder, understand how the processes in the stakeholder's department works, and to ensure that all relevant issues are addressed.

Stakeholder needs will undergo variability depending upon different situations. The quality of the data and services offered is essential for stakeholders to continue their involvement in data governance decision making. Trust between the IT department and stakeholder groups is important for these types of decisions to be made jointly. The IT management groups should endeavor to establish long-term relationships with stakeholder groups to minimize the amount of time they spend on negotiating. Complacency on the part of IT management puts at risk such long-term relationships with data governance stakeholders. Providing good services should increase the likelihood that a relationship will continue in the future. If IT department data managers can develop trust and keep their stakeholders satisfied, they will be less likely to search for other alternatives for their data needs.

Data governance is not a single event, but a continuous process. Data governance systems take time and effort to devise and implement. Business and IT management need to be fully informed on existing and changing customer and stakeholder expectations and determine the implications for organizational and data strategy. IT management needs to assess the resources and expertise the organization has to implement changes and determine whether it is necessary to outsource to external professionals. The data governance committee and stakeholders need to create or amend existing data policies to create a framework that meets the organization's specific needs. All the changes enacted need to be communicated to the stakeholders involved. Data governance is a cyclical process that needs continuous management involvement for a company to fully realize the advantages of a corporate data governance framework.

Excellent data liaising contributes significantly to building excellent stakeholders relationships. Data liaison responsibilities include:

- Developing working relationships with user, business, and stakeholder leadership
- Communicating the data issues and needs of stakeholders and users
- Working with stakeholders and user leadership to ensure appropriate data representation on task forces and committees
- Communicating data plans and policies with stakeholder and user leadership

SENIOR MANAGEMENT RESPONSIBILITIES

For the success of a data governance program and to provide for strategic deployment of resources, it is essential for the organization's leadership to be inspired, committed, and visionary. Data governance requires excellent leadership and management skills. Senior managers should understand that implementation of data governance policy is one of their major responsibilities and is part of their work plans. The responsibilities of the CIOs (chief information officers) are broadened well beyond management of information technology resources. CIOs have become strategic managers and their roles are likely to continue changing.

Senior management has several responsibilities in the data governance process, including:

- Ensuring that the organization has a data governance strategy
- Balancing the perspectives of stakeholders, users, and IT

- Establishing processes for budgeting, acquiring, and implementing applications and infrastructure
- Developing and modifying the responsibilities of IT and users
- Ensuring that IT applications and activities conform to relevant policies, procedures, regulations, and internal controls

Though, during normal operations, an organization follows regular processes and normal policies and procedures, the risk of data breaches and nonconformance of data policies rises during disaster recovery scenarios. A brief discussion of data governance during disaster recovery is below.

Disaster Recovery

Data governance also extends to the disaster recovery plans for an organization. IT systems are gaining ever greater prominence in the overall structure of many corporations. An organization's success depends on its ability to provide data and information to its customers and employees in a reliable manner. Establishing reliable disaster recovery capabilities is critical to ensuring that an organization will be able to survive significant events, such as computer outage due to natural calamities or power outage. A disaster could mean an outage of the entire IT infrastructure or some components for several hours to several days or months. Examples of such events are the earthquake and tsunamis in Japan, 2011, and Hurricane Katrina in New Orleans in 2005. Due to the ever-increasing complexity in today's computer networks, disaster recovery plans have to be well laid out so that an organization can reinstate its IT systems and services after a significant large-scale interruption. A disaster recovery plan describes the IT mechanisms for the purpose of bringing a functioning system back online (Robb, 2005). This applies to data loss and information components of the information systems (ISs), too. Creation of a remote disaster recovery center is often the first step in developing a well-organized plan. Other times multiple backup sites are established for business critical applications and resources are dedicated to data communication channels and external data storage. An appropriate plan depending on the organization should be created and the contents of the plan should be documented, tested, and updated. Effective documentation and procedures are extremely important in a disaster recovery plan for continuity of operations after the disaster.

USER RESPONSIBILITIES

Data governance is not just the responsibility of the senior leadership and management. The responsibility of successful data governance lies with the users as well. User responsibilities include:

- Understanding the data activities that support their function
- Ensuring that the goals of data initiatives reflect the function's needs
- Developing specifications for data-related governance and IT projects
- Providing feedback to data stewards on implementation issues, application enhancements, and data needs
- Ensuring that data-related applications function properly
- Participating in developing the data governance agenda and priorities

EMOTIONAL INTELLIGENCE AFFECTING DATA GOVERNANCE

For effective data governance, the level of emotional intelligence of its participants plays an important role. Emotional intelligence is one's ability to be aware of one's own feelings, be aware of others' feelings, to differentiate among them, and to use the information to guide one's thinking and behavior (Salovey and Mayer, 1990). A person's ability to exercise emotional intelligence (EQ) influences his/her ability to work across departments or functions. EQ has been linked to work outcomes and improved task performance (Lam and Kirby, 2002). Organizations around the world seek and analyze information to compete effectively. Managers use their skill sets and competencies to understand their organizational world and translate information into actionable strategies (Sparrow, 2000). Often managerial executives have unequal abilities to bring about or transfer new data or information. Unequal competencies exist in collecting or socializing information. These differences affect the performance of good data governance. They hinder the transfer of key information between the source of data or information and its recipient.

National and organizational culture has been found to affect managerial styles and behaviors (Marvel and Rahim, 2011). Managerial attitudes and beliefs reflect the views, norms, and assumptions embedded in organizational and national culture. In today's increasingly global economy, dimensions of empathy and social skills influence management's ability to successfully govern data and information across cross-cultural differences in national or organizational cultures. Emotional intelligence provides one with abilities to induce desirable responses in others and deal with problems without allowing one's own or others' negative feelings to inhibit collaboration. It allows one to negotiate and manage affective conflict with tack and diplomacy to achieve the desired goals. These skills become imperative when implementing data governance processes across multiple layers of an organization and across organizations.

CHANGE MANAGEMENT IN DATA GOVERNANCE

Data governance process develops and enforces policies for data ownership, control, and stewardship. With clear policies, it is easy to identify who or what business unit owns and has stewardship responsibility for key data entities throughout the enterprise. Formal corporate-wide data oversight processes and clearly defined data standards further augment ownership and stewardship policies. As a result, critical data is easily available in a timely fashion when it's needed.

To stay competitive in today's fast-paced environment, organizations are subject to reorganization, new business processes, technological advancements, and varying regulation and policy changes. These changes affect the information processes and assets within the organization. Business processes and procedures are updated and modified to meet the changing needs of the business. Organizational restructuring results in changes in the roles and responsibilities of its personnel. All of these result in changes in the informational needs of the organization.

Managing data and information in such a changing environment presents its own challenges. As business processes change, modifications to business applications cause different types of records and data to be generated. Data is transformed in different ways to meet the information needs of an evolving organization. Existing databases may be modified, data formats may be transformed, and other metadata changes may occur. Data retention requirements may change as well. A growth in the organization may result in a growth in the information domains of the organization. New data sources, systems, processes, and ways of delivering information imply changes in the underlying governance process. All the above reasons cause a change in the data governance policies and procedures of the organization.

For effective data governance, these changes have to be managed both proactively and reactively. Change control data policies and procedures have to developed and implemented. Along with change comes resistance to new policies and procedures. Resistance to change is a phenomenon widely seen in organizations today. People cling to the status quo, and to overcome resistance, data governance initiative leaders need to address change management early on. Rapid innovation in technology is forcing people to face change at an ever-quickening pace. Change affects people's ability to feel comfortable, capable, and confident because it means that they must learn new systems, work in new ways, and accept new responsibilities. It may result in reassignment, retraining, and reengineering. Clear communication and sharing of information can reduce the levels of anxiety and uncertainty. Successful change management processes involve key players and stakeholders and use a structured approach to implement and minimize resistance to change. Providing information about the purpose of the change, providing a vision of the expected outcomes and the future, and providing clear and specific expectations are some ways to overcome the resistance. With any change management process, the primary concern is to understand the change, assess the impact on existing processes, and develop ways to either minimize the impact or update existing processes to absorb that change (Vednere, 2010).

Data governance policies and procedures are subject to change and need to be reevaluated periodically. Organizational changes, transformations in business processes, audits, regulatory changes, or other circumstances leading to a change in data management can lead to a revision and updating of the current data governance policies and procedures. These updates to data governance policies should be made after proper assessment, evaluation, and understanding of the impact of the changes taking place. Data governance committees evaluate and approve all modifications. These modifications must be reflected in all documentation, procedure manuals, and training materials. This should be followed by training and communication of the policy changes or procedure changes to all stakeholders in the data governance process. If the change in the data governance policy is substantial, a slow and structured approach to implement the changes should be adopted. Rolling out all the changes at once may not be the optimal approach. Development of appropriate training and documentation emphasizing the reasons and benefits of the changes to the data governance policies and procedures ensures an effective and smooth transition.

Data is regarded as an important asset in organizations. It is an asset that is constantly undergoing change unlike a static asset. Data governance should consist of data management processes with appropriate checks and controls built in. Maintaining change control logs of data, the requesting and authorizing body of changes, and maintaining version history of the policies is helpful when dealing with data governance in diversified organizations. It also is useful during audit, enabling organizations to explain why, how, and when data was shared, transferred, deleted, or replaced. Change management also should address record retention policies and any changes to them. A change in the retention requirements due to change in a regulatory requirement or amendment of laws may not only result in a change in the duration of time data is retained, it may result as well in a change in how the data itself is fundamentally managed. It may affect the way data is retained electronically, its offsite storage, or data disposition requirements.

Organizations undergo reorganizations to avail of opportunities, expand their operations, or in the case of mergers and acquisitions. The impact of the reorganization should be evaluated carefully and appropriate changes in data governance plans must be incorporated. The data governance process should be tied into the organizational change management process. In case of business process changes that affect data and information processes, the data governance committee should try to secure a seat on the change management committee and provide the necessary expertise and guidance when discussion of and decisions about various business process changes occur. Many times changes in technology or in systems can affect the data governance process. When there is a change in one business system or application, it can have a rippling effect on other business applications or systems that lie downstream from it or feed into it. Having a plan to manage these changes and involving and keeping the application owners and stakeholders updated and informed contribute toward a good data governance process.

Changes in personnel also affect the data governance process in many ways. People leaving or changing roles could result in changes in the data custodianship, data ownership, data management, and points of contacts. During the period of change, identifying appropriate backup and contingency personnel, training the new personnel, and maintaining an appropriate level of communication and documentation leads to an easier transition and good data governance practices. A proactive change management plan, e.g., cross-training personnel, minimizes the risks associated with change. Being prepared for the unexpected ensures a successful data governance process.

ORGANIZATIONAL CULTURE AND ITS IMPACT ON DATA GOVERNANCE

Data governance is a dynamic, adaptive, and complex system that should be viewed as an organic whole, which includes people, technologies, rules, and relationships to support the information needs in the organization.

Organizational culture plays a large part in the success of a data governance plan. Organizations with a culture of openness, sharing, and exchanging information within and beyond the organization (as appropriate) understand the importance of data and information and are supportive of data governance policies. It is regarded as the norm and is supported and rewarded.

Commitment by all stakeholders of the data governance program and their continuing involvement is essential for a data governance program to succeed. Organizations that empower their employees, valuing initiative, encouraging employees to take responsibility for advancing organizational objectives, and providing people with the information resources to act, contribute to effective data governance.

The culture of the organization should be considered when setting expectations and plotting the course of progress for data governance. With data governance, a measure of structure is added where needed. In highly collaborative environments where decision making is drawn out, a level of rigor is added by introducing decision-making protocol in the organization.

Culture of Accountability

Data governance changes how an organization views its data. It involves a cultural shift away from thinking about data as a commodity toward thinking of data as one of the organization's most valuable assets, and creating an organizational mindset of accountability.

For data governance to be implemented successfully, the entire enterprise must be willing to be accountable for data governance success.

They must buy into the importance of data governance and acceptance of responsibility according to the role played by individuals for the continued success of the data governance effort. A culture of accountability would be required for continued success.

Accountability pertains to willingness to be answerable for something. Accountability is the acknowledgment and assumption of responsibility for actions, decisions, and policies for data governance and its implementation within the scope of the role of the individual, and encompasses the obligation to be answerable for resulting consequences.

A culture of accountability rests on awareness, buy-in, responsibility, and communication. Awareness involves educating employees of the data governance program. It creates a deeper level of understanding of the usage of data, the underlying processes that use data, and how that data impacts other processes downstream. It results in the realization of how data governance benefits the individual's job and how a lack of data governance impacts the individual's performance and the performance of others in the organization.

For example, if clinical data managers enter data into a clinical database and that data is later used by physicians to make decisions on the treatment of the patients, it is essential for the clinical data managers to understand how the quality of data they entered affects patient care. Educating them on the benefits of having data governance policies and procedures helps enforce data standardization and consistency. Once the benefits of the data governance program are clear, it leads to accountability and buy-in to the data governance program.

To instill an ethos of responsibility, it is necessary to incentivize people. A formal delineation of roles and tasks, tied to compensation along with data ownership, stewardship, and policies and procedures, should be established throughout the organization. Realistic metrics to measure the effectiveness of the data governance program should be developed and an incentive mechanism to reward those who meet or exceed their performance targets should be installed.

Communication is vital to getting buy-in from the organization as a whole. Communication from the executive sponsors is key to gathering buy-in from knowledge workers in the lines of business. It is not easy to build a culture of responsibility. Everyone in the organization from top to bottom must buy into the importance of data governance and they must accept responsibility according to the role they play for the continued success of the data governance effort.

WHAT MAKES DATA GOVERNANCE A SUCCESSFUL PROGRAM?

Organizations are constantly juggling with competing priorities and data governance is usually one of the initiatives underway, but not always the project in the forefront. Though data governance should form the foundation of the information management strategy, in many organizations, the value of data governance is recognized only when a serious problem involving data quality arises or when a breach in data governance affects the financial bottom line. Effectively managing the quality, consistency, usability, security, and availability of the organization's data plays a large part in the organization's information management. Successful data governance requires many pillars: clear ownership, value recognition, data policies and procedures, and data quality. These are discussed below.

Clear Ownership

A data governance program should be enterprise-wide and have clear ownership. If there is no ownership for the data governance effort, it will flounder for a lack of clear purpose and direction. Data governance is not an IT project. Its success lies in the joint ownership between business and IT. If IT alone owns the effort, the business may not feel that the data governance initiative meets its needs or requires its input. Establishing a data governance committee or council resolves this problem. The governance committee or council should be composed of representatives from all business units. The data governance council sets the data policies, procedures, and standards for the organization. These should be implemented throughout the organization and updated with council consensus when appropriate.

At the outset of the program, the data governance council should formally define and assign data governance roles and responsibilities. Data ownership, stewardship, and policies and procedures should be established throughout the enterprise. This is often achieved by implementing a RACI (responsible, accountable, consulted, and informed) chart of decision rights for a data governance program. It is necessary to incentivize people, along with a formal delineation of roles and tasks, with rewards tied to compensation. There must be empowerment of data stewards that includes valuing initiative, encouraging people to take responsibility for advancing organizational objectives, and providing people with the resources they need to act. Realistic metrics to measure the effectiveness of the data governance program should be developed and an incentive mechanism installed to reward those who meet or exceed their performance targets.

Value Recognition

For successful data governance, its value must be recognized. It is difficult to quantify the value of data in dollar terms, but data is one of the most important assets of any organization today and it has many intangible benefits. The organization cannot function effectively without data standards and quality. Poor-quality data leads to compromised information internally and dissatisfied customers externally. Therefore, in any data governance effort, appreciation for the true value of business data is critical, along with upper management's financial support for the time, effort, and expense to effectively manage that data.

Communication, especially from the upper management, including the CEO, COO, CIO, and CFO, is crucial to building awareness of the importance of a data governance program. It leads to a cultural shift in thinking about data as not just a commodity, but one of the organization's most valuable assets. It leads to the creation of an organizational mindset of accountability. Communication is vital to getting buy-in from the organization as a whole. The internalization of the value of data governance is reflected in the formal communication by the sponsors of the data governance program who are valued by the organization. Communication from the executive sponsors and the chief data officer is key to getting buy-in from the different quarters of the organization. The organization culture should be one that supports and rewards openness, sharing, and exchanging information within the organization.

Data Policies and Procedures

Effective data governance requires effective data policies and procedures. To be effective, the data policies and procedures must be cross-functional and not be dictated by the requirements of individual business units. The data policies should be enterprise-wide and apply to the business as a whole. If there is a lack of an enterprise-wide data governance model and vision, data chaos will likely follow, leading to immense data quality problems. A clear data governance strategy and consensus on what makes data governance successful should exist. This vision should be shared and be understood by all.

Data Quality

The final principle of successful data governance is data quality. It is critical for an organization's knowledge workers and management to be able to trust the data source. IT needs to know all sources of data, its completeness, quality, and lineage for both operational and regulatory purposes. However, in reality, it is a difficult task to accomplish. Few companies can absolutely trust their data. Organizations deal with it by implementing human middleware to fix and control data quality. Currently, the market offers a plethora of data quality tools and methodologies to address poor-quality data.

CHALLENGES OF DATA GOVERNANCE

The effort required to achieve data governance often seems far higher than the perceived benefits. This is because organizations may be more focused on the direct costs of data management in running their businesses and have overlooked the downstream impact of poor-quality information and missed opportunities. They may have data management initiatives in place, but not data governance strategies. Again, organizations may have a data governance policy and structure, but may not focus on the execution of these data policies. These could be some of the reasons they may not be seeing the return on their efforts in data governance.

Despite data policies and procedures in organizations, they are often unable to readily account for the various systems linkages and data-sharing arrangements, or provide an accurate inventory of the data assets, data exchanged, where data is hosted, or the sensitivity levels of the data. Data governance helps organizations effectively audit and manage data access control, identify and classify data owners, and oversee entitlement and authorization processes for their sensitive data. An effective data governance approach is often the solution to these problems.

With the explosion of mobile technology, records are now stored across platforms, including the cloud. This makes data security, safeguarding proprietary information, and keeping the integrity of information intact one of the main challenges. Aligning security with the business and taking a risk-based approach manages these threats through data governance. For example, one could implement data categorization and tagging rules using industry-specific best practices to support internal policies and external regulations, or implement risk-based enforcement, incorporating prompts, justifications, and blocks that support policy awareness and risk deterrence. Implementing a scalable taxonomy where document characteristics, including metadata, security, and retention requirements, are inherited in a content taxonomy also helps mitigate this threat by making it easier to identify where documents belong.

With the latest trends of "big data" and the innovative ways in which organizations are leveraging value from their data and information assets, data governance and data management are important in providing a competitive advantage to organizations. Without a data governance framework, organizations will be unable to effectively manage their valuable data assets and meet the increased demands for data to support management information systems and business decision making.

LESSONS LEARNED

Some of the lessons learned from organizations that have succeeded in sustained data governance are discussed above. For effective data governance, individuals and leadership skills matter. Skilled and experienced leaders must be the champions of data governance in an organization to ensure its success. These leaders must not only understand the vision but be able to communicate the vision throughout the organization and motivate the stakeholders and data stewards for effective data governance. Achieving and sustaining excellent working relationships between the various stakeholders, data custodians, and IT is critical. An open and transparent relationship contributes to the success of the data governance program. Building these relationships and a good data governance program takes time. The organization needs time to move through the different stages of maturity to achieve a sustained data governance program. The evaluation of data opportunities during the data governance processes must be thoughtful and aligned to the strategic goals of the organization. A mature and strong alignment between the data governance strategy and the organizational strategy leads to an effective and sustained data governance program in an organization.

REFERENCES

ARMA. 2010. *International's Information Governance Maturity Model*. Available online at: http://www.arma.org/garp/Garp%20maturity%20Model.pdf

IBM. 2007. *Data Governance Council Maturity Model: Building a road map for effective data governance*, October. Available online at: http://www-935.ibm.com/services/us/cio/pdf/leverage_wp_data_gov_council_maturity_model.pdf

Lam, L. T., and S. Kirby. 2002. Is EQ an advantage? An exploration of the impact of emotional and general intelligence on individual performance. *Journal of Social Psychology* 142: 133–143.

Marvel, M. R., and M. A. Rahim. 2011 The role of emotional intelligence in environmental scanning behavior: A cross-cultural study. *Academy of Strategic Management Journal* 10 (2) July: 83.

NASCIO. 2009. *Data Governance Part II: Maturity models—A path to progress*. March. Available online at: www.nascio.org/publications

Robb, D. 2005. Affording Disaster Recovery from the World Wide Web. www.cioupate.com

Salovey, P., and J. D. Mayer. 1990. EQ. *Journal of Imagination, Cognition, and Personality* 9 (3): 85–211.

Sparrow, P. R. 2000. Strategic management in a world turned upside down: The role of cognition, intuition and emotional intelligence. In *Managing strategy implementation*, eds. P. Flood, T. Dromgoole, S. Carroll, and L. Gorman, pp. 15–30. Oxford, U.K.: Blackwell.

Vednere, G. 2010. Harnessing the winds of change. *Information Management* 44 (6) November-December: 28.

FURTHER READINGS

Achrol, R., and P. Kotler. 1999. Marketing in the network economy. *Journal of Marketing* 63: 146–163.

Begg, C., and Caira, T. 2012. Exploring the SME quandary: Data governance in practice in the small to medium-sized enterprise sector. *The Electronic Journal Information Systems Evaluation* 15 (1): 1–12.

Blair, B. T. 2010. Governance for protecting information in the cloud. *Information Management* 44 (5): HT1–HT4.

Craine, K. 2007. Managing the cycle of change. *Information Management* 41 (5) September-October: 44.

Dearstyne, B. 2004. Strategic information management: Continuing need, continuing opportunities. *Information Management* 38 (2) March-April: 28.

Griffin, J. 2010. Four critical principles of data governance success. *Information Management* 20 (1) Feb 1: 28.

Khatri, V. and Brown C. V. 2010. Designing data governance. *Communications of the ACM* January 53 (1): 148–152.

Rindfleisch, A., and C. Moorman. 2001. The acquisition and utilization of information in new product alliances: Strength of ties perspective. *Journal of Marketing* 65 (2): 1z–18.

Waddington, B. 2010. Data governance, MDM and data quality. *Information Management* Sept/Oct. 10: 14–16.

3

Metadata Management and Data Governance

Michael Schrader

CONTENTS

WHAT IS GOVERNANCE?

Data governance is the process of creating and enforcing standards and policies concerning data. Data governance standards and policies are created and enforced by a single authoritative organization called the Governance Board.

The governance process isn't a transient, short-term project. The governance process is a continuing enterprise-focused program.

Governance provides standards and policies around the following in relation to processes and data:

- Software products
- Infrastructure
- Quality
- Security
- Dispute resolution
- Life cycle
- Best practices
- Architecture and future road maps
- Project prioritization
- Asset management
- Version control
- Evangelizing and communication
- Vendor relationship management
- Legal and corporate compliance

WHY GOVERNANCE?

A strong governance program is vital to the success of any enterprise architecture. It provides:

- Compliance: Governance programs allow for the compliance to regulatory requirements. We have all heard "I am too pretty to go to jail." Well, without governance, it's true; there exists no formalized process for proving for regulatory compliance with HIPAA (Health Insurance Portability and Accountability Act, 1996) and privacy laws. Data governance initiatives may be aimed at achieving a number of objectives including offering better visibility to internal and external customers and compliance with regulatory laws.

- Harmonizing: Governance provides for standard definitions. This allows developers, database administrations, end users, and data stewards to be working on the same page.
- Consistent Analysis: This allows the business to roll up (consolidated) values with consistent values comparing apples to apples.
- Faster Development: By providing standard definitions and models, we provide the infrastructure for extreme development. The most difficult part of the development of a BI (business intelligence) project is getting the data. If we do not need to add data elements, we can develop applications in days or hours.
- Confliction Resolution: Many organizations have evolved into isolated fathoms. We need an authority to resolve disputes across each of the fiefdoms.
- Asset Management: This is the harvesting and management of assets to maximum business returns. Asset management ensures prioritization with an enterprise view and allows reduction in costs through elimination of duplicate efforts.
- Security: Operational metadata. Who accesses what and when and how? This will not only allow for regulatory compliance, but for better data warehouse design. We can map the usage of each data mart. If one data mart is not being utilized, we can redesign or start an educational program on how to better utilize it.
- Better Data and Process Quality: By having clearly defined enterprise business rules all users will be able to understand. We can further empower end users through exposing them to the business rules. This allows for completing jobs at the speed of business.

FIT FOR PURPOSE VERSUS SINGLE VERSION OF THE TRUTH

In a Single Version of the Truth architecture, the Governance Boards agree upon one true definition of each attribute. Without a governance

Encounter ID	Source	Discharge Date	Enterprise Value
101	Clinical	12/1/2011	FFP
101	Billing	12/2/2011	SVOT

FIGURE 3.1
Fit for Purpose model.

process, the realization of a Single Version of the Truth architecture is nearly impossible. Even with a good governance process, the realization of this architecture is very difficult. With this realization, an alternative architecture called *Fit for Purpose* has emerged. In a Fit for Purpose architecture, we can have different definitions of some of the attributes. In reality, that means storing both an enterprise attribute as well as additional values for the same attribute. The appropriate value would be populated to the correct data mart for presentation.

For example, we may not be able to agree to a single definition for *discharge date*. We have a clinic discharge date and a billing discharge date.

Thus, in Figure 3.1, we would store both a Fit for Purpose value, which would be our Billing value. The Clinical value was chosen as the Single Version of the Truth value. The Clinical value would be utilized as the enterprise value; however, the billing discharge date would be transferred to the financial data mart for presentation.

In addition, we can support a Fit for Purpose architecture with peer tables or flexible columns added to tables. Peer tables (Figure 3.2) are tables that shadow the main tables. For example, the Clinical value would be stored in the main tables as the enterprise or Single Version of the Truth. The Billing or any other alternative Fit for Purpose value would be stored in the peer table.

Main Table

Encounter ID	Source	Discharge Date
101	Clinical	12/1/2011

Peer Table

Encounter ID	Source	Discharge Date
101	Billing	12/2/2012

FIGURE 3.2
Peer table.

Encounter ID	Clinical Discharge Date	Billing Discharge Date
101	12/1/2011	12/2/2011

FIGURE 3.3
Additional columns for Fit for Purpose model.

In addition, we can add additional columns to the main table to support a Fit for Purpose model (Figure 3.3).

GOVERNANCE BOARD

The Governance Board should be a group of key BI senior sponsors, project sponsors, and IT (information technology) personnel from each of the business units. IT should serve the Governance Board as trusted advisors, not the primary drivers of the board. The leadership of the board should come from the business side. The board is not expected to be involved in day-to-day management of the governance program, but is there to set policies and standards.

The Governance Board should meet regularly, e.g., every month or quarterly depending upon number of issues. When the governance program is first initiated, more frequent meeting will be required.

PROGRAM VERSUS PROJECT GOVERNANCE

The governance program should be program-managed as opposed to project-managed. A program-managed governance program forces the governance program to be enterprise-based. Figure 3.4 points out the differences between the two approaches.

METADATA FRAMEWORK DEFINED

Metadata provides context for data by describing data about data. It answers "who, what, when, where, how, and why" about every facet of

Program Governance	Project Governance
• Long-term focus	• Short-term focus
• Enterprise focus	• Specific project focus
• Requires architecture with the benefits of standards and reuse	• Does not require architecture with the benefits of standards and reuse

FIGURE 3.4
Program versus project governance.

the data. It is used to facilitate understanding, usage, and management of data. For example, in the past when we went to find a book at the library, we could search in the card catalog using metadata, i.e., by title, author, or subject. These attributes are metadata. Now, if you want to find a book on bicycling, you merely type in *bicycling* at a bookstore Web site and a list of books on bicycling would appear. This is an example of utilizing metadata.

A metadata framework describes how the metadata is stored and utilized. A strong metadata framework is critical for the successful implementation of a data governance program. If you do not have a strong metadata framework, you do not have the systems setup to query or otherwise utilize the metadata.

METADATA TYPES

Metadata can be classified into four types:

1. Business metadata
2. Technical metadata
3. Process metadata
4. Operational metadata

Business Metadata

Business metadata describes the business meaning of data. It includes business definitions of the objects and metrics, hierarchies, and business rules. An object is a data storage structure, such as the patient table. A metric is a measure of something such as age. A hierarchy organizes the relationships of the data, such as a geographical hierarchy making up different geographical regions of the United States (for example, the western region is made up of California, Oregon, and Washington). A business rule is a procedure or process that must be followed. For example, a business rule might say that there will be no patients that are over 200 years old in the database; anyone over 200 years old would be an error. Another example of a business rule would be that any order over $100,000 in value must have a vice president's approval. Business metadata provides the semantic definition of the business data element. Business data is an element that represents business values, such as patient demographics or encounters. Patient demographics may have attributes such as race, age, or address. Business metadata would provide the definition of race, age, or address. For example, age could be defined as the current date and time minus the birth date.

Business metadata should be:

- Searchable
- Easy to access and integrated
- Exposed

Searchable

Business metadata must be searchable to determine how many occurrences of the term exist. This search ability component is important to support Fit for Purpose architecture versus a Single Version of the Truth. Many corporations attempt to implement a Single Version of the Truth data warehouse. Thus, for example, we would have one definition of patient stay. However, the reality is that many healthcare environments cannot support just one version of a term, such as *patient stay*. Therefore, they implement a Fit for Purpose architecture where they have an enterprise definition of a term, such as *patient stay*. However, they also can keep additional definitions of a term, such as *patient stay*. For example, a patient checks into a hospital and registers; however, his treatment does not begin until later. A billing person might define *patient stay* as the difference in time between the start of the treatment and the end of the treatment. A clinical view might define *patient stay* as the difference in time between when the patient registered and when the patient checked out of the hospital. It is critical for the data Governance Board to know how many different versions of patient stay there are.

Easy to Access and Integrated

Business metadata must be integrated in the application so that it is easily accessible by the end user. For example, an end user must be able hover his cursor on top of a field on his computer screen for a help screen to appear. This help screen should describe the business data of the element that the end user has selected. The Business metadata should appear to give a clear definition of the data element as well as an example.

Exposed

Business metadata represented by business rules ideally needs to be held in a business repository and exposed to the business. The business users would be able to change the business rules without the need of an ETL (extract, transfer, and load) or IT programmer. This allows for speed of business processing.

Many tools provide for a data dictionary that supports Business metadata including metadata columns in the data model or a separate data dictionary. A data dictionary is a repository of definitions of the Business metadata. Often the data dictionary is stored in a database table or Excel® spreadsheet. The Business metadata should be stored in a centralized repository. This will provide a single data dictionary to manage. For example, in Figure 3.5, Informant Type is defined as "indicates the human source of the information."

Technical Metadata

Technical metadata describes the data structures and formats, such as table types, data types, indices, and partitioning method. For example,

Entity Name	Attribute Name	Attribute Description	Sample Values	Data Type	Length	Cardinality
Observation	Informant Type	Indicates the human source of the information.	For example, Patient, Caregiver	Code	80	0..1
Observation	Interpretation Code	An abbreviated interpretation of the observation	For example, Normal, Abnormal, High, etc	Code	80	0..1
Observation	Observation Code	Coded value representing the observation	For example, 99218, 99219, Active Drainage From Ear, ECG, Lower Extremity Neurological Exam, Urinary Incontinence Characterized	Code	80	1..1

FIGURE 3.5
Data dictionary example.

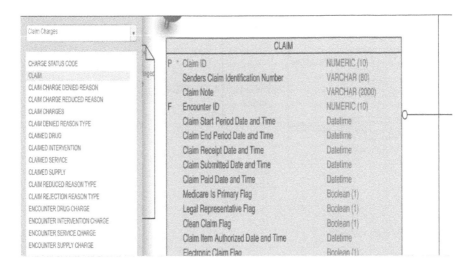

FIGURE 3.6
Technical metadata example.

in Figure 3.6, Encounter ID in the Claim table is a numeric (10) data type. Also, it describes the location of the data elements. Technical metadata is very critical in a federated architecture where a data model is implementing across many different servers in different locations. For example, on Server A, the patient's first name might be a 5-character field. On Server B, it may be a 20-character field. The patient's first name would not be consistent across these two servers because a patient's name could be truncated on Server A. For example, Michael would appear as Micha on Server A and Michael on Server B. The Governance Board needs to understand these technical data abnormities. The lack of enforcing consistent technical metadata across servers is the primary reason federated architectures fail.

Process Metadata

Process metadata describes the data input process. It includes source target maps, integration rules, validation rules, and consolidation rules. An integration rule could transform a 43 code to a standard code of Co (Colorado). A validation rule would verify that the Gender Code was an M or F or that the age of a patient was less than 200 years. A consolidation rule could combine North Zanesville and South Zanesville data into one Zanesville.

Process metadata tools need to support two important governance features: (1) data lineage and (2) impact analysis.

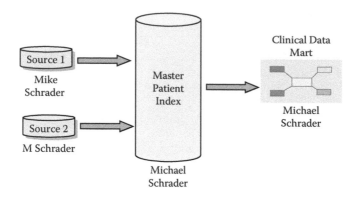

FIGURE 3.7
Data lineage chart example.

Data Lineage

The data lineage feature supports graphical visualization of complex data lineage relationships. We have the ability to track lineage of data from end user report/dashboard back to original data source elements. Data lineage will answer questions such as: Where did the data came from? What integration, transformation, or consolidation rules happened? What data source is the authoritative source? For example, in what system did the patient name of Michael Schrader originate and why was the original value of Mike Schrader and M Schrader changed to Michael Schrader? In Figure 3.7, we see an example of this type of data linage. We see that the original sources of Mike Schrader and M Schrader are changed in the Master Patient Index database. This is where Mike Schrader and M Schrader, with the assistance of other attributes, such as gender, Social Security Number (SSN), and birth date, are identified as the official record of Michael Schrader. These names are changed to the official name.

Impact Analysis

The impact analysis feature shows us what impact there would be if we changed a process. For example, the Governance Board has a question: What effort would it be to reduce down the number of different definitions of *patient stay* from four to two? The Business metadata would confirm that there are five different versions of *patient stay*. The Process metadata tool with impact analysis would tell us that 50 ETL programs would have to be modified. It would tell us that 15 easy ETL programs, 20 medium ETL programs, and 15 hard ETL programs would have to be modified. ETL is a set of tools utilized to move data from one system to another and change or transform the data to meet the requirements of integration and business rules. With this information, we can make estimates on the number of ETL programmers that we would need, the timeframe, and the total cost.

Process metadata, including data lineage and impact analysis, are supported by many tools including Informatica Metadata Manager.

Operational Metadata

Operational metadata stores information about who accessed what and when. This information is not only important for legal requirements, but for the design of the data warehouse itself. For example, we can identify that a particular data mart is not being utilized. This will enable us to develop a plan. Should we eliminate the data mart? Should we be providing better education for the end users? Should we redesign the application or the data mart?

The goal of data warehousing is to provide business users with a time-based, nonvolatile integrated view of cross-functional data. We integrate, transform, and consolidate the data to create an integrated view of the data. Data warehousing provides historical data. An Online Transactional Processing (OLTP) system has a current view of the data and can answer the question: How many patients are currently in the ER (emergency room)? A data warehouse could answer the question: How many patients were processed in May by the ER and how does that compare to last year?

Operational metadata is supported by many tools including Oracle® Audit Vault.

CASE STUDY OF METADATA USE
FOR DATA GOVERNANCE

Company XYZ wants to implement a data governance program, and attempts an Enterprise Data Warehouse. However, the company decides that it cannot implement a single version of the truth because some of its divisions utilize the same terms, though they have different meanings. So, it adopts a Fit for Purpose model. This presents the company with a serious issue. It created a data Governance Board represented mainly by the vice presidents of the various business areas, with IT as a technical adviser. IT is asked for the number of versions of *patient stay* defined in the model and where they are defined. IT quickly does a search in the metadata repository. It determines that there are five different versions of patient stay. The data Governance Board asks how much time and effort would be required to reduce the number from five versions to two versions of *patient stay*. IT quickly does an impact analysis through its metadata tool and determines that it would require modifying 50 easy ETL programs, 100 medium ETL programs, and 10 hard ETL programs at a cost of three man months. The board approves the changes.

MASTER DATA MANAGEMENT

Master data management (MDM) provides for special data quality processes on a limited number of objects. MDM utilizes metadata to assist in the cleansing of MDM data. However, it is a separate concept from metadata. All objects cannot be given MDM treatment. Usually, the MDM scope is limited to between 5 and 10 objects. These objects are very critical and need special treatment to ensure a higher data quality standard. For example, we need to know that a patient is the correct person in our database. We may have more than one Mary Smith. It is important to know the correct Mary Smith in order to deliver the correct treatment. One Mary Smith may be allergic to penicillin and another Mary Smith may not. Do we give Mary Smith a penicillin treatment? MDM repository contains one true version of each master entity created from multiple source systems and this "golden copy" is used by downstream systems. MDM tools are designed to identify duplicates, handle the variations of key entities across source systems, and standardize the data. Without MDM, the important data that links the subject areas of the data warehouse could not be relied upon. For example, are Michael Schrader, Mike Schrader, and MT Schrader the same person? With MDM, we can identify Michael Schrader, Mike Schrader, and MT Schrader as one person. MDM requires special attention from the governance process. For example, what degree of confidence is required for a match or, once patient records are merged, if there is a requirement to be able to break them apart again.

The following represent objects to consider for MDM in healthcare:

- Master patient index
- Units of measures
- ETS (enterprise terminology services)

In addition, the following represent objects for MDM that are not specific to healthcare:

- Location
- Time (months, quarters, and fiscal year)

METADATA REPOSITORY TYPES

There are several metadata repository strategies including:

1. Centralized Metadata Repository: An enterprise metadata solution where the metadata is stored in a single database.
2. Federated Metadata Repository: Metadata is stored in several databases. For example, the business metadata may be stored locally for each application.
3. Hybrid: Metadata is broken into categories, such as operational metadata, and stored in a central database.

Often Business, Technical, and Process metadata can be stored in the same physical database. They share many characters including less frequent inserts, frequent queries, and limited size.

Operational metadata should be stored in a separate database. It is much larger in size as compared to the Business, Technical, and Process metadata, and its characteristics are very different from the other metadata types including frequent inserts, not frequent queries, and large massive size. Operational metadata databases are often 10 to 1,000 times larger than Business, Technical, and Process metadata databases.

DATA PROFILING: INVESTIGATION AND ENFORCEMENT

Data profiling is a data investigation and quality monitoring process. It allows the business to assess the quality of its data through metrics, to discover or infer rules based on data, and to monitor historical metrics about data quality, such as range of values, frequency, patterns/formats, and sparseness. Data profiling is a key enforcement mechanism of data governance. Data profiling examines the data to validate the data. Often this process leads to the discovery of new business rules.

The following are types of data profiling:

- Integration Data Profiling: Integration means conforming data to a single enterprise value for the data element. For example, the state code for Colorado might be 23, C, or CO in three different source systems. There needs to be agreement on one enterprise value, such as CO for Colorado. We would then convert the 23 and C to a CO. This would allow the end user to run integrated queries in which CO will represent all of the Colorado data. We need to have data profiling process to verify that the integration rules are being implemented.
- Domain Validation Data Profiling: Domain validation data profiling process would confirm the valid possible values for a column. For example, the gender column can have only M, F, or null. If we see an X value, that would violate the domain validation rule.
- Format Validation Data Profiling: Format validation data profiling process would check to see if we are enforcing a specific standard format requirement, such as phone number or a Social Security Number (SSN). For example, SSN has the format 999-99-9999. The 9 value represents a number value. So 923-123-333X would be an invalid SSN number.
- Range Checking Data Profiling: Range checking data profiling checks the data to verify that data values fit within a boundary of data values. For example, a birth date value may be checked to verify that the person is no more than 200 years old. It is a common mistake for people to leave off the first two digits of the birth year. For example, a person who was born in 1959 might enter 59 instead of 1959 as the birth year value. This would make the person almost two thousand years.

- Sparseness Data Profiling: A sparseness data profiling checks to verify that a column is actually populated with a value as opposed to null values or missing values. Not only do we need to verify the percentage of null or missing values, but also the percentage of zero or blank values. Often users will enter a blank (spaces) value or zero value in an attempt to get around a requirement that a value must be entered.
- Uniqueness Data Profiling: Uniqueness data profiling is a process that verifies that each value is different. This is important because we need to be able to retrieve a single row by these data values.
- Frequency Distribution Data Profiling: Frequency distribution data profiling is a count of the distinct values in a column. Often we find that certain SSN values, such as 123-45-6789, are found many times in the database. This type of data profiling may lead to business rules that give certain values more validation, such as 111-11-1111 for an SSN.
- Overloading Data Profiling: Overloading data profiling is a process to check to verify that a column has multiple values in the same column. This may be an indication that we need to redesign the column into two or more columns. For example, Figure 3.8 shows 123XYZ and Wrench as values. 123XYZ might be a product code, whereas Wrench might be a product description.
- Authoritative Source Data Profiling: Authoritative source data profiling verifies that a column is being populated by the correct source. Often a column can be populated from multiple sources. Medaling is a concept where we have a gold source, a silver source, and a bronze source. In the medaling concept, we will take a silver source over a bronze source and a gold source over a silver source. Authoritative source data profiling verifies that we are populating a column with the correct source at a correct time. We may want to populate a column with a silver source until a gold source is available.
- Calculation Validation Data Profiling: Calculation validation data profiling is a process that validates the calculation of derived data values.

Product Code
123XYX
Wrench

FIGURE 3.8
Overloading column example.

- Hierarchy Validation Data Profiling: Hierarchy validation data profiling validates the hierarchies for aggregations. Hierarchy dimensions define the relationships between attributes. For example, geography has a hierarchy. In the geography dimension, we will find country, state, county, and city. A city will be located in a county, a county within a state, and a state will be in a country. Often different groups want to see different hierarchies. For example, they might want to see total sales being aggregated or rolled up differently. The organization might have had a major acquisition. The different groups might want to have a hierarchy with and without the major acquisition to compare apples to apples.
- Data Enrichment Data Profiling: Data enrichment data profiling validates that the process of adding or supplementing data from other sources is correct. For example, we have a physician's demographic information. We use this demographic information to search and obtain his/her license number.
- Matching Validation Data Profiling: Matching validation data profiling is validating that the matching process is correct. For example, we would verify that Michael Smith, Mike Smith, and Mikey Smith are the same person in the Master Patient Index.
- Dependency Data Profiling: Dependency data profiling investigates the relationships between columns. If we discover that one column is completely dependent upon another column, we may go back and design the data model or verify that the data is correct. For example, birth_date is always a lower date than death_date. So, if we have a person that was dead before they were born, we have a data error.

There are many data profiling tools, one of which is Oracle® Datanomics.

DATA LIFE CYCLE

Defining data life cycle rules is an important part of data governance.
Data life cycle rules answer questions, such as:

- What is the length of time that the data needs to be accessible?
- If the data is archived, what is the service level agreement for the amount of time in which we can retrieve the data back?

- Can we permanently remove the data?
- Do we need to retain mistakes? For example, a blood pressure machine short circuits and produces an incorrect reading that was used for the justification of a medical procedure that was performed. Do we need to retain this error data?

DATA RETENTION TECHNIQUES

There are many data retention techniques including:

- Soft Delete: A soft delete means that a data row is marked as deleted; however, the row is physically not removed from the data table.
- Permanent Delete: A permanent delete physically removes the data row from the data table. The data row can only be recovered from a backup tape.
- Archiving: Archiving takes the data from the normal access environment. There are three types of archiving: off-site archiving, offline archiving, and inline database archiving:
  - Off-site archiving removes the data from the server to a location for storage. This archiving strategy is for long-term storage. The main concern of off-site archiving is the cost of retrieval after many years or even decades. After many years, the operating system, the hardware and software, will be very different. Retrieving the data after an extended period can be very expensive and very difficult.
  - Offline archiving removes the data from the database; however, it keeps it local. For example, Oracle database provides a feature called Transportable Tablespace. A tablespace is a unit of storage. One can store each month's data in a different tablespace. After a period of time, you can unplug a tablespace and move it to tape. To retrieve the data, you restore the tablespace to online disk storage and plug it back into the database. The main concern is that the backup tablespace must be upgraded to the current database version.
  - Inline database archiving keeps the data in the database; however, it would compress the data. The data would still be accessible; however, the access times to retrieve the data would be much slower. For example, Oracle Exadata Database Machine has a

feature called Hybrid Columnar Compression. With this feature, one can compress the data by a factor of 10. The data is still available; however, access times are often over two times longer. The main advantage of this approach is that the data is available and stored in the database so that, when the database is upgraded, the compressed data is upgraded as well.

DATA VERSIONING

Data governance provides business rules for the versioning of data. There are different data versioning techniques depending upon the data format in which the data is stored—star dimensional model versus third normal form.

Data Versioning Techniques

Data versioning is different depending upon the data format. The two main data formats are star dimensional model and third normal form.

Star Dimensional Model Data Versioning

Star Dimensional model is very different from the 3rd normal form. It is a much flatter or simpler data model, and consists of fact and dimension tables. The fact tables represent the WHAT. A fact table consists of foreign keys from the dimension tables and measurements or metrics of a business process. It is the center of a star schema surrounded by dimension tables. For example, what are the total sales by product, by state, and by year? Total Sales is the fact (metric). The dimension tables are the HOW. A dimension is a category used to view/access the metrics. In our example, product, state, and year are the dimensions, or how we want to view the data.

In the Star Model in Figure 3.9, we have one large table called the Sales fact table and a set of smaller tables called Dimension tables: Product, Date, Customer, and Location.

Star Dimensional Model data versioning is supported through slowly changing dimensions, which are dimension data values that change over time. For example, the customer dimension stores information, such as a customer name. Often when a female marries, she will change her last name to that of her husband's last name. Data governance will give us the

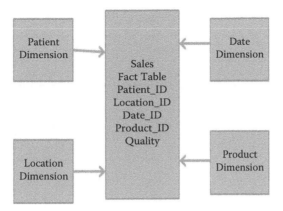

FIGURE 3.9
Star model example.

versioning policy as to whether we overwrite the data or keep all of the history. Each table could have a different versioning policy; however, the policies should have an enterprise view.

There are three basic slowly changing dimensions for handling data versioning in a star dimensional model:

- Type 1: Replace the value
- Type 2: Add a record with an effective start date and effective end date
- Type 3: Store the old value in addition to the new value on same row

Type 1

Type 1 simply writes over the previous value. The historical facts are lost. For example, in the customer dimension, Rachael Schrader marries William Smith. In this example, a Type 1 methodology overwrites Schrader to Smith. The fact that Rachael was once Rachael Schrader is lost. In this example, the data in the database would change as diagramed in Figure 3.10.

Type 2

In a Type 2 slowly changing dimension, we add an additional row to store the new data values with an effective start date and an effective end date, thereby saving the historical fact that before she was Rachael Smith, Rachael was Rachael Schrader (Figure 3.11).

Type 3

In a Type 3 slowly changing dimension, we add additional attributes to the row to store the prior information. In our example, a Type 3 slowly

Before

Patient ID	First Name	Last Name
12345	Rachael	Schrader

After

Patient ID	First Name	Last Name
12345	Rachael	*Smith*

FIGURE 3.10
Slowly changing dimension Type 1 example.

Patient ID	First Name	Last Name	Eff_Start_Date	Eff_End_Date
12345	Rachael	Schrader	1/18/1960	*8/27/2011*
78345	*Rachael*	*Smith*	*8/28/2011*	

FIGURE 3.11
Slowly changing dimension Type 2 example.

Patient ID	First Name	Last Name	Prior First Name	Prior Last Name	Effective Date
12345	*Rachael*	*Smith*	*Rachael*	*Schrader*	*8/28/2011*

FIGURE 3.12
Slowly changing dimension Type 3 example.

changing dimension change would add columns to the rows to store the old name. The prior last name field would be changed to Schrader, and the last name field would be changed to Smith. Also, there will be an effective date (Figure 3.12).

Type 3 slowly changing dimension is utilized less than Type 1 or Type 2 because of the overhead of additional columns. If we have a table with 60 columns and 36 columns would require versioning, the new column total would be 96. Another disadvantage of Type 3 slowly changing dimensions is that history is usually limited to one change. If we need more than one change stored, we would need to add additional rows.

The main advantage is that history is stored on a single row so that we can retrieve both the prior value and the current value at the same time.

Patient ID	Version #	First Name	Last Name	Eff_Start_ Date	Eff_End_ Date
12345	1	Rachael	Schrader	1/18/1960	8/27/2011
12345	2	Rachael	Smith	8/28/2011	

FIGURE 3.13
Data versioning Third Normal Form composite surrogate key example.

Third Normal Form Data Versioning

Normalization is the process of organizing data to minimize redundancy. Most Online Transaction Systems are in third normal data format or close to it. With third normal data format, there are many more tables than a Star Dimensional model.

Data versioning in a Third Normal Form (3NF) model is more complex than in a Star Dimensional model. There are many different ways to support data versioning in a Third Normal Form model. One approach is a composite surrogate key. This approach is far less complex: less effort to implement, performs well, and maintains referential integrity than the other approaches. The composite surrogate key has a primary key that is made up of two columns: the surrogate key and a version number. Multiple versions of a row share the same surrogate key. Multiple versions of the row will have different version numbers. In Figure 3.13, notice the additional row and the version number used to support our example.

ENFORCEMENT

There are many enforcement techniques for data governance, including:

- Data Profiling: The data profiling investigates the data to verify that business rules are enforced.
- Funding: If there are repeated major violations, the offending unit is fined by reducing their Business intelligence or overall IT budget.
- Training: One of the most important for enforcement is training. People will follow policies if they are trained to understand what the policies are and why they exist.

- Certification: Certification is much like a driver license. If you have a license, you have the right to access the data warehouse. And, just like drivers license, if you break the rules, your license could be revoked.
- Watermarking: Watermarking is the placing of an official seal or symbol on a report much like a watermark on currency. Unofficial reports would not have the official seal of approval.

CONCLUSION

Data governance is critical for the successful business operations. Governance provides standards and policies that allow us to harmonize resources and provide transparency for legal compliance. The governance process is an ongoing enterprise-focused program. At the heart of a data governance program is a metadata program, which needs to support Business metadata, Technical metadata, Process metadata, and Operational metadata. Data versioning requirements need to be specified by the data governance program. In addition, a data governance program relies on an enforcement program, such a data profiling. By implementing these pillars of data governance, the organization is able to manage its most important resource—data.

4

Operationalizing Data Quality through Data Governance

Julia Zhang

CONTENTS

A PHARMACEUTICAL INDUSTRY PERSPECTIVE

This chapter focuses the discussion on data quality through the data governance. It will include the discussion of data quality definition, the importance of data quality, standards enabled automation of data quality processes, and strategies of how to improve data quality.

WHAT IS DATA QUALITY?

The definition of data quality has been mentioned in one of the ISO standards on Quality Management and Quality Assurance as: "The total of

65

FIGURE 4.1
Data quality is demonstrated by different data dimensions.

characteristics of an entity that bear on its ability to satisfy stated and implied needs." Therefore, we can define data quality as the satisfaction of the requirements stated in a particular specification, which reflects the implied needs of the user. An acceptable level of quality has been achieved if the data conforms to a defined specification that correctly reflects the intended use. Data quality is reflected by multiple factors, such as the time and the way of data collection, the formats, and the types of data collected. High data quality should contain many dimensions like accuracy, completeness, integrity, consistency, timeliness, and traceability. As indicated in Figure 4.1, data quality is demonstrated by multiple data dimensions. Each data dimension will be addressed below.

Data Accuracy: Accuracy of data is the degree to which data correctly reflects the real world object or verifiable sources. All data values should be within the value domains specified by the business. In many cases, accuracy is measured by how the values agree with an identified source of correct information. The measurable characteristics of accuracy can include value precision (each value conforms to the defined level of precision), value acceptance (each value belongs to the allowed set of values for the observed attributes), and value accuracy (each data value is correct when assessed against a system of records).

Data Completeness: Completeness of data is the extent to which the expected attributes of data are provided. Competence rules can be assigned to a dataset in different levels of constraints, such as mandatory attributes (that require a value), optional attributes (which may have a value based on some set of conditions), and inapplicable attributes (which may not have a value). Completeness can be prescribed on a single attribute, or can be dependent on the values of other attributes within a record or a message. Data completeness definition is the "expected completeness." It is possible that data is not available, but it is still considered completed because it meets users' expectations. Every data requirement has "mandatory" and "optional" aspects. For example, a customer's mailing address is mandatory and it is available, while customer's office address is optional; it is okay if it is not available. Data can be complete, but inaccurate, e.g., all the customers' addresses are available, but many of them are not correct.

Data Integrity: Integrity of data means that data has a complete or whole structure. Data integrity is imposed within a database when it is designed and is authenticated through the ongoing use of error checking and validation routines. All characteristics of the data must be correct—including business rules, relations, dates, definitions, and lineage—for data to be complete. As a simple example, to maintain data integrity, numeric columns/cells should not accept alphabetic data.

Data Consistency: Consistency of data means that data should be synchronized across the enterprise. For example, data should be consistent between systems and no duplicate records should exist. Data can be accurate (i.e., it will represent what happened in real world), but still inconsistent. Data is inconsistent when it is in sync in the narrow domain of an organization, but not in sync across the organization. Data can be complete, but inconsistent, e.g., data from different therapeutic area studies using different data formats.

Data Timeliness: Data should be available at the time needed. Timeliness refers to the degree to which information is up-to-date with the corresponding real-world entities. "Data delayed" is "data denied." The timeliness of data is extremely important and it depends on user expectation. An example of data not being timely: The courier package status is delivered, but it will be updated in the system only in the night batch run. This means that online status will not be available.

Data Traceability: Data traceability means that any transaction, modification, and report can be tracked to its originating transaction. It is the property that enables the understanding of the data's lineage and/or the relationship between an element and its predecessor(s). Traceability facilitates transparency, which is an essential component in building confidence in a result or conclusion. It is built by clearly establishing the path between an element and its immediate predecessor and establishes across-dataset relationships as well as within-dataset relationships. There are two levels of traceability:

1. Metadata traceability enables the user to understand the relationship of the analysis variable to its source dataset(s) and variable(s) and is required for derived data compliance. This traceability is established by describing (via metadata) the algorithm used or steps taken to derive or populate an analysis value from its immediate predecessor. Metadata traceability also is used to establish the relationship between an analysis result and analysis dataset(s).
2. Data point traceability enables the user to go directly to the specific predecessor record(s) and should be implemented if practically feasible. This level of traceability can be very helpful when a reviewer is trying to trace a complex data manipulation path. This traceability is established by providing clear links in the data to the specific data values used as input for an analysis value.

None of the data quality dimensions is complete by itself, and, frequently, dimensions are overlapping. Data quality is not linear; having data quality on one dimension is as good as "no quality."

IMPORTANCE OF DATA QUALITY

Information/data penetrates into corporations' networks, systems, and storages, thus delivering volumes of data about customers, products, partners, and new opportunities. After analysis and review of that information is complete, data then flows back out in the form of new products and services, documents, and applications. Organizations invest heavily in mission-critical business software initiatives trying to capture each drop of information as it cascades into data centers around the clock. However, data typically resides in multiple sources with various data structures. There are inconsistent rules for changing, improving, or accessing it. No one can agree on which data quality measures should be applied; business users and IT personnel view information differently and do not speak a common language. To make matters worse, many companies use disparate, poorly integrated, data quality management tools and applications.

Organizations must not only address structured data, they also need to leverage unstructured text data from word processing documents, PDF files, email messages, blogs, and Web pages to gain significant insights into their business. They want to identify emerging trends, and proactively respond to opportunities or potential risks. Companies need to be able to sort through the noise of unstructured content and automatically identify what that text content is "about." To be competitive, large and midsize businesses must be able to access all types of data from throughout their organization, no matter which vendor's technology or solution houses the information. Companies need to respond quickly and effectively to the influx of new data, as well as prepare for and meet anticipated factors, such as federal or industry regulations governing information protection and control. To find a solution for achieving the right strategic decision, overcoming the competition in the market, efficiently and effectively using enterprise-wide information/data, and bringing back the high return-on-investment (ROI), data quality is a critical factor. For example, the drug development process can be treated as an international trip; data quality is the passport in this journey for reaching the final destination—an approved drug. Without a valid passport (i.e., high-quality data), you will not be able to reach your destination. Data quality represents the state of data completeness, consistency, accuracy, timeliness, integrity, and traceability that makes data appropriate for a specific use.[1,2] Improving enterprise data quality is critical for enterprise ROI. The London-based market research firm, BDRC Continental, did an Information Difference survey in 2009. It is indicated that poor data quality can have serious financial costs for organization.[3] For example, one respondent to the survey said that problems with data quality and consistency had led to the orphaning of about £20 million worth of product stock. The goods (values at $30.8 million at currency exchange rates) were sitting in a warehouse and couldn't be sold because they had been "lost" in the company's system.

Let us take an example from the biomedical world to illustrate the importance of data quality to the field of biomedicine. There have been phenomenal developments in the field of biomedicine over the past 15 to 20 years. Most of these have been in the form of incredible volume and/or diversity of biomedical information generation. There are thousands of clinical trials, tens of millions of polymorphisms identified, and billions of pairs of sequences. Expression profiles now are increasingly measured in the hundreds of thousands of structures, animal models, new modalities of data intensive imaging, and disease characterization.

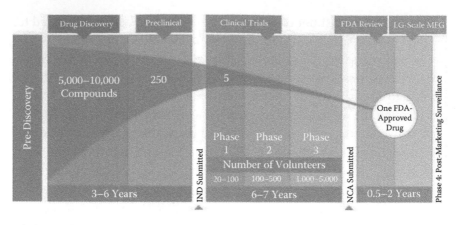

FIGURE 4.2
Unsustainable model of drug development.[4]

At the same time, the biopharmaceutical industry, private and public institutions, and government have invested heavily in a large number of research platforms and more research-specific initiatives than are practical to mention. It should be the best of times for drug development, but, alas, it is the worst of times. Despite increasing financial investment in pharmaceutical R&D (research and development), innovation has reached a plateau. This has been exacerbated by patent expirations, poor outcomes from R&D, increasing regulatory burden around the globe, and healthcare reimbursement issues. Figure 4.2 shows a model of drug development;[4] there is an ocean of research producing treatments by the drop. Indeed, in recent decades, one of the most sobering realities in the field of biomedical research has been the fact that, despite significant increases in funding (as well as extraordinary advances in things like "omics," computerized molecular modeling, and drug screening and synthesization), the number of new treatments for illnesses that make it to market each year has flatlined at historically low levels. Recent researches[5-7] summarize that one FDA-approved drug from start to finish lasts 10 to 15 years, costs about $1 billion, and involves 1,000 to 6,000 volunteers. To face all the current challenges, the real need is to improve innovation and pharmaceutical R&D productivity. Organizations make strategic and operational decisions based on data. As quoted by John Martin (Gilead CEO) at a *Fortune* magazine interview (May 16, 2011): "We tend to think of the pill as the drug. But, the drug is really the data that's been collected through clinical research that defines the best use of that drug."

As stated above, data is very important for organizations making strategic and operational decisions, therefore, poor quality data can negatively influence how a company is perceived in the marketplace. Business users cannot do their jobs when they are relying on information that is redundant or inaccurate. When enterprise information is complete, accurate, and accessible, it can empower users to make better decisions, drive operational excellence, ensure regulatory compliance, and minimize IT costs. Poor data quality increases costs through wasted resources (due to rework or lack of processes), a need to correct and deal with reported errors (rework), and an inability to optimize business processes. It will result in lost revenue through customer dissatisfaction, lowered employee morale, and poorer decision making. Reduced costs are often linked to increased efficiencies in day-to-day operations as well as improved performance-oriented organization. Studies have found[8] that if you don't have an enterprise information/data management in place, almost three-quarters of your users can waste their time searching for data. Data quality management can be used to seek out operational efficiencies for cost reduction, leading to increased margins, and, consequently, increased profits. Reducing expenses is more about being *smart* (Specific, Measurable, Achievable, Realistic, Timely) in understanding where costs have exceeded reasonable levels and determining ways to identify and eliminate excessive costs. How to achieve high data quality will be discussed in the following sections: data governance drives data quality, data standards enable automation of data quality control processes with metadata-driven enhancement, and best practices for improving data quality.

DATA GOVERNANCE DRIVES DATA QUALITY

Ensuring high-quality data is a complex process. To ensure a high data quality, we need to develop the data quality strategy, which includes data governance, technical strategy, enterprise-wide data culture, and more. Data governance is an organizational structure that creates and enforces policies, rules, processes, and procedures to ensure and improve enterprise data quality. For example, it is to set up a process in a clinical trial data life cycle for how the data can be exchanged, integrated, analyzed, and reported in drug development. It ensures that data can be trusted and that people can be made accountable for any business impact caused by poor data quality. Data governance is about putting people in charge of fixing and preventing data issues and using technology to help aid the process.

Any time data is synchronized, merged, and exchanged, there have to be ground rules guiding this. Data governance serves as the method to organize the people, processes, and technologies for data-driven programs like data quality; they are a necessary part of any data quality effort. The quality of a company's data dictates the effectiveness of the organization in driving new business opportunities, delivering state-of-the art customer service, managing risk and compliance, generating meaningful decision support models, and reducing operating costs. In turn, the overall condition of data assets is directly dependent on the company's ability to align people, processes, lines of business, and technologies. It requires that all of these things be working together to produce the desired outcomes that make data fit for its business purpose. The only way to align the interdependencies of disparate people, processes, lines of business, and technologies is through a well-orchestrated data governance program. Data governance includes the ability:

- To develop and implement data quality governing disciplines, guidance, and roadmaps for data processes enterprise-wide or globally.
- To force the organization to develop enterprise data quality culture, which helps people think more broadly about quality and to reexamine their day-to-day practices.
- To assist the organization in being more clear about its objectives with respect to reducing costs, increasing effectiveness and efficiency, and improving the decision-making process.
- To provide users with confidence and stability when accessing and using data arising from the organization.
- To improve relations and communication with the organization's clients (both data providers and data users).
- To improve the standing of the organization in the wider community.

Are data quality and data governance the same thing? They share the same goal, essentially striving for the same outcome of optimizing data and information results for business purposes. Data governance plays a very important role in achieving high data quality. It deals primarily with orchestrating the efforts of people, processes, objectives, technologies, and lines of business in order to optimize outcomes around enterprise data assets. This includes, among other things, the broader cross-functional oversight of standards, architecture, business processes, business integration, and risk and compliance. Data governance is an organizational structure that oversees the compliance and standards of enterprise data. Establishing and implementing good data governance practices, we can:

- Keep the enterprise-level data quality picture in mind and prevent the company from understanding and addressing upstream problems that impact data outcomes caused by people and processes and that cannot be fixed by technology alone.
- Avoid project silos or data quality silos in the data quality control development.
- Leverage data quality strength across the enterprise and apply right data standards, business rules, and data models, therefore reducing duplicating operational costs.
- Increase the process efficiency by leading the implementation of multiple technologies for the same purpose within the company, which raises the cost of software, training, and maintenance.
- Synergize enterprise-capable technologies, which are utilized in a single instance when they could be leveraged across multiple projects and data sources.

In other words, data governance drives enterprise data quality by breaking down the barriers associated with project-based data quality.

DATA STANDARDS ENABLES AUTOMATION OF DATA QUALITY CONTROL PROCESS

We live in an electronic age where information is captured every second and data volumes are growing exponentially. Every 1.2 years, the volume of business data worldwide doubles.[9] A research firm, IDC (Framingham, MA), predicted[10] in 2011 that global digital output is expected to increase tenfold from 2008's output of 180 exabytes (1 exabyte is a little over 1 billion gigabytes) and is projected to reach 35,000 exabytes by 2020. With emerging technologies and demanding of business needs, we are facing all kinds of challenges that block us in achieving business efficiency and productivity. In this section, we will discuss why standards are important through some challenges and address what standards can help and suggest how to implement standards.

Enterprise-wide challenges: In a collaborative environment, communication issues are everywhere; different dialects (technical language and business language) exist internally between research and development (R&D), across R, and across D, externally between internal and our partners, vendors, and regulatory authorities. For example, there is the representation of males versus females in clinical trials. The data may be presented in various ways, such as "male and female," "M and F," "1 and 2," or "0 and 1." The "language of gender" should be standardized in order for an efficient communication. As one can imagine, inconsistencies of this "gender language" usage across department, enterprise, or outside partners can cause communication and efficiency problems when trying to exchange data from multiple clinical studies and make assessments within and across therapeutic areas nearly impossible. On the other hand, information/data is stored in multiple or siloed systems with no "global" standards to use, there is no infrastructure for data sharing, and no common data model or formats or common terminology/vocabulary for data exchange. If globalization is the trend for business, then data collection, process, storage, analysis, and exchange should be globalized as well.

Economy challenges: With the current economic situation and drug R&D innovation reaching its plateau, resource and monetary constraints, and increased cost and complexity of trials (see Figure 4.2), we expect the budget increase to support the business needs. However, we face budgets cut, budgets limited, budgets unavailable, and budgets frozen all the time. We probably all feel that making cash stretch is like a rubber band.

People challenges: People's roles changed due to the business needs and changes in the economy, technology, etc. For example, a clinical trial data manager's previous role was reviewing protocol, developing case report forms (CRF), designing the database, collecting data, validating data (performing edit checks and quarries), and locking the database. With the turning of the business trend and its needs, the data manager's role now will not only cover the above functions, but also will be to manage different projects and other operational management. Most people act on change differently, such as resistance, avoidance, and complaining.

Technology challenges: Many technologies, such as XML, SOA, Public cloud, Private cloud, Hybrid cloud, Community cloud, SaaS (Software as a Services), PaaS (Platform as a Service), IssS (Infrastructure as a Service), and many more, are emerging. Which one you will need? We almost can see or hear new tools/e-tools often using emerging technology, but which one is good for us to use? There are many standards being developed by different standard organizations, such as HL7 (Health Level seven), CDISC (Clinical Data Interchange Standards Consortium), ICH (International Conference on Harmonization), ISO (International Organization for Standardization), etc. Which one is the right one to apply? With increasing outsourcing activities, issues from how to perform better on education, training, implementation, and communication are all popping up. How do we handle them?

How do we face all these challenges? How can we improve the data quality leading to business efficiency and effectiveness? The adoption of data standards will facilitate and enhance data sharing, analysis, and comparability across functional, jurisdictional, or geographical boundaries. Data standards are established rules, principles, or measures that are widely used and are recognized and accepted as having permanent value. The goal of a data standard is to enable the sharing or exchange of information between multiple parties in a way that guarantees that the interactive parties share the same understanding of what is represented within that information. For example, when fire engines come from other municipalities to put out a fire in our neighborhood, we aren't concerned with whether or not their trucks will be able to hook up to the local fire hydrants because all connections are standardized. Contrast this with the Great Baltimore Fire of 1904 where thousands of fire fighters from the surrounding cities and states were unable to assist as the fire raged for 30 hours, simply because their fire hoses were not compatible with the Baltimore hydrant connections.[11]

Standards are necessary for interoperability, portability, and reusability, and are the most efficient way to facilitate the development of cost-effective, interoperable systems. Standards lead the way to achieve interoperability, which provides a technical foundation for data integration ("reuse without rework," facilitates exchange of information between two or more parties with common interest), establishes data consistency, and facilitates communication that enforce a common language with others, ensuring integrity of data and meaning for every user. Standards also streamline business processes, from protocol development through reporting/submission activities; reduce time and cost of clinical trials including decreased learning times over time; compliance and risk reduction; reduce submission review times; and eliminate some proposed postmarketing studies because information and knowledge can be extracted from a standards-based repository. Standards improve data quality both from efficiency and effectiveness, making outsourcing easy to manage. They also increase people's morale (learn the job once and perform it consistently), enable "plug and play" tool/application selection, and facilitate retirement of old systems, plus the use of common viewing tools if data is in standard format.

Using standards can lead us to interoperability. Metadata-driven is an important approach to applying standards in a drug development process. Metadata describes data, which provides the descriptive information of the what, when, who, how, and where of geographic and spatial information concerning a particular set of data that was collected, and how the data is formatted. It is the information that describes the content, quality, condition, origin, and other characteristics of data or other pieces of information. It is difficult to distinguish between data and metadata because something can be data and metadata at the same time. For example, the "unit" is both metadata when it used as a terminology for code/codelist, and data when it acts as value of measurements. Data and metadata can change over time. In a study design, "protocol name" is treated as data, and in study data processing and analyzing, "protocol name" is treated as metadata. Therefore, metadata needs to be defined for the purpose. Metadata includes clear, unambiguous data element definitions used in the business development as well as in interfacing systems. How to apply metadata to drug development industry is a challenge. A well-designed metadata tool or system can help us implement standards appropriately to our daily work and will increase the work efficiency and effectiveness. Metadata is essential for understanding information stored in data warehouses.

A metadata-driven architecture (metadata repository (MDR)) contains information about data and status of various processes. The metadata provides a foundation for connecting multiple processes and systems, thereby allowing the creation of tools that largely automate the drug development process. Standards drive productivity enhancement for drug development based on metadata obtained from the development plan, protocols, and analysis plan. A well-designed metadata application is an asset for standard implementation and it is a good tool or methodology to apply standards to our daily work. MDR is the single source of truth for all information about data and process. It is not a static standard library, it is a dynamic standard application tool or system for creating, maintaining, archiving metadata. In a metadata repository, metadata flows bidirectionally from the source to the metadata repository and back to the source. The metadata repository acts as the center of the universe and it is an architecture to help organizations proactively manage data.

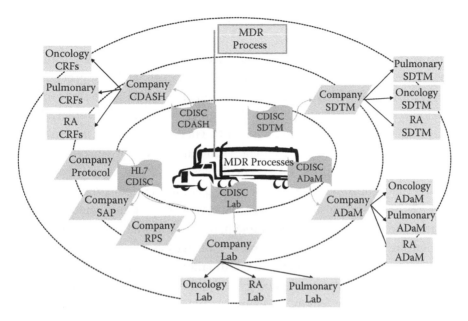

FIGURE 4.3
A suggestion for a metadata repository architecture.

Metadata has been used in the clinical data life cycle from protocol development, CRF design, data collection, validation, derivation, and reporting to submission and postmarketing research with or without realization. Implementing standards from protocol design to regulatory submission appropriately can streamline the clinical trial development process. In this streamline process, all standards used should be from a central source—MDR. This will ensure that the harmonized standards, including terminology, can be used effectively and efficiently throughout the entire life cycle of a clinical program. The structure of a metadata repository varies by business goals and objectives. A metadata repository can be defined at many different levels, e.g., global/industry standard level, compound/product level, therapeutic level, study level, dataset/domain level (description, structure, class, keys), and variable level (label, type, origin, length, controlled terminology). Figure 4.3 sketches an idea of an MDR structure at three levels using dotted oval shapes: industry level, company level, and therapeutic level. It contains a metadata dynamic governance process as a driving engine. When designing a metadata repository, a detailed and thorough requirement is critical for a particular business. For example, how can MDR help the statistician develop a study analysis plan, how can it help a statistical programmer to process clinical data, and how can it help a clinical trial study team develop protocol, CRF, etc., in a pharmaceutical company?

To ensure clinical data quality and business process efficiency, a metadata-driven method is a necessary methodology in clinical data processing. Using the metadata-driven method will allow all components to share information about the data as it moves through its life cycle, thereby enabling consistency, accountability, and true control of data. It also will increase the capability to share and manage data within and across organizations and reduce the impacts on the safety, effectiveness, and cost of healthcare by having the right information at the right place at the right time. Using an example of creating a study analysis data, we can see a tremendous waste of time and resources when not implementing a metadata-driven process.

There are three processes in a clinical trial analysis data derivation: documentation, SAS programming, and QC (quality control) processes. Without using metadata-driven methodology, variable name, variable label, variable format, variable length, and variable type will be manually typed in each process. Assuming there are 30 SDTM (study data tabulation model) datasets and 20 ADaM (analysis dataset model) datasets for each study, 30 variables per data set, 5 attributes per variable, plus about 500 elements of controlled terminology terms, the total data attributes can be as many as 5,000 per study. Without metadata to use, each attribute is manually typed *three times* (private communication). All information about clinical trial development can be driven by a standard-based, metadata-driven architecture—metadata repository. When completely implemented, a well-designed metadata repository can help industry to reduce time and cost, increase efficiency and quality, while remaining compliant and aligned with evolving regulatory and industry initiative in the product life cycle from clinical data collection, data processing, data analyzing, reporting data, and postmarketing research. Therefore, metadata and a metadata repository can help us to reach interoperability while ensuring data quality.

The metadata repository is the origination point for semantic changes and it manages metadata as an asset. Imagine every new development project starting with the metadata repository to determine what data currently exists, which can be reused, who owns the data, how comprehensive it is, what other processes affect it, and where it is currently reported. A well-designed metadata repository is like a high-quality engine in a vehicle; however, to specify a metadata repository requirement is a complicated topic, it varies by the business goals and objectives. Based on our working experiences, a suggested general requirement for metadata repository will contain, but is not limited to:

- Metadata management (governance and process): It will build the function to create new metadata, maintain existing metadata, and archive and retire metadata. Metadata is needed to ensure consistency in use and meaning of content within the business development and across the clinical data life cycle, from trial design through submission and beyond.
- Version control: The version control function should be built at the level of terminology and element content. Version control of programs, data, and output is needed to control process and provide transparency.
- Audit trail: It will consist of an audit function for traceability.
- Ability to create and use elements provisionally.
- Ability to choose when product standards or individual projects inherit changes to industry/company/therapeutic standards.
- Ability for external users, such as CROs (clinical research organizations) and other partners, to request, create, and download a standard element electronically for use in their standard systems.
- Ability for configuration: It permits customization based on existing business rules.
- Security: It can control access and permissions for objects and actions. The security requirements are established by 21 CFR Part 11, the regulation that directs organizations to have their electronic processes under control. This is just a good business practice.

Another standard application approach is master data management (MDM). Master data management is the practice of defining and maintaining consistent definitions of business entities and reference data to facilitate the accurate sharing of consistent data across multiple IT systems and possibly beyond the enterprise to partnering business. Master data objects are those core business objects that are used in different applications across the organization, along with their associated metadata, attributes, definitions, roles, connections, and taxonomies. They are those "things" on which successful business operations rely—what are logged in our transaction systems, drive operations, are measured and reported on in our reporting systems, and analyzed in our analytical systems. MDM integrates policies and procedures for centralized information

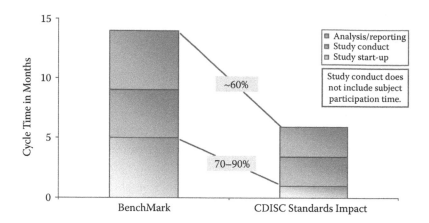

FIGURE 4.4
CDISC business case survey with Gartner.[12]

management with the business applications, methods, and infrastructure to support the integration and shared use of high-quality data. Master data management is essentially a data quality management.

Per the CDISC business case survey[12] (Figure 4.4), standards implemented from the beginning can significantly improve processes in a single clinical study and save about 80% of time, and save about 60% of time if standards are implemented in the analysis process. Appropriately applying MDR and MDM through standard implementation will bring business environment to interoperability.

DATA QUALITY STRATEGY

Having data quality as a focus is a business philosophy that aligns strategy, business culture, company information, and technology in order to manage data to the benefit of the enterprise. Data quality is an elusive subject that can defy measurement and yet be critical enough to derail a single IT project, strategic initiative, or even an entire company. Access to accurate and complete information is crucial for charting new markets and exploring new revenue opportunities. With achieving high data quality goals in mind, we need to develop a data quality strategy, which supports business processes that are critical to business success, such as organizational wide improvement programs, organizational data governance, metadata/master management, and standard implementation. Data quality cannot be achieved by oversight or monitoring alone; it should be built into the design and execution of studies. Quality approach includes quality as a rule, quality as a system, quality by design, and quality as a culture. Putting processes in place to capture/clean/maintain data will provide clear guidance on how you aim to achieve your goals and clear instructions to those working with you. Ensure that everyone in the organization is trained in the importance of maintaining good quality data, and hold regular review meetings to ensure that your data quality processes are up to date, efficient and effective, and remain that way. Quality planning, quality control, and quality improvement consist of different stages in quality strategy.

Stage 1: Quality Planning (steps involved in quality planning):
- Understand what matters most and start with the end in mind. Think of what your objectives are, what you want to do with the data, what it will be used for. Your objectives impact on the amount and type of data you need. Knowing what you are aiming to do at the beginning will ensure that you capture all of the fields you need, and that you have the ability to capture the data across the enterprise or all customer touch points.
- Develop a data governance package, including the data quality roadmap and data quality metrics, will help your organization truly treat its data as a corporate asset by enforcing consistent definitions, rules, policies, and procedures.
- Make the road to quality an enterprise culture.
- Win support for the investment. A good data quality program is an investment in the long-term success and profitability of your business. Like any investment, it needs to be justified to those holding the purse strings. Connecting the proposed investment to the company objectives and to the following areas should act as a good business case for investment: reputation, revenue, cost, profit, and compliance. Consider how improvement in data quality will affect these key board level objectives.

Stage 2: Quality Control (suggestions for QC):
- Develop mechanisms that will monitor, manage, and control what matters most.

- Use data standard and technology. The challenge of maintaining accurate data can sometimes seem like a daunting one, but standards and technology are out there to help you. The standards and technology you implement should be tailored to your specific organization's business needs; concentrating your business needs will provide you more sophisticated and effective solutions. Implement standards and use metadata-driven to design a quality control system.
- Keep data exchange interoperability in mind. With improved data quality procedures in place, you will be able to assess how much your data quality has improved over time against the targets you set for yourself.

Stage 3: Quality Improvement:

Data quality is a journey, not a destination. A data quality monitoring process should be in place to ensure if your data quality has been improved. Do you have systems in place that can measure how long these activities now take, and how long they took last year or the year before? Data quality metrics can help demonstrate what risks or issues might be presented by any decline in data quality levels as well as what opportunities might be gained by investing in improvements. It also can support objective judgment and reduce the influence of assumptions, politics, and vested interests. Metrics measure time savings, milestones, quality, and efficiency, e.g., how long it takes to complete a task, whether a milestone is achieved on time, the number of errors or how closely attributes align with a set of requirements, and the resources required to complete a task. Another way to measure the data quality is to set up a quality score measurement. Each quality score defines how well program processes and data attributes align with the tool's requirements and criteria. After developing the measure metrics, we need to know:

- Where to measure—Key processes. For most organizations, business KPIs (key performance indicators) and the executive decisions aligned with them will most likely relate to cost, revenue, profitability, logistics, products, customers, suppliers, and other important assets. Identifying the processes supporting these KPIs, the data required for these to operate effectively, and the quality of that data enables organizations to determine the impact or poor quality in tangible terms. The result is an improved ability to gain business understanding and support for building the business case for data quality.

- What to measure—Data dimensions. As stated previously: accuracy, completeness, integrity, consistency, timeliness, and traceability. We can measure on whether the data is in the right format for it to be usable. Does data comply with critical rules? Does data reflect the real world? Is business-required information present? Is it sufficiently current? Are duplicate records creating confusion? Is the data the same, regardless of where it resides? Is it useful to the business in its pursuit of objectives?
- How to Measure—Using rules. Data quality is the satisfaction of the requirements stated in specific business needs. Data quality metrics, when aligned to business KPIs, have the power to increase business user awareness, understanding, and support for data quality investments.

BEST PRACTICES FOR ACHIEVING DATA QUALITY IN THE PHARMACEUTICAL INDUSTRY

An enterprise's future, reputation, and financial well-being depend on the quality of information/data. Best practices demonstrate that a well-considered enterprise information/data management strategy, practice, and solutions turn information into a strategic corporate asset. It is only then that companies know their business, can decide with confidence, and can eventually act boldly by providing trust in the type and relevance of data from any source. In addition, they can empower business users to be in charge of their data, surround business initiatives with end-to-end data governance, and build on top of existing investments. Following the data strategy developed by the specific business needs, and reiterating the data improvement process to ensure the data strategy is well implemented, will enable you to achieve high-quality data. We will demonstrate below some best practices from data quality strategy development implementation in drug development area.

Step 1: To set up the data quality strategy, we begin with the planning stage. To improve data quality in a complicated clinical trial system, we need to understand the business needs and existing business processes. Assuming we begin with a new data quality system development, we need to identify how the data was designed, collected, and processed, and then gain a thorough understanding of the business needs in data quality from the clinical data life cycle. We will need to develop a data governance and data quality road map with vision and goals in mind.

Step 2: Following the data governance and data quality roadmap, we can start from the design, then development and finally implementation. To efficiently operate a clinical trial system that includes many different subsystems, tools, and functions, interoperability plays an important role. Assuming data governance has been developed and implemented, then quality data designing will be next. Quality by design drives clinical trial excellence by setting the right data quality systems under appropriate data governance; an organization can improve the process efficiency and reduce the cost, then increase the ROI. Quality by design makes for an integrated framework that effectively drives quality into the design, execution, analysis, and reporting of clinical trials to ensure protocol and regulatory compliance, patient safety, and data integrity. It also can proactively manage quality, focus on "what matters most," and detect/respond to threats to quality. For example, some protocol amendments are avoidable if the data quality is built into the design. To build quality into protocol, we first identify what matters most for the study, such as study risk factors, operational feasibility, scientific integrity and clarity of endpoints, and strategic alignment with clinical development plan. Secondly, we will guide protocol design using known quality criteria, such as a protocol quality control checklist and a protocol quality assessment tool, then we will assess protocol quality with clinicians, study teams, and investigative sites. Designing data is about discovering and completely defining your application's data characteristics and processes. It is a process of gradual refinement, from the rough stage of solving questions such as "what data does your application require?" to the more precise refinement of the data structures and processes that provide data. A data design defines data availability, manageability, performance, reliability, scalability, and security. It includes identifying the data, defining specific data types, storage mechanisms, and ensuring data integrity by using business rules and other run-time enforcement mechanisms. With a good data design, your application's data access will be fast, easily maintained, and able to gracefully accept future data enhancements.

Step 3: To establish enterprise data quality culture. Data quality can seem like a daunting task, but it is really all about having the right people, processes, and technology in place. The quality of data cannot be improved by only applying technology or only applying the process improvements. It requires a collaborative effort that arms business process experts with the right technical tools to make cost-effective decisions about identifying, reacting to, and anticipating the types of data errors that lead to negative business impact. If the organization has no quality culture, the concept of data quality will be abstract, distracting, and annoying. Simply writing new information capture procedures and putting them into a handbook will not be enough to change the culture of the company; it takes training, collaboration, and a willingness to make fundamental changes. Manuals will be put on the shelf and ignored without the cultural adoption.

Step 4: Develop and implement necessary industry and enterprise specific standards. In the pharmaceutical industry, CDISC standards are well known and accepted both by industry and regulatory bodies. CDISC has developed clinical trial standards from trial design, data collection, data processing, data analysis, to data submission. Implementing data standards in our clinical trial system allows for automation of data processing and validation, which leads to high efficiency. In addition, an organization needs to develop its specific standards according to its business needs that are based on the industry standard. Different organizations will have different specific situations when implementing standards, e.g., implementing CDISC standards end-to-end, including PROTOCOL, CDASH, LAB, SDTM, ADaM, define.xml, and Controlled Terminology, and also utilizing BRIDG (Biomedical Research Integrated Domain Group) as their underlying information model. To leverage the standards, we should build a metadata repository to govern data collection, data processing, and data submission, and to leverage the usage of different standards enterprise-wide. Taking a metadata-driven approach is an important way to apply standards in the drug development process.[1] The metadata provides a foundation for connecting multiple processes and systems, thereby allowing the creation of tools that largely automate the drug development process. The metadata repository acts as the center of the universe to help organizations proactively manage their data. Figure 4.5 illustrates how the MDR is a central source where data standards are applied throughout the clinical trial data life cycle. In this data life cycle, data collection, data processes, and analysis are all done with guidance from data standards, such as CDISC CDASH, CDISC LAB, SDTM, ADaM, and define.xml. We can streamline data processes under data governance, well-designed data semantics, and appropriately implemented standards.

Step 5: Develop a data quality tool/system. We have already discussed improving data quality by implementing data standards throughout governance, data design, and data processing. In order to increase efficiency and effectiveness, a data validation tool (DVT) is needed for improving data quality and ensuring data from multiple sources (both internal and

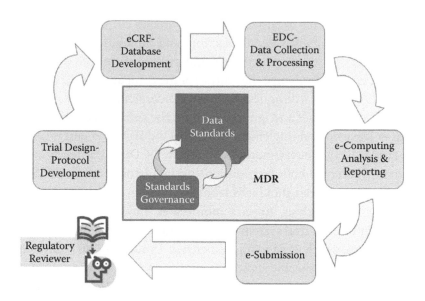

FIGURE 4.5
Streamline of the clinical trial data life cycle by implementing data standards.

external) matches all specified requirements. The data validation tool also ensures "quality by design." Data validation is the processes and technologies involved in ensuring the conformance of data values to business requirements and acceptance criteria. It uses routines, often called *validation rules* or *check routines*, that check for correctness, meaningfulness, and security of the data that is inputted in the system. The rules may be implemented through the automated facilities of a data dictionary or by the inclusion of explicit application program validation logic.

Data validation generally can be defined as a systematic process that compares a body of data to the requirements in a set of documented acceptance criteria. A data validation tool can provide data quality checks based on implemented standards and provide metrics to gauge data quality. The vision and ultimate goals of a data validation tool in drug development include:

- Be able to check CRF (Case Report Form), Central Lab, SDTM (Study Data Tabulation Model), ADaM (Analysis Data Model) data, and define.xml file against CDISC standards and company-specific requirements to ensure that the company receives, produces, and submits quality data.
- Align with the MDR to ensure metadata validation.
- Automate and streamline data validation processes.

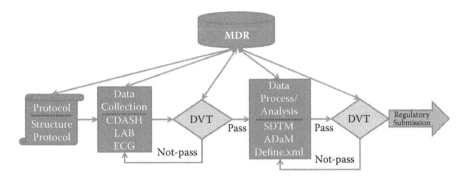

FIGURE 4.6
Data validation process through a streamlined drug development workflow.

To develop a successful data validation tool, a validation governance process and company-specific data validation requirements need to be set up and developed based on business needs and processes. For business applications, data validation can be defined through declarative data integrity rules, or procedure-based business rules. Data that does not conform to these rules will negatively affect business process execution. Therefore, data validation should start with business process definition and a set of business rules within this process. The data validation rules will be based on already developed industry standard data checks, such as SDTM data validation checks, ADaM data validation checks, define. xml checks, SEND data checks, plus will-be developed CDASH data validations checks, and Central Lab data validation checks. In addition, company-specific data validation requirements will be developed based on the company's business needs. Figure 4.6 illustrates interactions between drug development life cycle and data validation tools using MDR. The DVT can play a role as a gateway guard for outsourced study activities. For an example, before CROs, EDC (electronic data capture) vendors, or other third parties are able to deliver data to an analyst, the data must be loaded into the data validation tool, and pass the DVT checks. If the data does not pass the validation rules, the loaded data will be returned to the sender. The senders are responsible for ensuring that the data satisfies all data requirements and then correcting any data issues. The DVT also can help an enterprise to improve the communications among different functional groups, CROs, EDC vendors, and central labs.

The example of DVT's capabilities, possible rules, and users is demonstrated in Figure 4.7. To build an efficient DVT tool, we can leverage CDISC standard checks, which are developed by CDISC with our specific

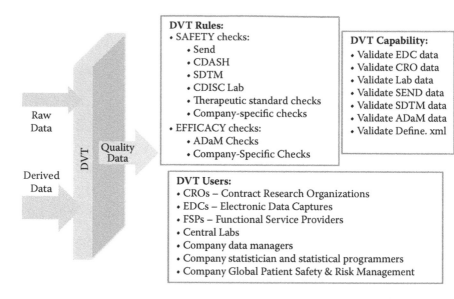

Raw
Data

Derived
Data

DVT

Quality
Data

DVT Rules:
- SAFETY checks:
  - Send
  - CDASH
  - SDTM
  - CDISC Lab
  - Therapeutic standard checks
  - Company-specific checks
- EFFICACY checks:
  - ADaM Checks
  - Company-Specific Checks

DVT Capability:
- Validate EDC data
- Validate CRO data
- Validate Lab data
- Validate SEND data
- Validate SDTM data
- Validate ADaM data
- Validate Define. xml

DVT Users:
- CROs – Contract Research Organizations
- EDCs – Electronic Data Captures
- FSPs – Functional Service Providers
- Central Labs
- Company data managers
- Company statistician and statistical programmers
- Company Global Patient Safety & Risk Management

FIGURE 4.7
Data validation tool's (DVT) basic capabilities, potential users, and some requirements.
CROs, EDCs, FSPs, and Central Labs are external activities.

validations rules. This will include checks from SEND, CDASH, SDTM, ADaM, and define.xml, plus the company's specific data checks. This DVT will be able to check data from EDC, CROs, and different central labs. The possible users can be in-house users, such as data managers, statistical programmers, statisticians, clinicians, and program/project managers; in addition, the outsourced partners are possible users. With the efficient DVT tools designed, developed, and implemented, we can achieve high-quality data goals with the help of data governance and standards.

Next, we would like to summarize some experiences and lessons learned from quality data management.

Experiences and Lessons Learned

To solve root cause data quality problems: Organizations spend lots of valuable time cleaning up data quality problems in the data warehouse and business intelligence environment, when a more proactive strategy could save time, ensure more reliable information, and ultimately help business workers make better decisions. You should solve the root cause data quality problem and focus on being more proactive when designing or updating data quality management strategies. The decision to design a more proactive data quality management strategy comes from upstream data quality management. It is difficult to justify an investment in improving the data capture and validation processes that occur "upstream" from the data warehouse. The ROI may be difficult to measure; instead, most organizations opt for data quality tools that are geared toward normalizing data in the warehouse. Such "downstream" tools are easier to justify because they produce tangible results more quickly. This downstream data quality strategy will not solve the root problem; it is just chasing its tail when implementing batch data quality within the data warehouse. Another possible root cause is likely a lack of proper training.

Maintain/update the data quality system: To focus on the system/application that is causing the most data quality issues. When you are trying to be proactive, don't try to identify every single point of data capture and update them. Try to identify which systems or applications or processes or teams are impacting the highest volume of valuable data and start using that as your pilot. Be careful not to take a siloed approach. When focusing on individual processes, be sure to keep enterprise-wide data governance goals in mind.

Realize the importance of data governance for achieving a high quality data: If the data definitions, business rules, and KPIs are created but not used in any business processes, a data governance effort won't produce business value. The governance process needs to be a complete feedback loop in which data is defined, monitored, processed, and changed when appropriate. Creating data governance without implementing these items is like getting blueprints drawn, but never building a house. Data governance sponsorship should have buy-in from business executives; however, the people from the business side need to do more, such as to create the data definitions, business rules, and KPIs for a data governance problem; achieve agreement on them across an organization; enforce usage and compliance; and ensure that the definitions, rules, and KPIs are updated on an ongoing basis as business needs evolve and change. The reality is that, in the vast majority of cases, data governance tasks are merely tacked on to the already overloaded schedules of business managers instead of being made a priority, with other responsibilities correspondingly getting taken off their to-do lists. Without a real business resource commitment, data governance will take a back seat to the daily firefight and will never be implemented effectively. One thing most organizations have gotten right on the enterprise data governance efforts is creating a governance steering committee and a separate governance working group. However, it is important to set them up at the right time when your business needs it. Do not overload committees; the more people on each committee, the more politics come into play and the more watered down governance responsibilities become. To be successful, try to limit the size of a committee to between 6 and 12 people and make sure that committee members have the required decision-making authority.

Do not try to boil the ocean: The significant trap that many data quality efforts fall into is trying to solve all of an organization's data problems in the initial phase of the project. You need to think globally and act locally; in other words, data problems need to be broken down into incremental deliverables. "Too big, too fast" will not help you to resolve data quality problems. It is much more costly to fix data quality errors downstream than it is at the point of origin. Usually a specific data quality problem was identified and project initiated and delivered to be resolved. This approach was characterized by a heavy emphasis on data cleansing, a one-off process where shortcomings were recognized and quantified and improvements made. The end result was that data cleanse became a regular, reactive, routine activity, with some data sources cleansed again and again. Often the data quality improvement achieved was not sustainable. Moreover, these tactical approaches failed to recognize a critical truth about data quality—the places in the organization where the problems originated.

Technology alone will not solve data quality issues: People may think that buying a master data management, data integration, or data quality software will solve enterprise data quality problems. However, this is not always true. You still need internal interactions, such as setting up data governance guidance and processes, creating your own data validation rules, and change management and many more, in place. Let the business drive the data quality implementation. All too often, an organization will move rapidly from a business imperative to a technology imperative. Soon, the organization is purchasing software, hiring systems integrators, and starting toward a data quality initiative. However, improving data quality is a complex project; it is the quality culture within an organization. Successful data quality efforts have two goals in mind: (1) planning for a long-term success (the organization must establish a vision for high-quality data and establish the long-term objectives), and (2) delivering against short-term goals.

Quality data requires a dedicated culture shift across the enterprise: Quality data requires a cross-functional effort involving resources (both people and monetary) and mindshare. The problem will involve key stakeholders from across the organization.

Data quality measuring: You cannot improve what you cannot measure, so we need a means for measuring the data quality. Once the systems and the data quality rules are identified and the data is characterized, scoring the data quality needs to be performed. Scoring represents the state of the data quality for identified data quality rules, and it is a relative measure of conformance to rules.

Responsibility of data stewards: The data steward is responsible for tracking and improving data across the company supply chain, ensuring the trustworthiness of business data. This includes monitoring data quality and fitness for purpose, and demonstrating measurable benefits of data management to lines of business, business processes, and systems. Data stewards also participate in data governance activities, serving as the connectors between data governance and data management communities within the organization. Without strict controls, an organization has no idea when or how changes were made, who made them, or why an original entry was altered. Thus, corporations run the risk of owning multiple versions of the same information or building a business model on faulty data. To avoid errors and confusion, and to ensure corporations create and adhere to stringent information governance controls, best practices suggest that leading organizations employ data stewards who determine, describe, and administer the company's business policies and data definitions. Data stewards steer their company's information policies and pilot employees through the deluge of data housed in multiple databases throughout the corporation.

CONCLUSIONS

In this chapter, we have defined data quality and suggested some data quality strategies under data governance by implementing data standards. We also introduced some standard implementation methodologies and shared some data quality best practices. To achieve high data quality, we need the right governance, strategy, methodology, technology, and culture, and we should think globally, act locally, start from small, and scale up to create values.

REFERENCES

1. Zhang, J. Z., and S. Dubman. 2011. Quality by design: Automating validation of standards-based data, end to end. *Contract Pharma*: 88–93.
2. Zhang, J. Z., and S. Dubman. 2011. Quality data depends on quality governance. *Pharmaceutical Executive* (June): 2–14.
3. SearchDataManagement. 2010. Uncover the real costs behind poor data quality, E-Guide. Online at searchdatamanagement@techtarget.com
4. Esserman, L. 2011. Putting precompetitive/new trial models into practice: The I SPY-2 experience. Paper presented at the NCI Translational Science Meeting, Washington, D.C., July 28–29.
5. Munos, B. 2009. Lessons from 60 years of pharmaceutical innovation. *Nature Reviews Drug Discovery* 8: 959–968.
6. Paul, S. M., D. S. Mytelka, C. T. Dunwiddie, C. C. Persinger, B. H. Munos, S. R. Lindborg, and A. L. Schacht. 2010. How to improve R&D productivity: The pharmaceutical industry's grand challenges. *Nature Reviews Drug Discovery* 9: 203–214.
7. Collins, F. S. 2011. Reengineering translational science: The time is right. *Science Translational Medicine* 3 (90): 6.
8. Financial Services Technology. Online at: http://www.usfst.com/article/Enterprise-Content-Management-getting-started/
9. MIT Sloan Experts. Online at: http://mitsloanexperts.wordpress.com/2011/05/18/riding-the-rising-information-wave-are-you-swamped-or-swimming-mit-hosts-experts/
10. *Christian Science Monitor*. Online at: http://www.csmonitor.com/Business/The-Reformed-Broker/2011/0609/Big-Data-hits-Wall-Street
11. Seck, M., and D. D. Evans. 2004. *Major U.S. cities using national standard fire hydrants: One century after the great Baltimore fire (NISTIR 7158)*. Gaithersburg, MD: National Institute of Standards and Technology.
12. CDISC Business Case for Standards. Online at: http://www.cdisc.org/stuff/contentmgr/files/0/ff2953ea8dbc8e81080f0e44ba6714c7/misc/businesscasesummarywebmar09.pdf

5

Semantic Analytics and Ontologies

O. Takaki, N. Izumi, K. Murata, and K. Hasida

CONTENTS

INTRODUCTION

This chapter explains semantic analytics in data governance (DG) by introducing a framework to define quality indicators and to calculate their values based on medical databases, where quality indicators are measures of medical service quality, which are represented by numerical values. Most importantly, we introduce an ontology called Medical Service Ontology (MSO) as an example of an ontology that plays the central role in semantic analytics.

Semantic analytics plays an important role in DG. The term *semantic analytics* in this chapter refers to a technique used for semantically analyzing, retrieving, integrating, or managing data resources in several databases and on the Internet using ontologies. In fact, it is one of DG's primary roles to manage and utilize the data accumulated by an organization and to use that data for the organizational decision making. However, for this purpose, it is essential to be able to deal with data in an integrated manner beyond differences in data formats or expressions. Semantic analytics judges the semantic identity or similarity between data beyond syntactic differences, making it possible to collectively deal with the same or similar data from data resources in various formats. Moreover, ontologies are important as the fundamental tools of current semantic analysis.

We here explain a role of ontology in semantic analytics by natural language processing (NLP). NLP is an area of research and application that explores how computers can be used to understand and manipulate natural language text or speech to do useful things [Chowdhury, 2003]. NLP can be regarded as a basic theory of semantic analytics. Knowledge used in the four stages of analysis in NLP—morphological analysis, syntactic analysis, semantic analysis, and context analysis—can roughly be divided into the following two types: constraints and preferences. Constraints judge whether a given document satisfies the requirements, whereas preferences are used for selecting the analysis result of a given sentence that is considered the best. Further, while reasoning is considered a major approach for realizing constraints, ontologies are considered a major approach for realizing preferences. In other words, while constraints regard the structural analysis of a document as important, the analysis of the vocabulary comprising a document plays an important role in determining the preferences. Because the structural analysis of sentences and a vocabulary analysis, in fact, could be conducted with reference to the analysis results of each other, both the techniques (reasoning and ontologies) are required for analysis in natural language processing. This chapter presents, in particular, a discussion on the topic with a focus on ontologies.

Below, we explain the MSO that is introduced in [Takaki et al., 2012] to define quality indicators. We also briefly explain a framework to define quality indicators by using MSO and to calculate its value based on medical databases as an example of semantic analytics in medical service domains. We call the framework *QI-framework*. MSO provides unified vocabulary to describe assessment of medical service quality and to define quality indicators, and QI-framework helps accurately compare medical service quality among multiple hospitals based on databases of the hospitals. Medical staffs, including managers of hospitals, have to make judgments based on values of quality indicators, which provide a benchmark of hospitals based on data in medical databases. Thus, one can consider QI-framework to be a typical example of semantic analytics in medical service domains.

The first section (Ontology) will present an overview of this subject. The next section (Semantic Analytics) will provide a brief overview of semantic analytics in natural language processing and a semantic web. The following section is A Framework for Definition and Calculation of Quality Indications, which will explain the MSO and QI-framework. In the final two sections, we will introduce several related works and explain the results.

ONTOLOGY

In this chapter, ontology is explained. First, is a simple definition of ontologies and purposes for constructing ontologies from the viewpoint of knowledge co-creations. Next, referring to [Noy and McGuinness, 2001] and [Mizoguchi 2003], we will briefly explain the construction of ontology. Finally, we will briefly explain a standard ontology language for a semantic web.

Definition of Ontologies

Although the definitions of ontology vary according to different publications, the most well known is that of ontology being "explicit formal specifications of the terms in the domain and relations among them" [Gruber, 1993]. In this chapter, we adopt this definition and explain ontology as either a discipline that appropriately clarifies important concepts and their origins in order to achieve a given purpose or a corresponding research, or a product of this clarification. However, the scope and extent of clarification stated here is limited; it is important to the extent that it fulfills one purpose appropriately.

Purposes for Constructing Ontologies

The reasons for constructing ontologies are diverse, and only a small number of these reasons, the typical or the essential ones, are mentioned here. First, the direct purposes of ontology construction are "knowledge co-creation," that is, creation, sharing, and management of specific knowledge. To elaborate, they are as follows:

1. Clarification and systematization of knowledge
2. Sharing of knowledge
3. Reuse and appropriation of knowledge
4. Agreement with respect to the considered knowledge

The term *knowledge* refers to information that can be clarified, systematized, and shared, and the knowledge directly dealt with in ontology construction is explicitly expressed and is named.

Data governance is a process by which organizations control the definition, usage, access, and security of the information they own and manage by using metadata, taxonomies, and ontologies, and it contributes to organizational success through repeatable and compliant practices. So, knowledge co-creation forms the basis for data governance. We will discuss next how this "knowledge" is expressed using ontologies.

The aforementioned four purposes, in many cases, are achieved not individually but together because they seem to have a symbiotic relationship. In particular, in the case of agreement with respect to the considered knowledge (point 4), not only is the agreement on the contents or definitions of individual pieces of knowledge but also the agreement on the handling of knowledge is reached through ontology construction in parallel with points 1, 2, and 3 given above. Here, the agreement on the handling of knowledge means that on how extensive the domain that should be recognized as knowledge is, how thorough the knowledge to be analyzed or clarified is, and how the considered knowledge should be used.

In addition, the creation, sharing, and management of knowledge is carried out by a single person or by several people and in collaboration with a single computer or multiple computer systems (or something that can deal with knowledge in the same way as computer systems).

Further, the purposes of such acts as the creation, sharing, and management of knowledge are numerous. Following are some of the typical ones:

1. Building and management of systems in a broad sense (models, databases, information systems, processes, protocols, etc.)
2. Collaboration by a number of people or over a long period of time
3. Integration and standardization of the existing systems and work

Here, we will cover the building of a medical information retrieval system as an example of the purpose of ontology construction. The objective is to build a system that searches across multiple medical databases for specific patient records, etc., or across multiple medical information systems for files pertinent to specific patient records. Further, this retrieval system should retrieve not only what matches the given keywords textually, but also what is semantically related.

It is important to be able to assume on a semantic level what keywords are used in the retrieval system. That is, it is important to know the domains of keywords searched by users and the meanings that these keywords are assumed to have. For instance, it is necessary to decide among pertinent healthcare domains of the medically established concepts which of the basic information to deal with as a search criteria. For example concepts of illnesses, drugs, etc., of patients or concepts pertinent to medical acts (processes and records of acts), to deal with as search criteria. In addition, the systematization of the individual concepts of illnesses, drugs, etc., namely, the positioning of concepts and the giving of meaning to concepts, is necessary in dealing with semantic relations between key-words. Furthermore, it then may be necessary to clarify concepts that have not been clarified or have not gained a common consensus, such as "patient notation information" and "medical acts." On the other hand, it also would be necessary to decide what aspects of the established concepts of illnesses, drugs, etc., to systematize and in how much detail, etc.

In the next section, we will discuss what is built through ontologies for such creation, sharing, and management of knowledge including the systematization and clarification of knowledge.

Construction of Ontologies

In this section, the construction of ontology (in other words, what ontology represents and how it is built) will be explained.

It was stated previously that the direct purpose of building an ontology is the creation, sharing, and management of knowledge. Furthermore, even though we did not clearly define the term *knowledge*, we did state that it is an intermediary wherein the creation, sharing, and management is carried out through the cooperation of individuals and systems. Therefore, in this section, we will assume that ontology is represented by this intermediary.

Ontology as an expression of the above-mentioned knowledge is formed by a series of parts. These parts also can be defined in various ways. In this section, we will introduce one of the most well-known definitions, the definition of a component, according to [Noy and McGuinness, 2001].

- Concepts (also often referred to as classes)
- Properties (also often referred to as slots)
- Axioms (also often referred to as facets or constraints)
- Instance

Concepts (Classes)

Concepts are entities that are recognized as parts having a certain consistency or can be seen as existing independently. For example, in ontology related to medical treatment, the words *patient* (in relation to the person who receives the medical services) or *operation* (in relation to a form of medical service) can be considered to be typical concepts. A name (or label) is assigned to each class.

When knowledge is created, shared, and managed, it is important to clarify where this knowledge is aimed (with respect to the size, scope, and level of detail). Concepts should be treated as the main point of knowledge, and the range and scope of this knowledge can be clarified further by noting these concepts.

Concepts are the key parts of ontology. The other elements can be considered to be parts that define these concepts. In fact, if a concept name is known as *vocabulary*, the vocabulary is determined by writing down the concepts, while the meaning of the vocabulary is determined by writing down properties and axioms, which will be explained in the following sections. For this reason, ontology is often called a *concept dictionary* or a *vocabulary system.*

The concepts in ontology are often equated with sets. However, this does not mean that concepts necessarily have to be interpreted as a set. For example, there exists a debate on what elements concepts, such as "time" or "space," relate to.

Properties (Slots)

The definition of concepts is implemented by the relation of other concepts. A group of relation R and concept D, which has a relation with concept C, is known as properties of C. Relations are often considered important from the perspective of concepts. Therefore, properties are often equated with relations.

Some of the typical properties include:

- "Is-a" relation: For two concepts C and D, in cases where D is a special form of C, it is said that D has an is-a relation to C. In cases where C and D are seen as a set, as D becomes a partial set of C, frequently, it is called a subclassOf relation. For certain concepts, the base concept must be considered. This is a very basic question related to concept definition. Hence, this property is one of the most fundamental ones.
- "Has-a" relation: This is one of the most representative methods used while trying to define some concepts and then trying to define the other concepts depending on these concept parts. In cases where concept C has parts of concept D, C and D are said to have a has-a relation. C is also said to have D as a part of C.

- Attribute: Most concepts, when seen from certain aspects, have certain characteristics. For example, when one considers the concept of a [Human], it has certain characteristics, such as [sex] and [birth date], that are innate. These characteristics are known as base concepts and attributes. Frequently in this section, when C has attributes (R, D) against the relation R, R is known as a (C, D) attribute relation.

Axioms

Here, axiom refers to the conditioning constraints for the definitions of concepts and properties.

Ontology is an expression of knowledge, and the most important parts of ontology are concepts. Through properties and axioms, it is said that the meaning of these concepts (details) is defined. Commonly, while defining something, it is important to provide an example. Here, instances serve as an example of concepts.

The above is an explanation of ontological parts. Ontology is frequently described using graphs. In these cases, a graph's nodes represent the concepts, and the graph's edges represent the properties (for the relation). Furthermore, ontology is composed of concepts, properties, and axioms, while instances are examples of ontology. Hence, in this discourse, often instances are provided as ontology examples and are considered different from ontology.

Representation of Linguistic Vocabulary on a Semantic Web

The World Wide Web was developed as a framework for actualizing the creation, sharing, and management of knowledge through the Internet. Through the association of hypermedia documents, the Web has provided a series of foundations for the integrated management of decentralized information ([W3C, 2012] and [Berners-Lee and Cailliau, 1990]). In a semantic web, the system will interpret the information in the hypermedia documents, and such a framework can make possible the collaboration and the joint manipulation of information between humans and a computer system (cf. [W3C, 2012]). In order to achieve the integration of knowledge on the basis of a semantic web, it is necessary to decide upon a framework for compiling the vocabulary to be used as part of this information. In this section, we will provide short descriptions of RDF, RDFS, and OWL, which serve as the fundamental parts of the framework related to the vocabulary proposed for a semantic web.

Data governance is a process by which online marketing and Web analytics organizations define and manage different types and categories of data related to behavior tracking, audience measurement, e-commerce, and other aspects of online business. Synonymous with "quality control," data governance strives to ensure companies have reliable and consistent datasets to assess performance and make management decisions. While data governance is one of the least visible aspects of Web analytics, it's easily one of the most impactful [Hassert, 2011]. RDF, RDFS, and OWL provide a standard framework of vocabulary for the Web analytics or the semantic analytics on a semantic web.

RDF (Resource Description Framework)

RDF is a mechanism for describing resources. Here, the term *resource* refers to all the concepts that can be identified on the Web.

RDF is represented by triples, indicating the subject (who), the predicate (what), and the value. These representations are often confronted with the table data in the relation database. In other words, it is a representation method showing "from which item," "in which lines," and "having what value." On the basis of an RDF triple, information constructed by hypermedia documents can be described using charts.

RDFS (Resource Description Framework Schema)

RDFS is the framework that defines the vocabulary in an RDF graph. The nodes in an RDF graph, namely, subjects and objects in RDF triples, are defined by the classes or literals. On the other hand, edges are defined by properties. Therefore, the definition of the expression of classes and properties in RDFS is important.

The foundational vocabulary for an RDF schema has the following classes as a basis ([Brickley and Guha, 2004] and [Kanzaki, 2005]):

rdfs:Resource	Class for all the resources described by RDF
rdfs:Class	Entirety of classes in RDF
rdfs:Literal	Entirety of literals described by RDF
rdfs:Datatype	Entirety of RDF data types
rdf:XMLLiteral	Entirety of data types of XLM character string

At the same time, as these classes have rdfs:Datatype instances, there also exist rdfs:Literal subclasses.

rdf:Property Entirety of properties in RDF

The following basic properties also are defined as the fundamental relationships between classes [Brickley and Guha, 2004]:

rdfs:range	Relationship between property and community class
rdfs:domain	Relationship between property and domain class
rdfs:type	Relationship between resources and their data types
rdfs:subClassOf	Relationship between classes and their upper classes
rdfs:subPropertyOf	Relationship between properties and upper properties
rdfs:label	Relationship between labels relative to the resources
rdfs:comment	Relationship between comments relative to the resources

These representations are obtained by constructing the basic classes at the beginning and then built upon by a hierarchy structure of classes, extension of classes, etc. In other words, they are obtained by constructing a set of instance classes.

Figure 5.1 shows an example of a patient's hospitalization as defined using RDF.

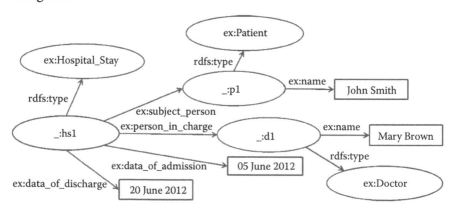

FIGURE 5.1
RDF graph defining hospitalization (graphical representation).

The chart in Figure 5.1 is created by focusing on three blank nodes of _:hs1, _:p1, and _:d1, which denote "admission," "admitted subject," and "person in-charge," respectively. It is constructed with two RDF triples from the relations of these three nodes: "datatype," "admission," and "date of admission and discharge" of each of the three blank nodes, and seven RDF triples formed by the names of "admitted subject," "person in-charge," and so on. Furthermore, in this chart, there are uniquely defined properties that have the "prefix" of two basic properties mentioned earlier: "rdfs:type" and "ex" properties.

OWL (Web Ontology Language)

Although RDFS provides the basis for building ontology in an RDF framework, in order to perform a series of operations (such as the deduction of ontology), an enhanced framework is required, such as that which ensures the possibility of calculations related to such operations. For these purposes, OWL is used as a framework for defining the constraint conditions, such as a more specific method to construct classes and properties, the number of units, or the comparability among classes and instances.

OWL can be divided into three languages—OWL Lite, OWL DL, and OWL Full—in accordance with the computability of the classes and properties structured by these frameworks. OWL DL consists of expressiveness; in other words, it has the same level of expressiveness as the description logic SHOIN(D) with respect to the definability of classes and properties. This implies that the compatibility of a series of managements of classes and properties defined on the basis of OWL DL and the limit of complexity are assured.* In contrast, even though OWL Full consists of higher levels of expressiveness as compared to OWL DL, compatibility is not assured. On the other hand, OWL Lite is considered to be simpler and more legible than OWL DL, and it consists of the same level of expressiveness as the description logic SHIF(D) that has less complexity than SHOIN(D).

The vocabulary of OWL is given by defining *axioms* based on the following basic class descriptions: "owl:Class," "owl:Thing," and "owl:Nothing"

---

* Complexity here refers to the complexity in inferring inclusive relations among constructed classes. In this book, we will not discuss the definition of Compatibility, Complexity, or Description Logic. (Horrocks et al., 2003) and (Horrocks et al., 2007).

and other class descriptions, where an axiom denotes a definition of a class, a property, or an individual of OWL.

owl:Class   It is used to define a concept. Each individual should belong to a subclass of this class.

owl:Thing   It denotes the set of individuals in OWL.

owl:Nothing   It denotes the empty set. It should be a subclass of every class of OWL.

Axioms in OWL can be divided into class axioms, property axioms, individual axioms, restrictions, descriptions, and data types. They are defined to construct concepts and properties, to restrict classes, properties, or individuals, or to verify their consistency. In OWL, each axiom is usually described as a RDF triple.

See Table 5.1 for class and property axioms of OWL Lite. For other axioms, we refer the interested reader to the language specification [Hitzler et al., 2009].

SEMANTIC ANALYTICS

In this section, we will briefly introduce semantic analytics, mainly that of text described by natural language and charts, and semantic analysis on a semantic web. All of these technologies make use of ontologies.

One of the major challenges when integrating information systems in any domain, especially in healthcare, is the challenge of interoperability, such as integration of vocabulary for electronic health records or semantic integration of biomedical data warehouses. There are three aspects of interoperability: technical, semantic, and organizational. The semantic analytics deals with sharing the same understanding (semantics) of exchanged information among all applications and services.

With respect to DG, semantic analytics plays an important role in referring to the data in multiple databases; however, in order to do this, it is necessary to search and identify the data that have to be referred to and managed for a specific condition. To accomplish this, the semasiological analytics of condition text or data is needed. Here, the semantic analytics of language processing and semantic web plays an important role.

TABLE 5.1

Class and Property Axioms of OWL Lite

Class axioms of OWL Lite as RDF triples	Short explanation in the first order logic
Class (A partial S1,...,Sn)	The extension of A is included in each extension of Si (i = 1,...,n); here the extension of A denotes the set of instances of A.
Class (A complete S1,...,Sn)	The extension of A is the same as the intersection of all extensions of S1, ..., Sn.
EquivalentClasses(A1,...,An)	A1, ..., An-1 and An share the same extension.

Property axioms of OWL Lite as RDF triples	
DatatypeProperty (T	Short explanation in the first order logic
super(T1)...super(Tn)	The extension of T is included in every extension of Ti (i = 1,...,n).
[Functional]	For each x, y, and z, if T(x, y) and T(x,z), then y = z, where T(x,y) denotes that the extension of T contains (x,y).
domain(d1)...domain(dm)	For each i = 1,...,m and for each x and y, if T(x, y), then di(x), where di(x) denotes that the extension of di' contains x.
range(d'1)...range(d'l))	For each i = 1,...,l and for each x and y, if T(x, y), then d'i(y).
ObjectProperty (R	
super(R1)...super(Rn)	The extension of R is included in every extension of Ri (i = 1,...,n).
[InverseOf R0]	For each x and y, R(x, y) if and only if R0(y, x).
[Symmetric]	For each x and y, if R(x, y), then R(y, x).
[Functional]	For each x, y, and z, if R(x, y) and R(x,z), then y = z.
[InverseFunctional]	For each x, y, and z, if R(x, z) and R(y,z), then x = y.
domain(A1)...domain(Am)	For each i = 1,...,m and for each x and y, if R(x, y), then Ai(x).
range(A'1)...range(A'l))	For each i = 1,...,l and for each x and y, if R(x, y), then A'i(y).
EquivalentProperties(X1,...,Xn)	X1, ..., Xn-1 and Xn share the same extension.
Subproperty(X1, X2)	The extension of X1 is included in that of X2.

In the following subsections, we first will explain semantic analytics, which uses natural language text as input data. Then, we will briefly explain the semantic web and semantic analytics, which use the conditional expressions of a chart's description as input data. Finally, we will explain semantic analysis on a semantic web.

Semantic Analysis Based on Natural Language Text

Below, we explain semantic analysis on natural language texts. It becomes a basic theory of NLP and semantic analytics on a semantic web.

In data governance, it is important to identify relevant data and to reason similarity and equivalence of given data among data. To this end, it needs to analyze data in different formats or vocabularies in a coherent manner. A semantic approach of analyzing data is one of the most standard approaches for such analysis.

Several previous studies have been conducted on semantic analytics in which natural language text is used as the input data. Semantic analytics is part of a four-step analysis in natural language management: morpheme analytics, syntax analytics, semantic analytics, and context analytics. In this section, we will briefly explain existing semantic analytics in natural language management on the basis of [Allen, 1995] and [Okumura, 2012].

Morpheme analytics and syntax analytics analyze and structure the grammar of natural language text. On the other hand, semantic analytics analyzes and structures the meaning of this text. This is similar to assigning semantic analytics to structured text that is based on grammar through syntax analysis. Here, the term *semantic structure* means that it is structured on the basis of the semantic relations among words.

The relations among words in a text are known as cases. The relations of syntax are called *surface cases*, and the relations of semantics are called *deep cases*. [Fillmore, 1969] concentrated on specific words expressing the behavior of words centered in a text and suggested a series of major deep cases by focusing on the word relations. Semantic analytics can be defined using conceptual cases as follows: If each word (basic form) that leads to the formation of text S and the cases of these words are obtainable, semantic analytics can be defined as the revelation of the deep cases of each word and the meaning of each word simultaneously. In real-life languages, such as Japanese and English, a word or its surface case that are characterized by grammar structures generally may have multiple deep cases or meanings.

This is known as ambiguity in word interpretation. In order to analyze the definition from surface case to deep case on the basis of other information in each word, an ontology to record the relations of "surface case–deep case–definition" (also known as a corpus or a case frame) is applied.

There are several studies on semantic analysis using ontology. However, the most well-known study deals with the application of an ontology, such as the one mentioned above, by calculating the "relativity of each word W and the surrounding word V" and "the repetition or possibilities" to the derivation of the deep case of W and the likely meaning. For more details, refer to [Allen, 1995], [Fillmore, 1969], or [Jurafsky and Martin, 2009].

Semantic Analysis Based on Conditional Expression of Graph-Based Representation

In current natural language management technology, it is still difficult to efficiently conduct semantic analytics on the general text of a natural language. Therefore, instead of using natural language text, we are considering executing semantic analytics and syntax analytics in parallel with the structure of "representation and the meaning," which are designed without any interpretation ambiguity. "Structure analytics" and "semantic analytics" of these kinds of artificial text probably have a different meaning with respect to the essential structure analytics and semantic analytics in the field of natural language management. However, in this section, we have broadened these meanings and we still consider conducting a structure analysis on the text with these kinds of artificial language as "structure analytics" and "semantic analytics."

Artificial language texts usually have a representation "tree" or a "more commonly used chart." Semantic analytics can be easily carried out for this kind of artificial text representation because such text can be said to have a unique meaning.

In the fourth section (A Framework for Definition and Calculation of Quality Indications) of this chapter, a graph-based representation, such as the one mentioned above, will be used to signify the conditional statement of a quality indicator, where a care quality indicator means an indicator of a medical service quality. Further, we will introduce a framework for performing a calculation on the quality indicator value from several medical care databases on the basis of the semantic analytics of these quality indicators from the graph-based representation. Furthermore, in the last part of the fourth section, we will introduce a method for calculating the quality indicator value and the semantic analytics of quality indicators from conditional statements where the representation is close to a natural language.

Semantic Analytics on a Semantic Web

The essence of semantic analytics on a semantic web is to detect *semantic associations* in information over the Internet, analyze them from every point of view, and organize them. Here, semantic associations are "meaningful and relevant complex relationships between entities, events and concepts" [Aleman-Meza et al., 2005]. Semantic associations help figure out or characterize a lot of entities on the Web as those carrying inherent meanings.

For semantic associations over information in certain languages, one can give more formal definitions to semantic associations based on the languages. For example, in [Anyanwu and Sheth, 2003], semantic associations in an RDF graph are given a formal definition that two entities e1 and en are semantically associated if there exists a sequence e1, p1, e2, p2, e3, …, en-1, pn-1, en in an RDF graph where ei, $1 \leq i \leq n$, are entities and pj, $1 \leq j < n$, are properties (see also [Aleman-Meza et al., 2005]).

Semantic associations enable the analyzing of data on the Web at the semantic level and the utilization of the data for more sophisticated purposes including data checking, ranking, retrieving, discovering hidden patterns of data, and detecting inconsistency in data. For example, [Aleman-Meza et al., 2005] apply semantic association to the insider threat application, which involves validation of legitimate access of documents. On the other hand, [Aleman-Meta et al., 2006] and [Aleman-Meta et al., 2008] address conflict of interest detection by using semantic association. Furthermore, [Anyanwu, Maduko, and Sheth, 2005] rank search results on a semantic web that have complex relationships based on semantic association.

A FRAMEWORK FOR DEFINITION AND CALCULATION OF QUALITY INDICATIONS

In this section, we will introduce a representation system of quality indicators that is based on MSO as an example of ontology and semantic analytics for data governance in the medical service domain.

Quality Indicators

Quality indicators are measures of medical service quality that are represented numerically. A quality indicator consists of a name (or a label) and a calculating formula. For example, "fracture rate among in-patients aged 75 or older" is the name of a quality indicator [NHO, 2009], and its calculating formula is given as follows:

Calculating Formula (CF1): The data of the quality indicator above is obtained by calculating the proportion of the following values.

Numerator: The number of in-patients that satisfy the condition defined in the denominator and that broke their bones in a hospital and received treatment for the fractures.

Denominator: The number of patients that were hospitalized for three days or more, and aged 75 or older when they were admitted into the hospital.

The value that is obtained from a quality indicator by using the calculating formula and data in a hospital (or hospitals) is called "the value of a quality indicator (in a hospital (or hospitals))" or "the data of a quality indicator (in a hospital (or hospitals))." We assume that the values of quality indicators are basically calculated from data in medical databases. Though we here distinguish a quality indicator and its calculating formula, we simply will often call the calculating formula of a quality indicator by "a quality indicator," unless it makes readers get confused.

In decision making about medical services in a hospital, it needs to assess medical service quality in the hospital or to compare them among the hospital and other ones. In comparison and/or assessment of medical service quality, quality indicators play an important role as evidences of the comparison and assessment. However, it is not easy to realize appropriate comparison of medical service quality of multiple hospitals based on quality indicators. In fact, it is not straightforward to properly share the definition of a quality indicator. For example, the calculating formula CF1 has at least the following two problematic points:

1. What data should be a fact that an in-patient broke his/her bone checked by?
2. What is the definition of "treatment of bone fracture?"

These problems above cannot be solved by only the calculating formula in natural language (cf. [NHO, 2009]). Moreover, we should consider a problem of unification of structures of quality indicators. For example, in practice, CF1 should be defined to be a proportion of the numbers of hospital stays (not in-patients). In fact, there are quality indicators that have ambiguities of their structures (cf. [NHO, 2009]) or ambiguous reasons to have their structures.

To address the problems above, it is significant to establish a way to unify vocabulary of quality indicators and their interpretation including their whole structures, that is, it is significant to establish a way to develop quality indicators with easily self-checking vocabulary words, combinations of words, and whole structures of quality indicators. In such a case, natural language is not suitable for developing quality indicators with ensuring unambiguity and reasonability of their definitions. Thus, in this chapter, we introduce a representation system that enables the development of quality indicators with explicitly checking their definitions toward solving the problem.

Overview of QI-Framework

Though the purpose of this section is to introduce a representation system QI-RS of quality indicators, we briefly explain an overview of a framework QI-FW to develop quality indicators and to calculate their values based on medical databases before entering upon a discussion of QI-RS.

QI-FW consists of (1) QI-RS, (2) medical databases in hospitals, and (3) mapping systems (Figure 5.2). Moreover, QI-RS has Medical Service Ontology (MSO) as the main component. Medical staffs and system engineers who administer medical databases (and knowledge engineers, if necessary) collaborate in developing and improving MSO. We will explain QI-RS and mapping systems later.

Users of QI-FW are assessors of the medical service quality of a hospital (or hospitals) based on data in medical databases, who are supposed to be patients, medical staffs, and so forth. They can develop quality indicators in QI-RS via some interface of QI-FW. A quality indicator Q in QI-RS is expressed as a graph. Some nodes in Q are concepts in MSO, while edges in Q are properties in MSO. On the other hand, main concepts and properties in MSO are automatically translated to entities or terms in entities in Global Data Model (GDM), which is a virtual data model, under certain rules. According to the translation, Q is translated to a data $(Q_1,..., Q_n, A)$

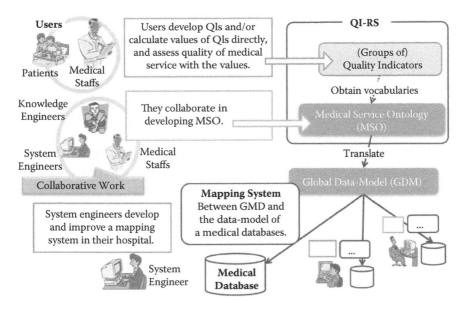

FIGURE 5.2
The overview of QI-framework.

consisting of queries $Q_1,\ldots, Q_n$ on GDM and an algorithm A on the data obtained from $Q_1,\ldots, Q_n$.

On the other hand, system engineers, who administrate a medical database *DB*, develop and improve a mapping system between GDM and the data model *DM* in *DB*. Through the mapping system, the data $(Q_1,\ldots, Q_n, A)$ above is translated to data $(Q_1^*,\ldots, Q_n^*, A^*)$ consisting of queries on *DM* and algorithms on the data obtained from the queries. By the data $(Q_1^*,\ldots, Q_n^*, A^*)$, a user can automatically obtain the values of Q in the medical databases.

Outline of QI-RS

The representation system QI-RS is developed based on an idea to regard a quality indicator as a combination of a target of quantification and a way to quantify the target and to develop the target and the way independently. For example, the calculating formula CF1, in the Quality Indicators section above, is regarded as a combination of the following components:

- The set of hospital stays of patients aged 75 or over in which they broke their bones and received treatments of bone fractures.
- The rate of the number of the hospital stays above that of hospital stays of patients aged 75 or over.

These components indicate that CF1 is determined by defining what the rate is or how the rate should be calculated as well as what the target of calculation is. Thus, we represent the target of the calculation or the quantification as a graph that we call an *objective graph*, while we represent the way to calculate it or quantify it by a concept that we call a *quantifying concept*. Moreover, objective graphs are constructed based on an ontology that we call Medical Service Ontology (MSO).

We first define MSO below, and then we briefly explain objective graphs and quantifying concepts. In this chapter, we focus on MSO, therefore, we won't go beyond briefly mentioning objective graphs and quantifying concepts.

Medical Service Ontology

In this section, we define MSO as vocabulary for calculating formulas of quality indicators. For example, the calculating formula in the above section on Quality Indicators uses several words, such as "patients," "hospitalize (hospitalization)," and "aged." In fact, to define quality indicators, it needs words for describing characters of patients, events (medical services) in hospitals, predicates about patients, and so forth.

MSO is originally introduced in [Takaki et al., 2012] and it is developed in an ontology developing tool "semantic editor" [Hasida, 2012].

Outline of MSO Concepts

We will first show main concepts in MSO and their main attributes. To describe results of assessment of medical service quality, the following vocabulary words are especially important: patients and their states, medical services in hospitals to such patients, and outcomes of such medical services. In many cases, an outcome is represented as an event that happens in a hospital. For example, death of a patient as an outcome of a surgery is represented by an event of a death discharge of a hospital. Therefore, we regard concepts related to patients, states of patients, and events in hospitals as main concepts in MSO. In the following, we will explain the main concepts and properties.

Patients

First, we show basic concepts related to patients and their attributes, as seen in Figure 5.3.

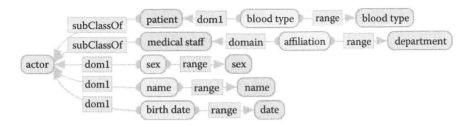

FIGURE 5.3
Basic concepts and attributes related to patients.

In this figure, dark softly-colored rounded rectangles denote concepts, and pink rounded rectangles denote attributes. In general, pink rounded rectangles in diagrams on semantic editor denote properties. In this chapter, we classify properties between concepts into attributes of concepts and relations between concepts. The concept [patient] has attributes {blood type}, {sex}, {name}, {birth}, where we describe a concept by brackets and labels and an attribute by angle brackets and labels. The values of these attributes are supposed to be basically eternal for one patient.

In defining quality indicators, it is often useful to classify patients from the viewpoint of assessment of medical service quality. The following diagram classifies patients by the aspects of states of pregnancy and childbirth, a grown process, a degree of psychosomatic disorder, and positions as hospital staffs.

A "+" mark in the diagram of Figure 5.4 denotes that there are subdiagrams from the concepts (dark rounded rectangles) with "+" marks,

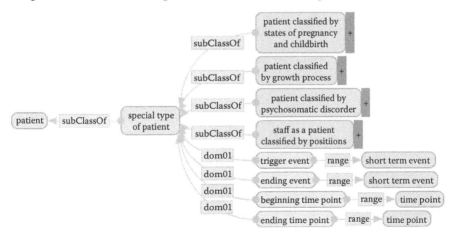

FIGURE 5.4
Patients classified by four aspects (partial).

and they are abbreviated. We omit showing the subdiagrams due to limitation of space.

Events

Next, we explain basic concepts related to events in a hospital. An event is defined to be what a medical staff or a hospital executes for a patient or what happens to him/her. Events are classified into long-term events and short-term events, and short-term events are classified into scheduled events and unscheduled events in Figure 5.5.

A long-term event usually takes multiple days. (For example, a hospital stay (a hospitalization) is a long-term event.) Basically, a long-term event is executed by a medical staff or a hospital for a patient. On the one hand, a short-term event does not basically take more than two days. For example, admission, discharge, diagnosis, examination, and operation (surgery) are typical scheduled short-term events, while death, falling, and bone fracture are typical unscheduled short-term events. In MSO, usual medical services are regarded as scheduled events, while accidents, such as deaths, are regarded as unscheduled events. Each typical event is furthermore classified into detailed classes. For example, examination events are classified into about 30 types of examinations.

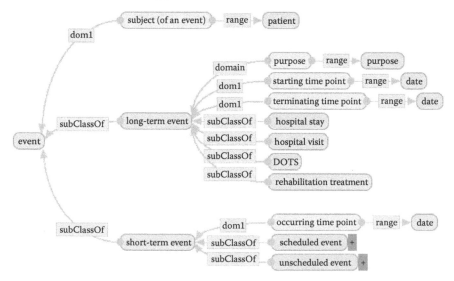

FIGURE 5.5
Basis concepts and attributes related to events (partial).

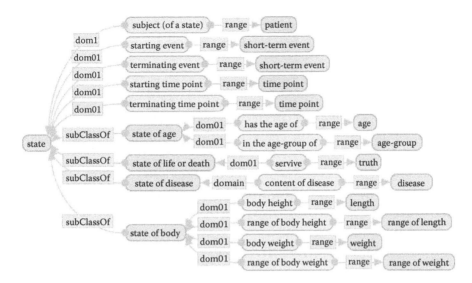

FIGURE 5.6
Basis concepts and attributes related to states of patients.

Each long-term event has attributes: the subject (target patient), purposes, the starting date, and the ending date, while each short-term event has the subject and occurring time point (see Figure 5.5). Though scheduled and unscheduled events have their own attributes, we omit their explanation due to space limitation.

States of Patients

A state of patient denotes a health state or a condition of a patient at a time point. The diagram in Figure 5.6 defines main states: age, state of life or death, state of disease that a patient possesses, and basic body properties. These states are used to describe a feature of a patient as a target of a medical service or an outcome of a patient that cannot be represented by any event.

Main Relations in MSO

In this section, we define properties in MSO that are not attributes. We call them *relations*. We define the primary relations between concepts as follows.

Relations of patients and events: The relations are defined between the concept [patient] and concepts of events. For example, the following relation denotes the relations between patients and their hospital stays (we describe a relation by angle brackets and a label).

{subject (of an event)} ≤ [patient] × [hospital stay]

Note that these relations share the same name "subject (of an event)." We omit the explanation of the relations between patients and other events due to limitation of space.

Relations of patients and states: The relations also are defined between [patient] and concepts of patients' states. For example, the following relation denotes the relationship between patients and their states of diseases.

{subject (of a state)} ≤ [patient] × [state of disease]

These relations also share the same name "subject (of a state)" and all concepts of patients' states have the attributes of starting time points and terminating time points. We also omit the explanation of the relations between patients and other states.

Relations of time ordering: The relations are also defined between the concepts of events and patients' states. For example, the following relations denote the relationships between operations.

{more than <p> before} ≤ [operation] × [operation]
{less than <p> before} ≤ [operation] × [operation]
{less than <p> after} ≤ [operation] × [operation]
{more than <p> after} ≤ [operation] × [operation]

Here, "<p>" denotes a parameter. For example, the relation {before more than <2 weeks>} consists of a pair <op_1, op_2> if op_1 and op_2 are performed and if op_1 is performed more than two weeks before op_2.

Belonging relations of events: The relations are defined between concepts of events with no term and events with terms. For example, the following relation denotes the relations between operations and hospital stays that have operations.

{belonging} ≤ [operation] × [hospital stay]

The relation contains a pair (op, sty) of an event of an operation (op) and that of a hospital stay (sty) if op is performed in the duration of sty.

Objective Graphs and Quantifying Concepts

Objective Graphs

An objective graph is defined as a finite and labeled directed graph. A node in an objective graph is labeled by a concept in MSO, a value of an attribute of a concept, or another objective graph, while an edge in an objective graph is labeled by a property in MSO. An objective graph G has a unique node called the *root node*. The label of the root node is a concept in MSO, which is called the *base concept* of the objective graph.

As an example, in Figure 5.7 and Figure 5.8, we describe the objective graphs that correspond to the sets of patients that satisfy the conditions defined in the numerator part and the denominator part, respectively, in the calculating formula in the above section on Quality Indicators.

Quantifying Concepts

A quantifying concept is a function that denotes how to extract the value from a given target that is expressed to be an objective graph. The function may have input data that are some attributes of the base concept of a given objective graph and another function on the values of the attributes above. Here, each concept is regarded as a set obtained from the concept under some circumstance. For example, in a hospital A, the concept "in-patient" is regarded as the set of in-patients in A.

There are mainly three types of quantifying concepts: (1) summation of attribute values of elements of a given objective graph, (2) ratio of the summation of attributes' values of elements of a given objective graph to that of a generalized objective graph, respectively, and (3) average of attribute values of elements of a given objective graph.

Example of a Quality Indicator in QI-RS

As an example, we describe the calculating formula of the quality indicator in the first part of this section by using QI-RS, as seen in Figure 5.9.

Note that the quality indicator in Figure 5.9 uses graphs in Figure 5.7 and Figure 5.8. Here, "rate of numbers of patients" is a quantifying concept that denotes the ratio of the sets corresponding to the patient-concepts that are targets of the event-concepts described in Figure 5.3 and Figure 5.4. We also remark that the event-concept described in Figure 5.3 is a generalized graph of another event-concept described in Figure 5.4.

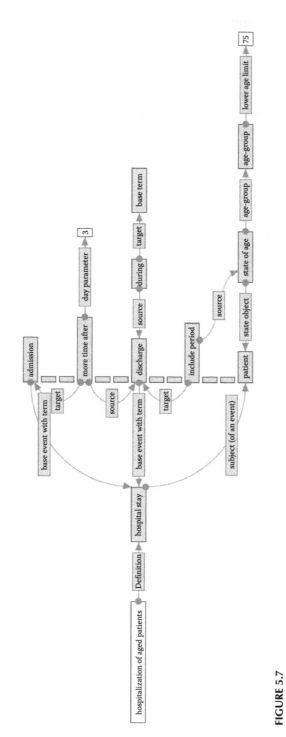

FIGURE 5.7
Hospitalization of aged patients.

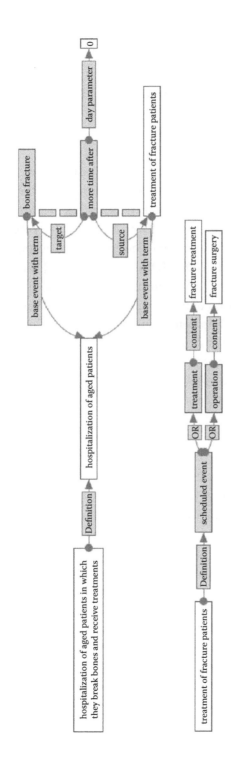

FIGURE 5.8
Hospitalization of aged patients in which they break bones and receive treatments for fractures.

FIGURE 5.9
The quality indicator in Section 1.1.1 expressed with QI-RS.

RELATED WORK

Research of quality indicators has a long history, and one can see a starting point in Nightingale's work [Nightingale, 1859]. One can see researches on the ways to define quality indicators in [Donabedian, 1980], [Mainz, 2003], and [Mainz et al., 2004]. Moreover, in recent years, comparison results of quality indicators among multiple hospitals or countries are seen in [Mainz et al., 2004], [OECD, 2006], and [Mainz et al., 2009]. Though these researches are important for actual definition of quality indicators for comparison of medical service quality, they have been done from the viewpoints of epidemiology. On the other hand, because this chapter focuses on how to describe quality indicators from the viewpoint of knowledge representation, especially, we focus on a representation of a quality indicator that satisfies understandability and formality.

Formality and understandability of ontology-based representation for medical services have been researched in [Huser et al., 2010] and [Mabotuwana and Warren, 2009]. The later authors propose a framework to indentify hypertensive patients who satisfy evidence-based criteria for quality improvement potential. They propose three issues for domain modeling: (1) shareability, (2) extensibility, and (3) easy visualization of a knowledge base for domain modeling. On the other hand, [Huser et al., 2010] establish a query system of an electronic health record data based on a flowchart that indicates processes to treat patients. The authors propose a tradeoff problem of readability and expressiveness of query representation. [Huser et al., 2010] and [Mabotuwana and Warren, 2009] focus on how to represent queries correctly and/or easily on the basis of considerably restricting the domain of the query, and their approaches are not easy to extend for evaluation of general medical service quality. This chapter enhances formality and understandability of QI-RS by MSO that provides sufficient vocabulary words to define quality indicators and by establishing a general framework of ontology-based graph representation.

For more general medical information, there are a lot of researches for ontology-based information retrieval, or ontology-based information integration (e.g., see [Hartel et al., 2005], [Kaiser, Akkaya, and Miksch, 2007], and [Serban et al., 2007]). However, to define quality indicators, it is important to provide sufficient vocabulary not only to represent concepts in medical domain, but also to cover description patterns of medical service assessment, such as "how a certain medical service was executed" or "what results were obtained from a contain medical service." In this chapter, we provide MSO and object graphs, by which we specify description patterns of medical service quality assessment, and quantifying concepts, by which we stipulate how to quantitatively represent medical service quality.

CONCLUSIONS

In this chapter, we introduce a framework QI-FW for defining and calculating quality indicators for assessment of medical services qualities in hospitals as a semantic analytics in medical service domains. In particular, we explain Medical Service Ontology (MSO) and a representation system QI-RS of quality indicators based on MSO. QI-RS is the main component of QI-FW and it helps develop quality indicators with unified vocabulary and structures. Like other semantic analytics, the ontology plays the central role to consider how to represent assessment of medical service quality and how to define quality indicators. Medical staffs including managers of hospitals have to make judgments based on values of quality indicators, which provide a benchmark of hospitals based on data in medical databases. So, one can consider QI-framework to be a typical example of semantic analytics in medical service domains.

ACKNOWLEDGEMENT

This work was supported by a JSPS KAKENHI Grant Number 24500167. The authors would like to thank Dr. Neera Bhansali for her helpful comments.

REFERENCES

[Aleman-Meza et al., 2005] Boanerges Aleman-Meza, Amit P. Sheth, Devanand Palaniswami, Matthew Eavenson, and I. Budak Arpinar. 2006. Semantic analytics in intelligence:

Applying semantic association discovery to determine relevance of heterogeneous documents. In *Advanced topics in database research*, ed. Keng Siau, pp. 401–419. Hershey, PA: Idea Group, Inc.

[Aleman-Meta et al., 2006] Boanerges Aleman-Meza, Meenakshi Nagarajan, Cartic Ramakrishnan, Li Ding, Pranam Kolari, Amit P. Sheth, I. Budak Arpinar, Anupam Joshi, and Tim Finin. 2006. Semantic analytics on social networks: Experiences in addressing the problem of conflict of interest detection. Paper presented at the proceedings of the 15th International Conference on World Wide Web (WWW '06). ACM, New York, pp. 407–416.

[Aleman-Meta et al., 2008] Boanerges Aleman-Meza, Meenakshi Nagarajan, Li Ding, Amit Sheth, I. Budak Arpinar, Anupam Joshi, and Tim Finin. 2008. Scalable semantic analytics on social networks for addressing the problem of conflict of interest detection. *ACM Transactions* Web 2, 1, Article 7 (March): 1–29.

[Allen, 1995] Allen, J. F. 1995. *Natural language understanding*. Wokingham, U.K.: Benjamin Cummings.

[Anyanwu, Maduko, and Sheth, 2005] Kemafor Anyanwu, Angela Maduko, and Amit Sheth. 2005. SemRank: Ranking complex relationship search results on the semantic web. Paper presented at the proceedings of the 14th International Conference on World Wide Web (WWW '05). ACM, New York, pp. 117–127.

[Anyanwu and Sheth, 2003] Kemafor Anyanwu and Amit Sheth. 2003. P-Queries: Enabling querying for semantic associations on the semantic web. Paper presented at the proceedings of the 12th International Conference on World Wide Web (WWW '03). ACM, New York, pp. 690–699.

[Berners-Lee and Cailliau, 1990] T. Berners-Lee and R. Cailliau. 1990. WorldWideWeb: Proposal for a HyperText project. Online at: http://www.w3.org/pub/WWW/Proposal.html

[Brickley and Guha, 2004] Dan Brickley and R. V. Guha (eds.). 2003. RDF Vocabulary Description Language 1.0: RDF Schema. Online at: http://www.w3.org/TR/rdf-schema/

[Chowdhury, 2003] Gobinda G. Chowdhury. 2003. Natural language processing. *Annual Review of Information Science and Technology* 37 (1): 51–89.

[Donabedian, 1980] A. Donabedian. 1980. *Explorations in quality assessment and monitoring, Vol. 1. The definition of quality and approaches to its assessment*. Ann Arbor, MI: Health Administration Press.

[Fillmore, 1969] Charles J. Fillmore. 1969. Toward a modern theory of case. In *Modern studies in English: Readings in transformational grammar*, eds. David A. Reibel and Sanford A. Schane. Englewood Cliffs, NJ.: Prentice-Hall.

[Gruber, 1993] Thomas R. Gruber. 1993. Toward principles for the design of ontologies used for knowledge sharing. *International Journal Human-Computer Studies* 43: 907–928.

[Hartel et al., 2005] W. Hartel, S. de Coronado, R. Dionne, G. Fragoso, and J. Golbeck. 2005. Modeling a description logic vocabulary for cancer research. *Journal of Biomedical Informatics* 38 (2): 114–129.

[Hasida, 2012] Koiti Hasida. 2012. Introduction to semantic editor. Online at: http://i-content. org/semauth/intro/index.html (in Japanese).

[Hassert, 2011] Jim Hassert. 2011. 5 reasons why data governance matters. Online at:http://analytics.infinitive.com/2011/10/13/5-reasons-why-data-governance-matters-to-your-online-business/

[Hitzler et al., 2009] Pascal Hitzler, Markus Krötzsch, Bijan Parsia, Peter F. Patel-Schneider, and Sebastian Rudolph (eds.). 2009. OWL 2 Web ontology language primer. Online at: http://www.w3.org/TR/owl2-primer/

[Horrocks et al., 2003] Ian Horrocks, Peter F. Patel-Schneider, and Frank van Harmelen. 2003. From SHIQ and RDF to OWL: The making of a web ontology language. *Journal of Web Semantics* 1(1):7–26.

[Horrocks et al., 2007] Ian Horrocks, Peter F. Patel-schneider, Deborah L. Mcguinness, and Christopher A. Welty. 2007. OWL: a description logic based ontology language for the semantic web. *The Description Logic Handbook 2nd Edition*: 458–486.

[Huser et al., 2010] V. Huser, S. P. Narus, and R. A. Rocha. 2010. Evaluation of a flowchart-based EHR query system: A case study of RetroGuide. *Journal of Biomedical Informatics* 43 (1): 41–50.

[Jurafsky and Martin, 2009] Daniel Jurafsky and James H. Martin. 2009. *Speech and language processing: An introduction to natural language processing, speech recognition, and computational linguistics*, 2nd ed. Upper Saddle River, NJ: Prentice-Hall.

[Kaiser, Akkaya, and Miksch, 2007] K. Kaiser, C. Akkaya, and S. Miksch. 2007. How can information extraction ease formalizing treatment processes in clinical practice guidelines? A method and its evaluation. *Artificial Intelligence in Medicine* 39 (2): 151–163.

[Kanzaki, 2005] Masahide Kanzaki. 2005. *Introduction of RDF/OWL for the semantic web*. Chiyoda, Japan: Morikita Shuppan Co., Ltd. (in Japanese).

[Mabotuwana and Warren, 2009] T. Mabotuwana and J. Warren. 2009. An ontology-based approach to enhance querying capabilities of general practice medicine for better management of hypertension. *Artificial Intelligence in Medicine* 47 (2): 87–103.

[Mainz, 2003] J. Mainz. 2003. Developing evidence-based clinical indicators: A state of the art methods primer. *International Journal for Quality in Health Care* 15 (1): i5–i11.

[Mainz et al., 2004] J. Mainz, B. R. Krog, B. Bjørnshave, and P. Bartels. 2004. Nationwide continuous quality improvement using clinical indicators: The Danish National Indicator Project. *International Journal for Quality in Health Care* 16 (1): i45–i50.

[Mainz et al., 2009] J. Mainz, A. M. Hansen, T. Palshof, and P. D. Bartels. 2009. National quality measurement using clinical indicators: The Danish National Indicator Project. *Journal of Surgical Oncology* 99 (8): 500–504.

[Mizoguchi, 2003] Riichiro Mizoguchi. 2003. Part 1: Introduction to ontological engineering. *New Generation Computing* 21 (4): 365–384.

[Nightingale, 1859] F. Nightingale. 1859. *A contribution to the sanitary history of the British army during the late war with Russia*. London: John W. Parker and Son.

[NHO, 2009] Nihon Hospital Organization. 2009. Clinical indicators 2009. Online at: http://www.hosp.go.jp/7,7018,61.html (in Japanese).

[Noy and McGuinness, 2001] Natalya F. Noy and Deborah L. McGuinness. 2001. *Ontology development 101: A guide to creating your first ontology*. Stanford Knowledge Systems Laboratory Technical Report KSL-01-05 and Stanford Medical Informatics Technical Report SMI-2001-0880, Stanford, CA.

[OECD, 2006] OECD. 2006. *Health care indicators project initial indicators report*. OECD (Organisation for Economic Co-operation and Development) Health Working Paper 22, Paris.

[Okumura, 2012] Manabu Okumura. 2010. *Introduction to natural language processing*. Tokyo: Corona-sha (in Japanese).

[Serban et al., 2007] R. Serban, A. ten Teije, F. van Harmelen, M. Marcos, and C. Polo-Conde. 2007. Extraction and use of linguistic patterns for modelling medical guidelines. *Artificial Intelligence in Medicine* 39 (2): 137–149.

[Takaki et al., 2012] O. Takaki, I. Takeuti, K. Takahashi, N. Izumi, K. Murata, and K. Hasida. 2012. Representation system of quality indicators towards accurate evaluation of medical services based on medical databases. Paper presented at the proceedings of the 4th International Conference on eHealth, Telemedicine, and Social Medicine (eTELEMED 2012), February 4, Valencia, Spain.

[W3C 2012] World Wide Web Consortium. 2012. The World Wide Web Consortium (W3C). Online at: http://www.w3.org/

6

Data Privacy, Security, and Compliance through Data Governance

Charlyn A. Hilliman

CONTENTS

INTRODUCTION

This chapter will provide a framework for developing data privacy, security, and compliance through a systematic data governance structure. An effective data governance initiative within an organization should be focused on issues related to data management. There are several aspects of data management, for example, designing, warehousing, and ensuring the quality of the data. This chapter will provide a foundation for protecting data and complying with the federal regulations that govern data usage and accountability. There are risks related to warehousing data; therefore, this aspect of data usage is heavily regulated and must comply with industry standards. The data governance committee must develop strategies for regulatory compliance and adherence to determined policies.

For the purposes of this chapter, we will focus on privacy as it relates to the most basic yet comprehensive definitions of privacy. According to the *Merriam-Webster Dictionary* (2012), "privacy is the freedom from unauthorized intrusion or the state of being apart/secluded." The basic right of privacy is the right or freedom to which all human beings are entitled to be free from government interference. Individuals have the right of basic liberties and freedom of thought or expression and equality of the law. Although the right to privacy is not mentioned directly in the Constitution, the Supreme Court has used constitutional amendments to infer that individuals have the right to privacy and that it should be protected by law. In order to present the most comprehensive definition, privacy will be separated into three aspects of privacy: personal behavioral privacy, personal communications privacy, and personal data privacy.

Privacy Aspect One, the personal behavior privacy, relates directly to an individual's expectation of the privacy of sensitive matters. In general, when addressing privacy of computer systems, developers focus on the technical limitations or infrastructure related to privacy and often overlook the personal connections to privacy. Privacy must be inherent in systems, through the use of technology, because of the personal expectations that people ascribe to the protection of their private information. When customers share their most intimate details with an organization, they expect it to be regarded as such. Moreover, the organization's responsibilities should be linked more to the needs and expectation of its customers than simple regulatory compliance. Individuals have the right to choose what should be shared with others. Individuals do not expect that their personal information will be shared with the media or other individuals not related to the provision of services. Alan F. Westin describes information privacy as the "the claim of individuals, groups, or institutions to determine for themselves when, how, and to what extent information about them is communicated to others" (Lederer et al., 2004, p. 441). For example, when applying for a loan, a customer expects that his or her annual salary will remain confidential.

In Privacy Aspect Two, the personal communications privacy, individuals expect that their personal information will be free from interception and accidental disclosure to nonrelevant personnel. According to the

National Institute of Standards and Technology (NIST, 2010), organization personal communication privacy relates to "the right to communication without undue surveillance, monitoring, or censorship." When interacting with organizations, individuals expect that the telephones are free from listening devices or other intrusion paraphernalia. There is also an expectation that organizations have sufficient monitoring in place to provide training and quality improvement to staff taking information over the telephone or using telephones to communicate personal information. In some instances, technical safeguards that are built in to protect systems can cause customers to become concerned about the interception of the electronic medium. For example, scanning programs, such as email scanning for spam, can leave some individuals uncomfortable. Consumers may question how the program really distinguishes spam from nonspam. Does identifying spam include some form of electronic data interception before the email arrives to the customer's inbox? There has to be an intersection between privacy and protection where the customer continues to feel secure and at ease with the system while actually being protected by the system. Of course, customers expect that their communications are free from intrusion and external monitoring. However, should the employee have the same expectation? These are all interesting questions that this chapter will not address completely, but should all be kept in the forefront of your understanding of privacy as data privacy, security, and compliance under the purview of a data governance committee are addressed.

The final Privacy Aspect, personal data privacy, relates to the protection of data stored via computer, server, or any other form of electronic media. There is an expectation that such data are stored safely with sufficient backups and that the data are accurate. In the most basic terms, individuals expect that their data will always be kept confidential, have integrity or accuracy, and be available when needed to provide them with service. Additionally, collected data should be used only for the specified purpose by authorized personnel. For example, in a university payroll system, confidentiality requirements would expect that those with access to the database would refrain from prying into the salary of the university's deans and senior leadership within the organization; integrity of the data would require that the staff members with access cannot alter their own pay rate or that of a colleague; and, finally, availability would require that pay information is available for payroll in a timely manner without incident. The aforementioned aspects of privacy lend themselves to the need for continued data security and compliance.

Data security refers to the processes that are used to ensure that data are not only available to those who need it for servicing customers, but that such data are private and include aspects of access controls and other measures to ensure privacy and compliance. Data security requires that personal data are protected through safekeeping, free from corruption and unauthorized access. Many computer systems and databases used throughout the business world, educational institutions, and healthcare facilities encompass information containing names, addresses, telephone numbers, birthdates, social security numbers, and other financial or personal health information, depending on the agency or organization's mission. While these data elements are essential components for the day-to-day operations, such data can be used to harass, steal a person's identity, sell to the media, or simply learn embarrassing information regarding the customer. Therefore, many organizations choose to encrypt its data or use various layers of control to protect the data used for business purposes. Even though organizations should consider privacy and data security as essential components of doing business, the rationale behind adherence to these basic needs have not always been based on altruism. Therefore, the state and federal government have mandated several regulations that require compliance as part of doing business.

Compliance with regulations is not an arbitrary concept and noncompliance is not inconsequential. Regulatory compliance, in terms of institutional compliance, is the process to ensure that laws and regulations that govern how business is conducted are followed. Throughout the data governance discourse, techniques on improving compliance and mechanisms for doing so efficiently and effectively are deliberated. There are ever-increasing regulations that can govern a single organization and each must be adhered to while under not only internal scrutiny, but that of the general public, shareholders, and governmental entities. As the needs for compliance grow and the penalties associated with noncompliance also increase, organizations are adding compliance officers to the staff and relying on their expert guidance as internal policies and procedures are created. These individuals are legally trained and experts in interpreting the regulatory codes that impact the organization's business model. The compliance officer's role is one of great importance within the data governance committee.

The data governance committee is focused primarily on defining and understanding data as an asset and must develop policies and procedures that not only align with the organization's mission, but with regulatory agencies. Moreover, the data governance committee is focused on developing ways to improve the confidentiality, integrity, and availability of the organization's sensitive data. This chapter will use five primary perspectives to define data privacy, data security, and compliance plan through data governance. They include:

1. People management: This requires the data governance committee to identify appropriate stakeholders to manage privacy and compliance.
2. Process management: This requires the data governance committee to define and implement a data governance strategy through appropriate policies and strategies for achieving privacy, security, and compliance.
3. Technology management: This requires that the data governance committee use technology frameworks and initiatives to ensure appropriate access control across systems.
4. Risk management: This relies on the data governance committee to define and manage risks and mitigate risks to ensure security and regulatory compliance.
5. Enforcement: This requires that the data governance committee develop appropriate regulatory and contractual compliance enforcement strategies for those within the organization who have violated one of the aforementioned perspectives within the data governance committee's purview.

PEOPLE MANAGEMENT: IDENTIFYING APPROPRIATE STAKEHOLDERS TO MANAGE PRIVACY AND COMPLIANCE

As organizations begin to realize that data are an important asset, just as important and in some cases more important than the revenue cycle itself, the need for defining data governance strategies has become paramount to success and longevity. Data governance strategies are directly related to developing appropriate stakeholders and project managers that are focused on managing privacy and compliance. Identifying appropriate stakeholders and managers is imperative to ensuring appropriate decisions are made in terms of identifying privacy concerns, mostly around access controls, and, eventually, leading to compliance with the complex regulations instituted to protect personally identifiable data. Project managers must remain vigilant and provide consistent oversight to ensure appropriate and timely response to privacy and compliance concerns that may arise within an organization.

As part of the overall objectives of the data governance committee, the committee must ensure that the organization's personnel not only complies with its policies and procedures, but also is well educated on the requirements of the regulators. As such, the committee is required to define privacy, security, and compliance within the organization. Data privacy represents the relationship between the types of data the organization collects, stores, and creates, and the expectation of the public, its constituents, and regulators for those data to remain confidential and free from unexpected disclosure. Based on this, the data governance committee is responsible as well for the security of these data by technical and physical safeguards. Ultimately, the data governance committee is responsible for compliance or adhering to the standards and regulations set forth to protect individuals' data and ensure its appropriate use.

Before an organization can determine what strategies are needed to manage privacy and compliance, there has to be a hierarchy of upper echelon organizational leaders who understand and determine what data are relevant and assign appropriate policies and procedures around those data. The accountability for privacy and compliance must rest sufficiently high enough in an organization to ensure its values are not overshadowed by other mission criteria, while, at the same time, privacy and compliance cannot render the mission inert. Finding the balance between effective policies and procedures to maintain privacy and compliance and efficient consistency of business operations can be a conundrum. For example, the Health Insurance Portability and Accountability Act of 1996 (HIPAA) requires an organization to maintain, publish, and educate its personnel on the primary components of the HIPAA regulation through the implementation of policies and procedures related to protecting a patient's protected health information (PHI). The HIPAA policies regulate everything from the responsibilities of an organization's security officer to the use of PHI for treatment, payment, and operations (TPO). Table 6.1 lists an example of 20 important components of HIPAA that each organization must implement as well as policies and procedures to address.

There are several parameters to be considered when determining appropriate stakeholders for managing data and ensuring that an organization is compliant with the appropriate regulations. The primary question that each organization needs to answer is: Who owns the data?

TABLE 6.1

Example of 20 HIPAA Policies

Policy Number	HIPAA Policy Title
HIPAA-1	Responsibility of IT Security Office or Administrator
HIPAA-2	Sanctions for Unauthorized Use or Disclosure of PHI
HIPAA-3	Disclosing PHI to Business Associates
HIPAA-4	Use of PHI for Purposes of Treatment, Payment and Healthcare Operations
HIPAA-5	Required Education for Covered Workforce
HIPAA–6	Providing Notice of Privacy Practices
HIPAA-7	Obtaining Individual Authorization for Use and Disclosure of PHI
HIPAA-8	Minimum Necessary Standard
HIPAA-9	Access Controls to Systems Containing Electronic PHI
HIPAA-10	Authentication and Audit Controls for Electronic PHI
HIPAA-11	Inventory of Hardware and Software Containing Electronic PHI
HIPAA-12	Technical Security Measures for the Transmission of Electronic PHI
HIPAA-13	Responsibility for Conducting Risk Assessment of PHI
HIPAA-14	Duty to Report Security Incidents Involving Electronic PHI
HIPAA-15	Access to Facilities Warehousing Electronic PHI
HIPAA-16	Use of De-Identified PHI
HIPAA-17	Use of PHI for Research
HIPAA-18	Use of PHI for Marketing
HIPAA-19	Use of PHI for Fundraising
HIPAA-20	Operating Contingency Planning for Electronic PHI

Some organizations want to believe that the Information Technology (IT) department has the ultimate responsibility for data and its integrity. This is not necessarily true and I would argue that this is contradictory to best practices. The chief executive officer (CEO) and chief financial officer (CFO) of an organization are responsible for the financial reports and, thus, are the appropriate stakeholders for financial data. In clinical venues, the chief medical officer (CMO), chief medical information officer (CMIO), and the chief operating officer (COO) are responsible for patient care and the overall operations of the organization and, thus, should hold the ultimate responsibility for clinical data. In research organizations, the primary investigator (PI) is responsible for the data collected and holds the ultimate responsibility for the research data. The secondary question is: Should the person who owns the data be responsible for its integrity, quality, and overall compliance to regulatory guidelines? This is where organizations may waver. Some would argue that those members of the organization who access the data and use it should hold this responsibility.

And, finally: Where does the IT department fit into all of this? IT should be tasked with using all available technologies to implement and enforce the policies (policy compliance) set forth by the executive sponsors and regulatory agencies. The business side of an organization in conjunction with IT also should be responsible for defining the data dictionary and standards through the use of data governance subcommittees that report back to the larger data governance committee. IT is responsible for the actual implementation of the data dictionary within the relational database management system.

If each of the aforementioned parameters are considered when determining the requisite stakeholders for ensuring compliance, a model for data governance can be constructed using an interorganizational group, with each member holding various responsibilities for data governance and privacy and security. Table 6.1 depicts four scenarios for executive sponsorship. In each scenario, a different group member within the data governance committee assumes responsibility for the data based on the type of data. This structure offers a solution to the dilemma detailed above by reassigning primary responsibility for privacy, compliance, data integrity, and quality based on the data type and the user of the data.

In this model, we will assume that the organization has a clear financial hierarchy, includes clinical care, and has a strong research component. This may be a hospital, a medical school, or another healthcare organization with research interests. Within scenario 1, the primary focus of the data will be financial data used for business intelligence and overall organizational management. In this model, the CEO/CFO hold the primary responsibility for the data; the CMO/CMIO/COO also have a high level of responsibility for the data, its integrity, and quality based on the clinical care aspects of the organization; the PIs of the organization have little responsibility and will serve an ancillary role within the data governance committee; and IT will serve as the implementation arm of the committee. In scenario 2, the focus of the data is research driven. Despite the research nature, the CEO/CFO should still maintain a high level of responsibility followed by the CMO/CFO, and overall research compliance rests with the Institutional Review Board (IRB), which may not be represented within the organization's data governance structure. In the absence of IRB membership within the committee, the IT/Compliance member will serve as a liaison and provide advisory functionality within this scenario.

In scenario 3, IT/Compliance is considered the executive sponsor for the data. An example of such data would be an IT asset management system.

In this scenario, IT/Compliance will ensure that privacy and security receive institutional support and would champion the policies and procedures around compliance. The CEO/CFO also would hold a high level of responsibility, followed by the CMO/CMIO/COO; research will have only an advisory role within this scenario. The final scenario would involve the responsibility for the medical data, such as that created within an EMR (electronic medical record). The CMO/CMIO/COO would be the executive sponsors for this type of data followed by IT/Compliance. The role of IT/Compliance is elevated due to the strict regulations governing medical data. Regulations, such as HIPAA and the Health Information Technology for Economic and Clinical Health (HITECH) Act, require access and audit controls of the clinical systems. These requirements elevate the role of IT within scenario 4. The CEO/CFO would have an important consultant role within the clinical data scenario, but primary responsibilities reside with the CMO/CMIO/COO and IT/Compliance. In this scenario, research would serve only the advisory role with no responsibilities for the data. This is not to say that the research representative is not interested in the data because, most often, clinical organizations with a research role often create a mirrored data warehouse for research purposes. Therefore, the research representative's presence on the committee is valuable and should not be taken lightly.

In the model depicted in Table 6.2, each member of the data compliance committee at one time or another will be responsible for or sponsoring the

TABLE 6.2

Four-Scenario Model

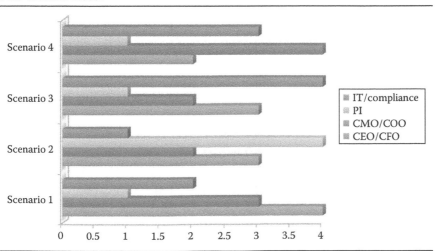

institution's data. Thus, the roles within the committee change from scenario 1 all the way to scenario 4. Each member will share responsibility for data privacy and compliance based on his or her role as the executive sponsor. There is a greater level of accountability for compliance as roles vary, and interorganizational membership to the data governance committee assures this. Using this model will help identify the key stakeholders to help an organization adhere to privacy, security, and compliance regulations.

The Four-Scenario Model provides examples of key stakeholders that should govern a data governance committee based on the type of data presented. This strategy distributes responsibilities equitably across the committee. Nonetheless, a great concern in issues related to security and compliance still remains: What is the role of IT? Should the data governance committee create a hierarchical structure that reports to the board on issues of privacy, security, and compliance? What would the hierarchy look like? In Figure 6.1 through Figure 6.3, there are three potential hierarchical models within the committee that may produce the level of accountability desired by organizations. In scenario 1, the CIO/Compliance officer lead the organization followed by the CEO/CFO and the COM/COO. In this model, other committee members would be ancillary and provide supporting functionality and advise as needed. The CIO/Compliance

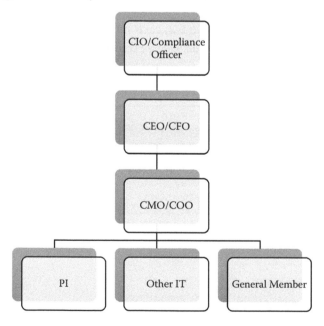

FIGURE 6.1
Hierarchical model 1.

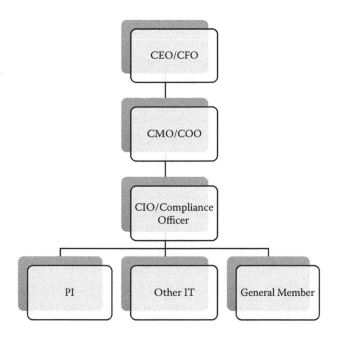

FIGURE 6.2
Hierarchical model 2.

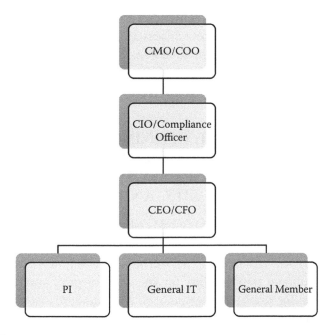

FIGURE 6.3
Hierarchical model 3.

officer has ultimate responsibility for data compliance and would report directly to the board. An example of this scenario would be an organization where the CIO has implemented a new data model, such as an IT asset management/tracking system. The CIO ultimately owns all IT assets and is the appropriate person to lead the data governance committee.

In scenario 2, the CEO and CFO have the responsibility for the data and report directly to the board, followed by the CMO/CMIO/COO and the CIO. As is the case in scenario 1, the other data governance committee members are ancillary to the hierarchical body represented and have no real reporting responsibilities. This scenario places the responsibility on the CMO/CMIO/COO, followed by the CIO/Compliance officer and the CEO/CFO. While these scenarios depict reasonable hierarchical models within the data governance committee organizations that would leave a single person or group of people within the committee responsible to the board, organizations must be careful in adopting such hierarchy within the committee as the interdisciplinary nature of the committee may be lost and true oversight may cease to exist. Data governance oversight should exist in an interdisciplinary and accountable setting and provide organizations with the guidance and oversight needed to ensure regulatory compliance. In Figure 6.4, you will find a model for data governance and compliance oversight where each member works as a team and the leader varies based on the type of data addressed. The committee membership reflects the scenarios depicted in Table 6.2.

PROCESS MANAGEMENT: DEFINING DATA GOVERNANCE THROUGH IMPLEMENTING POLICY STANDARDS AND APPROPRIATE STRATEGIES TO ACHIEVE PRIVACY, SECURITY, AND COMPLIANCE

Within each organization there is a body of authorized users or key stakeholders who are responsible for ensuring the successful implementation of policies and procedures needed to govern data. This governance committee has institutional responsibility for the data integrity and as such will be responsible for implementing policies and standards to ensure organizational adherence to regulations and standard operating procedures. While the committee will face many challenges related to data governance,

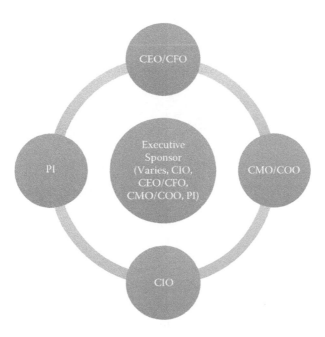

FIGURE 6.4
Hierarchical model 4.

adherence to privacy standards, information security, and regulatory compliance can only be achieved through effective and efficient policies. A successful policy implementation will require clear priorities and formalization of policies through documentation. In an effort to formalize and standardize data policies, stakeholders must reconcile gaps and inconsistencies and define requirements relative to the organizational mission.

There are three primary challenges related to implementing a data governance adherence strategy. The first primary challenge relates directly to the implementation of a comprehensive data governance process. Information technology implementations are challenging in themselves especially when they involve interdisciplinary workgroups and stakeholders; placed on top of these complex processes is the need to overlay a data governance strategy that outlines privacy, security, and compliance with the appropriate regulations. The second relates to obtaining organizational approval and authority to develop and approve policies and procedures. The third challenge relates to evaluating the success of the policies and procedures in a timely and efficient manner before unforeseen problems arise. This all must be considered during the writing of operationally pertinent policy and procedures.

TABLE 6.3

Policymaking Process for Data Governance

Policy Standards and Compliance

- Organizational data needs
- Policy and procedure writing process
- Organizational risk assessments
- Policy changes
- Date governance oversight

The policymaking process within an organization is ultimately the responsibility of the data governance committee. Largely, the policymaking process is a strategic initiative to provide a layer of control over an organization's most fundamental asset. An organization's data drives business decisions, allows the organization to demonstrate regulatory compliance, and helps key decision makers determine long-term business viability. Thus, the policymaking process has to be part of the overall strategic plans and must be meticulous in nature. The policymaking process in any organization is a cyclical process and has many stages that impact the final policies and procedures. In Table 6.3, the policymaking process is divided into its fundamental components. The largest component of the policymaking process is determining the data needs of an organization; this is also the first step in the policymaking process. The second component is the policy and procedure writing step, which is driven by organizational data needs. The third component is the risk assessment step. Organizations, through regulatory requirements, are expected to conduct regular risk assessments of their operations, which include their data, systems, assets, and financial viability. Risk assessments often lead to policy and procedural revisions to mitigate discovered risks and the overall protection of organizations' data. Throughout this process, but particularly after a completed risk assessment, the data governance committee must provide oversight of the policymaking process, which is the final component in the process. This component can occur at any time within the policymaking process. The fourth component deals with instituting changes as deemed necessary either through organizational changes or through the findings from the risk assessments. The final step (organizational oversight), while consistent throughout, may alter phases within the policymaking cycle.

The ultimate goals of the policymaking process and the governance committee are to ensure business continuity, data integrity, adherence to standards, and regulatory compliance. These goals make the role of the data governance committee one of the most crucial in any organization. In the unlikely event that an organization is found noncompliant in any of the many regulations that govern that industry, the mere presence of a governing committee provides a layer of internal credibility to outside auditors. Moreover, the governance committee holds the responsibility of maintaining overall documentation and procedures that can be examined and that will help an organization avoid hefty fines. The presence of oversight reassures regulators and provides a level of organizational transparency. Within the Florida state agencies there are frequent internal audits that through the Freedom of Information Act are readily available on the respective agencies' Web sites. For example, the Broward County auditors publish several reports regarding the county's internal auditing process (http://www.broward.org/AUDITOR/Pages/reports.aspx). These types of internal audits provide insight to internal findings related to IT risks, physical security risks, financial risks, fraud within the agencies, and ethics violations.

TECHNOLOGY MANAGEMENT: USING TECHNOLOGY FRAMEWORKS AND INITIATIVES TO ENSURE APPROPRIATE ACCESS ACROSS SYSTEMS

Information needs, primarily driven by regulations and changes in storage requirements, are suggested as the drivers of data governance. As a result, technology has to enable appropriate data governance. An appropriate data management solution will require applicable tracking, measurement, and protection of data. Data governance stakeholders and project managers rely on technical solutions to enable timely and appropriate response to data needs. Technical solutions facilitate effective communication, measurement, and monitoring needed for enforcement of policies and procedures. A software solution utilized by a data governance committee would provide several functions including:

- Identifying and addressing critical data quality management issues
- Monitoring and improving data quality in an iterative environment (constantly checking the same systems using the same metrics)
- Allowing a malleable solution where flexible rules can be defined to measure appropriate use thresholds
- Allowing access controls for data monitoring to C-level executives (CIOs, CEOs, CFOs, CMO, and CMIOs), IT and Compliance Officer, PIs, and other data governance committee members along with real-time feedback and quality reporting and alerts
- Providing logical interfaces between systems and other data reporting tools

A major responsibility of a data governance committee that is focused on privacy and regulatory compliance includes oversight of technology acquisitions that enable smart and accurate data management. As technology changes, the tools used to ensure appropriate access, timely access, and controlled access are constantly evolving; i.e., data monitoring was previously conducted on a system-by-system basis and required personnel to import data results from each system and compile the results. Today organizations can purchase applications that reside on top of each system through the use of interfaces and integration allowing data extraction, in real time, and for the quality reporting and analysis. An effective data governance committee will remain focused on acquiring such technologies and implementing polices appropriately. This can be costly and may create barriers for implementation. Nonetheless, if the governance committee uses technological solutions to communicate initiatives, enforce policies and procedures, monitor data issues, and correct data discrepancies, the overall organizational momentum will help empower the committee. Data issues can derive from incorrectly formatted data to out-of-date information, improperly accessed, allowing erroneous business decisions and affecting overall business intelligence. Figure 6.5 depicts a circular technology management solution where each circle initiates the next process in a linked pattern. Moreover, the process can begin in any of the circles. In this model, technology management will initiate a process for architecture management, change management, privacy and security access

FIGURE 6.5
Technology Management Solution

management, data quality management, and, finally, policy and procedural management. Architecture management includes, but is not limited to, the design of technology solutions, network management solutions, and database solutions. Within this technical architecture, changes will be made that affect data and systems designs based on the policymaking process, business growth, and regulatory changes. As such, an appropriate process to make these changes must be instituted through a change management committee and policy. While the data governance committee many not necessarily be the same committee that approves systems and software changes, the committee must be aware of the changes and modify policies and processes accordingly. These functions will allow the data governance committee to effectively manage technology within the organization.

RISK MANAGEMENT: DEFINING AND MANAGING RISKS USING DATA-RELATED CONTROLS TO ENSURE SECURITY AND COMPLIANCE

Organizations and key stakeholders must focus attention and resources toward ensuring the security of personally identifiable data and mitigating the risks of disclosure of those data. Protecting data from disclosure and protecting the privacy of personally identifiable data is directly correlated to compliance with various federal, state, and local regulations. Stakeholders and risk managers have to conduct comprehensive vulnerability and risk assessments related to intentional and unintentional use of data and develop strategies for mitigating such risks. This will require investments in technological tools for conducting effective assessments and proactive data governance strategies.

The need for managing risks, ensuring privacy, and compliance are largely driven by stricter regulations by the government over the public and private sectors. Examples of a few key regulations that impact the need for managing data and the associated risks are:

- Sarbanes-Oxley (SOX) of 2002, which calls for stricter financial governance and accountability. This act (Corporate responsibility, 15 USC 7201) was enacted after the infamous Enron and WorldCom scandals. The act called for the implementation of the Securities and Exchange Commission, which regulates corporate and financial records. There are now huge penalties associated with incidences of abuse and failure to disclose pertinent financial data to regulators upon request.
- Health Information Portability and Accountability Act (HIPAA) of 1996, revised in 2010, regulates the use and disclosure of Protected Health Information (PHI). HIPAA (Public Law 140-191, 104th Congress) forced the healthcare industry to establish national standards for the use of electronic data during care delivery. Not only does HIPAA mandate that health plans, providers, and their respective employees develop and implement specific procedures for securing the privacy of patients' protected health information (PHI), but the act mandates that these entities notify patients about their privacy rights and any unintended disclosures of their PHI. Thus, all applicable organizations are required to adopt policies and procedures, implement and track these policies, and educate their respective workforce on these policies. As

such, the data governance committee is ultimately responsible for ensuring that data are protected through physical safeguards, technical safeguards, and institute appropriate auditing capabilities to ensure compliance with HIPAA and other requisite regulations.

- Uniting (and) Strengthening America (by) Providing Appropriate Tools Required (to) Intercept (and) Obstruct Terrorism Act of 2001 (USA Patriot Act, 2001, HR 3162 RDS, 107th Congress), extended in 2011, allowed law enforcement to search telephone records, email communications, medical records, and financial records in response to the September 11, 2001 terrorist attacks on the United States. As a result, organizations are required to maintain accurate records that can readily be provided to state and federal organizations upon request.

- Electronic Signature in Global and National Commerce (ESIGN) Act of 2000 (15 USC 7001) allowed the use of electronic signature and other electronic records for use in business transactions. This act regulates the use of electronic transfer of records and electronic signatures for foreign and domestic commerce. While this act expedites commerce and business transactions by allowing electronic signature and use of data, the consumers' right to sign things the old fashioned way has been preserved. Moreover, this law now places data retention requirements on the use of this electronica data. As with other examples of increased reliance on electronica data, the need for additional governance and compliance has increased. Organizations that use these forms of data as part of their standard operating procedures must remain vigilant that their data are not only accurate, but accessible and auditable.

- Uniform Preservation of Private Business Records Act (UPPBRA) of 1994 provides regulations on the length of time businesses are required to maintain records. These regulations span across various industries and require that organizations retain data longer, are more susceptible to government inquiries and requests for data, assess the vulnerability of consumer data regularly, document the findings, and assess risks associated with data storage. Organizations must realize that consumer data are vulnerable to identity theft, Internet and telephone scams, and other forms of fraud, and data governance initiatives must keep this assumption at the forefront of their policy-making processes. As a result, organizations must realize the importance of being proactive in risk management. Proactive protection of data should include vulnerability scans and assessments by the organizations IT security team, firewalls, three-level authentication whenever possible, and use of a systematic intrusion detection system. The section on Enforcement below will elaborate on the different enforcement techniques used for protecting consumer and patient data within the healthcare environment.

Security threats can come from internal and external sources. Hackers, competitors, partners, such as vendors and suppliers, and consultants may cause intentional or unintentional loss of data, data breaches, or other forms of security risks to an organization. Similarly, employees can cause intentional or unintentional security risks to an organization. Thus, organizations are responsible for assessing their risks regularly and mitigating all known or discovered risks.

Organizations that realize that information security and risk management are simply a part of doing business and have deep financial implications will develop comprehensive risk management processes that not only examine IT resources and systems, but all aspects of risks within the organization. While risk management may be viewed as an organizational albatross, the data governance committee can turn the process into a major asset, educating the organization on documenting and mitigating risks. Risk documentation and mitigation provides a level of transparency and is just smart business. Table 6.4 defines the data governance committee risk management process.

Although risk management can be initiated from any level of an organization, the data governance committee can assume responsibility for developing policies and procedures around risk management. In doing so, they can define a process such as the example used in Table 6.4. Within this process, the data governance committee would determine the goals for the risk assessment and may decide to develop the tools or simply approve tools presented by the designated organizational representative. Once the governance committee initiates the risk assessment, the assessment team will identify the risks, and use an approved tool for determining the likelihood of occurrence and the associated consequences of this risk as part of the risk analysis. The next phase will include a complete evaluation of the risks, mitigation of the risks, and a report back to the data governance committee. In the final step, the data governance committee will develop a monitoring and review process to ensure that avoidable risks are mitigated and controlled and unavoidable risks are contained.

TABLE 6.4

Risk Assessment through Data Governance

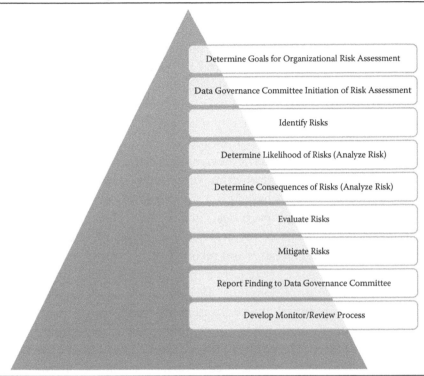

Comprehensive risk assessments protect the organization's mission critical data (its assets), and valuable consumer data, once lost, can affect the organization's market share and leave its consumers vulnerable. An organization's data also impacts its branding and overall business viability. With laws, such as HIPAA, which require public disclosure of lost consumer data, the organization's brand may be permanently and detrimentally affected by lost data or breaches. Additionally, there can be significant loss in employee productivity as a result of lost data or improperly accessed data.

ENFORCEMENT: ENFORCING REGULATORY AND CONTRACTUAL COMPLIANCE

Enforcing regulatory and contractual compliance based on external mandates requires a complex internal data governance structure and technical framework. Within this process are policies and procedures that require management and technical solutions for implementation and enforcement. The ability to apply physical security, network solutions, asset tracking, appropriate authentication, approved privacy layers for defense, and role definitions for access control are all needed to ensure an organization's ability to enforce regulations and respond to lapses in compliance. HIPAA, one among the many regulations previously discussed, requires that consumer data and PHI are not only protected through technical safeguards, but through obvious physical controls, such as double locked doors or doors accessed through employee credentials and biometrics. Thus, the demand for biometric devices increases, and so are the data requirements for storing information on who is allowed access to particular devices and rooms based on a fingerprint or retinal scan. These techniques satisfy multiple purposes, such as physical security, appropriate authentication, role based access, and a layered security defense. Asset tracking of technical purchases and resources where protected consumer information is stored is a key requirement of the regulations around data. Data governance organizations must have policies and procedures around how such assets are tagged, tracked, and monitored.

A layered security approach is a commonly used strategy for assuring security and enforcement within an organization. In a layered IT security approach, there are application level controls, access controls, firewall controls, policy controls, and detection and mitigation controls. Application level controls and firewall controls often accomplish the same goal of controlling the input, output, and/or access to a specific application or service. An organization also may use firewall policies, such as prohibiting access to specific types of Web site, e.g., pornography or game sites, to protect against unwanted viruses or other malware from entering the organization's intranet. If the preventative measures fail to achieve the appropriate security, the data governance committee is responsible for ensuring that appropriate mitigation/solutions or controls exist. Each layer helps organizations achieve robust information security over their data. The data governance committee is ultimately responsible for policies and procedures to help IT and Compliance achieve the overall mission. The data governance committee is responsible for using available technologies and other organizational resources to communicate policies and procedures throughout the organization. The data governance committee provides the appropriate institutional credence to those responsible for implementing and enforcing aspects of regulatory and contractual compliance. Once the data governance committee ensures that all policies and procedures are adhered to, violators can be appropriately sanctioned as per institutional policies and regulatory requirements. However, the enforcement standards must be publically available.

CONCLUSIONS

This chapter provided a comprehensive background for developing data privacy, security, and compliance through a systematic data governance structure. The chapter focused on issues related to stakeholder and people management to ensure privacy, security, and regulatory compliance. There was an emphasis on process management that included data management, the policymaking process, and strategies to achieve privacy, security, and compliance. Important challenges to this process were outlined along with its causes. Technology management through the use of software solutions and the creation of a robust system architecture was addressed along with processes for conducting risk management and enforcement as mandated by regulation.

REFERENCES

Lederer, S., J. I. Hong, A. K. Dey, and J. A. Landay. 2004. Personal privacy through understanding and action: Five pitfalls for designers. *Personal Ubiquitous Computing* 8 (6): 440–454.

National Institute of Standards and Technology (NIST). *NISTIR 7628. Guidelines for smart grid cyber security: Vol. 2, Privacy and the smart grid.* The smart grid interoperability panel—Cyber security working group. Washington, D.C.: U. S. Department of Commerce. Online at: www.csrc.nist.gov/publications/nistir-7628-vol2.pdf (accessed February 13, 2013).

FURTHER READINGS

Cheong, L., and V. Chang. 2007. The need for data governance: A case study. Paper presented at the ACIS 2007 Proceedings, no. 100. Online at: http://aisel.aisnet.org/acis2007/100 (accessed on January 12, 2012).

Khatari, V., and C. V. Brown. 2010. Designing data governance. *Communication of the ACM* 53 (1): 148–152.

NASCIO. 2009. Data governance: Managing information as an enterprise asset. Representing Chief Information Offices of the States. Online at: www.nascio.org/publications/documents/NASCIO-DataGovernance-Part1.pdf (accessed January 12, 2012).

Rosenbaum, S. 2010. Data governance and stewardship: Designing data stewardship entities and advancing data access. *Health Services Research* 45 (5): 1442–1455.

Solomon, M. D. 2005. Ensuring a successful data warehouse initiative. *Information Systems Management* (Winter): 26–26. Online at: www.ibm.journal.com

von Solms, B., and R. von Solms. 2004. The 10 deadly sins of information security management. *Computer & Security* 23: 371–376.

7

Adaptive Data Governance: The AT-EASE Change Management Approach

Dasaratha Rama

CONTENTS

INTRODUCTION

This chapter presents the AT-EASE change management approach for adaptive data governance. The term *adaptive data governance* is based on the notion of adaptive challenges. In adaptive challenges, problem definition, solution, and implementation of solutions are not clearly defined at the outset and require new learning (Heifetz, Grashow, and Linsky, 2009a). Given the rapid changes in the technology and business environment, as well as the continuously expanding knowledge base of data governance standards and best practices, data governance requires an adaptive process of ongoing learning and problem solving for leaders as well as for employees. Further, data governance requires people to change their values, beliefs, and behaviors related to data collection, protection, and use. Accordingly, data governance requires a sustained commitment to change management (Harris, 2011).

Recent change management approaches recognize that people do not change based on logical analysis and facts alone, and that the way people feel about the change affects the extent to which they embrace change. Leaders should assess the emotional and behavioral factors that affect people's willingness to change, and take steps to guide and support them through the change process over an extended period of time. Rather than using a universal checklist, organizations need an intentional and systematic process that can help them assess potential pitfalls in their IT initiatives, and develop appropriate strategies for managing change (McAfee, 2003). Such a process can help organizations overcome pitfalls and realize the value of data governance initiatives.

While many approaches incorporate ideas, such as emotion and motivation, the notion of at ease is the pivotal organizing idea for the AT-EASE approach. The AT-EASE learning model provides a systemic model that supports integration of technical and adaptive elements of data governance in a way that maintains a consistent focus on helping individuals toward greater at ease as they move through the change process over time.

The AT-EASE model is based on the premise that feeling at ease supports engagement and participation in learning and change (Ciborra, 2004; Immordino-Yang and Damasio, 2007; Kahn, 1990; Porges, 2004; Schore, 2009). Based on an extensive review of recent neuroscience findings, Rock (2009) suggests that the brain's over-arching principle in responding to the environment is to seek to reduce threats and increase rewards. Porges's (2004, p. 23) polyvagal theory suggests that the nervous system continuously "evaluates risk in the environment and regulates the expression of adaptive behavior." Thus, helping people to be at ease involves (1) helping people cope with negative emotions arising from uncertainty, lack of knowledge and skills, and fear of loss; and (2) motivating people and helping them understand the relevance of the change and developing their ability to implement the change.

Being at ease also can be visualized in terms of the three psychological conditions of personal engagement (Kahn, 1990): (1) meaningfulness, (2) safety, and (3) availability. The AT-EASE mnemonic reinforces the core message of AT-EASE learning: Make people feel more comfortable in implementing new data governance practices by:

1. Helping them understand the relevance of change
2. Helping them feel safe in the learning process
3. Creating conditions that help them be more available to new learning

GETTING TO AT EASE

In addition to the notion of adaptive challenges, the choice of the term *adaptive data governance* is motivated by two other central ideas from adaptive leadership (Heifetz, Grashow, and Linsky, 2009b): promoting employee ownership and regulating distress. Adaptive leadership is rooted in the idea that the responsibility for the solution to adaptive challenges lies with followers rather than leaders. Many data governance practices, such as those related to security and privacy, affect all employees. Further, many employees are involved with defining, collecting, and using data in organizations. The recent trend toward big data governance (Evans, 2012) further underscores the pervasive nature of data-related activities in organizations. Hence, creating ownership of data management practices and helping employees embed and sustain such practices may be critical for successful data governance.

The adaptive leadership model also recognizes disequilibrium as an expected and natural part of the change process. Accordingly, regulating distress is identified as one of the core practices of adaptive leadership. The notion of productive zone of disequilibrium (PZD) in adaptive leadership provides a useful lens to think about helping people be at ease. The PZD is the zone where people experience a productive level of tension and can be mobilized to engage the problem. If the level of tension is too low, people are comfortable, but they may avoid tackling the difficult issues that the adaptive change is seeking to address. If the disequilibrium is too high, people may be overwhelmed and unwilling to engage.

The adaptive leadership lens implies that the level of at ease changes over time. For many people, the initial focus of change management might be on helping them cope with stresses and engage change in an adaptive manner. It may take time for people to develop motivation through understanding the benefits as well as through developing the skills needed to adapt to the change. Viewing change consistently through the at ease lens and considering ideas, such as the PZD, can shape leaders' mental models of change management and associated practices. As discussed in later sections, different models often implicitly incorporate different underlying notions of at ease. Becoming aware of the underlying notions of at ease can enhance change management practices for data governance.

The rest of this chapter is organized as follows. The next two sections distinguish the AT-EASE model from other change management approaches and discuss the elements of the AT-EASE model. This is followed by a discussion of the use of systems thinking tools and practices as a vehicle for adapting the AT-EASE model to different contexts. The chapter concludes with a summary and implications for practice.

THE AT-EASE MODEL AND CHANGE MANAGEMENT

Recent change management approaches recognize that it takes time to implement and sustain change. For example, Kotter's (1996) eight-step model of change conveys the long-term nature of change in terms of "not letting up" and "making it stick." Kotter's model frames the long-term nature of change in terms of driving the change deeper into the organization through new projects and continued changes to structures, policies, and processes, and sustaining change through anchoring it in organizational culture. Like many change management approaches, this model emphasizes the organizational level of analysis and focuses on how a change is introduced and sustained in the organization as a whole rather than on how different individuals experience change.

In contrast, some change management models, such as the ADKAR (Awareness-Desire-Knowledge-Ability-Reinforcement), are based on the notion that, ultimately, sustainable change is about changing how individuals do their jobs (Hiatt, 2006). The ADKAR model views change management in terms of five outcomes including creating an **A**wareness of the need for change, creating a **D**esire for implementing the change, enhancing **K**nowledge about how to change, developing the **A**bility to implement new skills and behaviors, and **R**einforcement to sustain the change after it is implemented.

The AT-EASE model also describes the progression of one individual through the process of learning and change. In contrast to change management approaches that focus on the leaders' actions or on the employees' experiences, the AT-EASE model is a systemic view that focuses on interaction between stakeholders as they progress through the change process. This focus on interactions arose because the original purpose of the model was to describe the process of guided participation. The AT-EASE model grew out of the recognition that learners may not be at ease with new learning because of uncertainty, ambiguity, confusion, not knowing what to do, and not having adequate skills. Its purpose was to describe how guides support learners' progression from initial awareness to independent learning and competence.

Given the emphasis on helping employees assume responsibility for assuming change under adaptive leadership, the relationship between adaptive leaders and employees is analogous to the relationship between guides and learners. The AT-EASE model highlights the fact that, while employee ownership may be the goal, transferring responsibility to employees takes time. Change management entails a similar set of interactions between change agents and employees as the interactions between guides and learners.

Finally, the AT-EASE model also explicitly focuses on the guide's learning. Thus, the AT-EASE components can be used to describe the leader's learning process as well as the employee's learning process. The use of the same set of components to describe the actions of leaders and employees is a unique feature of the AT-EASE model. This feature supports the use of AT-EASE as building blocks for constructing models of complex organizational systems involving a variety of stakeholders.

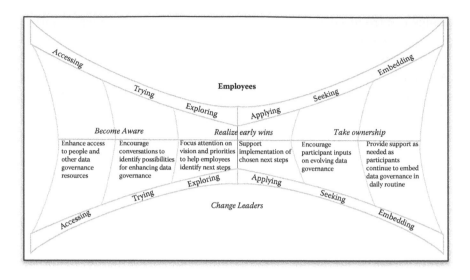

FIGURE 7.1
Helping employees get to AT-EASE with data governance.

THE AT-EASE ELEMENTS

The AT-EASE model (Figure 7.1) breaks down the learning process into six components (**A**ccessing-**T**rying-**E**xploring-**A**pplying-**S**eeking-**E**mbedding) that represent a progression from initial awareness and disequilibrium to competence and at ease. The six AT-EASE elements can be used as building blocks to describe the learning process for any individual regardless of his/her role or specific learning needs, and to construct systemic models to visualize stakeholders' influence on other individuals' learning and problem solving.

From a change management perspective, these six elements are grouped into three categories:

1. Develop awareness
2. Realize early wins
3. Develop ownership

These three phases correspond to different levels of at ease. The first phase corresponds to disequilibrium. During the second phase, employees gain confidence and begin to implement specific steps to enhance data governance. The third phase represents the highest level of at ease that arises when employees have internalized new practices and successfully embedded them in routine work. Leaders' priorities evolve depending on the level of at ease. The six components are described below.

Develop Awareness: Accessing and Trying

During the accessing and trying steps, employees become aware of data governance and its relevance to the organization and to the employees' own activities. During this awareness phase, employees may not be at ease. The next section presents two examples that show differing perspectives on helping people become more at ease.

Each individual starts the learning process by accessing people, information, and other resources (**Accessing**). Leaders can shape employee access to resources, such as relevant and up-to-date information about data governance best practices, organizational policies and procedures, and technologies and tools. More importantly, leaders can create a network of connections to provide a space for stakeholders to engage each other in the change process (Figure 7.2). However, simply creating a social network to enhance access to people and disseminating information may not be sufficient to engage people. The three psychological conditions of personal engagement (meaningfulness, safety, and availability) discussed by Kahn (1990) should be considered in designing access.

Leaders can help employees feel more at ease by structuring connections and providing access to relevant information targeted to the needs of different employees. They can create a holding environment (Heifetz, Grashow, and Linsky, 2009b) that binds people together in order to help them maintain collective focus on the problem being addressed. The holding environment provides safety and structure for people to surface and discuss diverse views on the problem and possible solutions. A holding environment can include elements such as shared goal and vision, history of working together, and procedures and rules.

Figure 7.2 highlights the fact that the accessing step is applicable to leaders as well as employees. However, the nature of accessing can be quite different for leaders. The idea of "getting on the balcony" underscores the need for the leader to step away from the details and discern patterns and reflect on the big picture. While the leader's accessing may be much

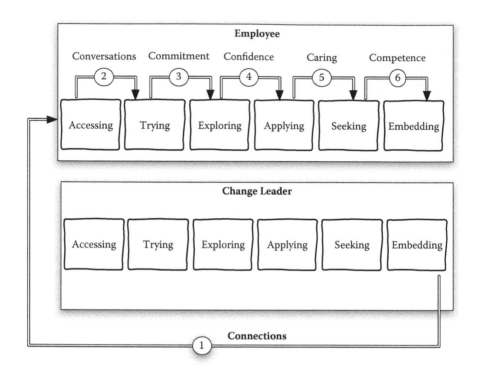

FIGURE 7.2
AT-EASE elements.

broader than those of other individuals affected by the change, access to people and other resources influences learning for all individuals.

As seen in Figure 7.1, information obtained during Accessing is narrowed down during Trying, as stakeholders consider different possibilities for aligning their current activities with the organization's data governance requirements and practices. Trying requires an experimental mindset (Heifetz, Grashow, and Linsky, 2009b) of viewing any potential approach to an adaptive problem as the starting point of an iterative process that will take shape and evolve over time. Figure 7.2 highlights that trying is an important part of the learning process for both leaders and employees. For an adaptive challenge, both leaders and employees need an experimental mindset. Leaders can encourage conversations to surface and evaluate different possibilities. While conversations can ensure that diverse views are considered, they also can result in conflicts. The adaptive leadership (Heifetz, Grashow, and Linsky, 2009b) approach provides detailed recommendations for "orchestrating conflict."

Figure 7.2 shows conversations as a link between accessing and trying to convey the idea that creating access to connections in a safe and structured environment supports productive conversations. In turn, conversations influence each individual's trying. The quantity and quality of the conversations can be seen as an indicator of at ease and of the safety and structure afforded by the holding environment. The "pressure cooker" metaphor (Heifetz, Grashow, and Linsky, 2009b) is used to describe a holding environment strong enough to contain disequilibrium of an adaptive process. This metaphor conveys the idea that leaders can turn up the heat as well or let the steam out as needed. However, the pressure cooker will not work if there is no heat. In addition to creating a safe environment, leaders have to hold employees accountable for conversations and for trying.

Realize Early Wins: Exploring and Applying

Under Exploring, stakeholders narrow the focus in order to identify next steps appropriate to their current level of data governance, and to prepare for implementing these steps. Connections and conversations can help people understand the need for data governance as well as the importance of engaging in data governance. However, employees also need to know the specific next steps that they need to take in the immediate future. Leaders must balance the need for inviting diverse input and stimulating conversations with the need for realizing early wins. For example, agile data governance recognizes that executives responsible for data governance programs may be too busy trying to meet short-term business objectives and, thus, unable to focus on the time-consuming process of implementing data governance (Ambler, 2012). Agile data governance thus emphasizes narrowing down scope and realizing quick wins as a way to motivate people.

In Figure 7.2, the link between Trying and Exploring is labeled *commitment*. This link highlights the fact that the process of trying out different ideas and engaging in conversations can help ensure that the organization commits to the appropriate next steps. While it may be more efficient if leaders themselves decide on the next steps, investing time in conversations may result in the identification of more valuable steps for the organization to take at any given time, and promote stakeholder buy-in.

Applying refers to the use of information learned in exploration in order to implement small steps to enhance data governance. Exploring implies that employees know specific steps that they need to take to implement data governance. However, they also need confidence in their ability to implement ideas in practice. In other words, confidence in implementing the selected steps helps individuals progress from Exploring to Applying. During Exploring and Applying, information needs are narrower and relate to specific data governance issues and practices rather than the broader range of information provided during accessing and trying. Leaders can assist employees in this phase through providing training and support, and by providing access to information and tools.

Develop Ownership: Seeking and Embedding

Seeking and Embedding lead to a broadening of perspective as stakeholders continue to learn more and integrate new information and insights. Unlike the initial stages, employees are more at ease with the new practices. The link between Applying and Seeking is labeled *caring* to convey the shift toward greater ownership and initiative.

The adaptive lens results in a subtle, but important, shift in the focus of embedding and sustaining stages to the actions of those affected by the change. Change agents still need to sustain communication and maintain stakeholder attention on change for an extended period of time. As new ideas, practices, and policies seep through the organization, employees embed them in their routines. However, the focus of the change process is on fostering ownership in those who will be affected by the change and how they embed data governance ideas and practices.

This idea of embedding is reflected in some current data governance approaches. For example, Corcoran (2009) frames the change process in terms of infusing data governance policies and procedures and letting it seep. The change management process described for IBM's Data Security and Privacy (DS&P) (Schell 2012) is based on a mental model of each individual's journey from initial awareness to general and personal understanding resulting in a willingness to accept change. As buy-in increases, individuals take greater responsibility for changing their own behavior. In contrast to the change agents' efforts to embed in earlier stages of the implementation process, end users create their own ways to embed and improve data governance practices. As stakeholders continue application of data governance practices, their knowledge about data governance expands. Change agents can foster communication to encourage knowledge sharing. In other words, stakeholder learning during one period of time provides information that can be leveraged during subsequent Accessing.

USING THE AT-EASE MODEL

The discussion above introduced the six AT-EASE components as well as some key relationships between them. As noted earlier, the AT-EASE model is a systemic model that emphasizes the bidirectional relationships between change agents and employees rather than the actions of either the leader or the employee. There are many potential relationships between the AT-EASE elements. As shown in later sections, different data governance and leadership approaches emphasize different subsets of these relationships.

The six AT-EASE relationships for one individual are related to each other. For example, access to a safe environment affects individuals' trying. There are also relationships that connect the AT-EASE components for different stakeholders. Six key interdependencies have been made explicit and labeled in a way that makes it easier for groups to maintain attention on these links. The six key relationships have been labeled with the six Cs (connections, conversations, commitment, confidence, caring, and competence). These six relationships represent factors that contribute to the level of at ease at each stage in a way that is likely to nudge individuals to the next step of the AT-EASE process. The six Cs provide a starting point for the use of the model.

The Six Cs and AT-EASE

In the initial disequilibrium stage, connections (a safe network of relationships) can help people feel more at ease. At this stage, they may not know exactly how the change will affect them or what they need to learn, but the holding environment provides reassurance that support will be forthcoming. This sense of safety can help employees feel comfortable in engaging in conversations, expressing their views, and contributing to the process of implementing data governance.

The quantity and quality of conversations affect trying. Productive conversations help people identify feasible choices that are meaningful to their context. In turn, thinking about possible actions during trying helps employees commit to a specific course of action.

If the conversation is not focused, people may be too overwhelmed to try and committing to a specific course of action may be difficult. Note that the word *commitment* is used in a narrow sense of settling on a particular course of action that seems most promising at that particular time. On the other hand, committing to a specific course of action does not necessarily result in at ease because a few individuals may drive the process and decide on a course of action without adequate buy-in from others.

Individuals need to feel confidence to feel at ease with a specific course for a chosen course of action to be translated into application. Thus, confidence is shown as the link between exploration and application. Confidence also means that employees have the knowledge and skills required to implement this action plan. Over time, individuals evolve to a different level of at ease where they are comfortable initiating ideas and actions because they personally care about data governance and understand its personal relevance. Finally, integrating and evolving new learning over time helps develop competence and a higher level of at ease.

Six Cs and AT-EASE Change Management Practices

The six Cs clarify the nature of the holding environment and reveal actions that leaders can take to evolve the holding environment to meet the needs of individuals as they progress to higher levels of at ease. Six key AT-EASE practices based on the six Cs include:

Accessing: Strengthen *connections* to help employees identify relevant information about data governance.

Trying: Encourage ongoing participation in *conversations* on data governance that help employees understand relevance and to align data governance practices with employees' work requirements.

Exploring: Strengthen *commitment* to data governance through helping employees see the path ahead and figuring out next steps.

Applying: Help employees develop *confidence* through supporting employees in their efforts to incorporate data governance.

Seeking: Strengthen *caring* through helping employees explore personal relevance.

Embedding: Help employees develop *competence* by evolving data governance practices and integrating them in routine practice over time.

ENHANCING AT-EASE APPLICATION
WITH SYSTEMS THINKING

Emerging data governance models are complex and encompass a wide range of issues. For example, the Data Management Body of Knowledge (DMBOK) consists of 10 data management functions and 7 environmental elements (Moseley, 2008). It uses graphical representations to organize these components. DMBOK provides context diagrams showing the detailed steps in each of the data management areas. The implementation of any of these 10 areas involves considerable complexity. Thus, organizations may need to prioritize and address a few data governance issues at any given time. While DMBOK uses graphical representations to organize information, these representations are geared toward conveying the comprehensive nature of the standards themselves rather than to serve as a tool for organizations to develop their own models.

Tailoring the general graphical representations in existing data governance approaches to the organization's specific situation can enhance the use of representations for communication and problem solving. Given the complexity of data governance issues, no one model is likely to completely meet an organization's needs at all times. Systems thinking and associated diagramming techniques can help adapt guidance from various standards to a particular organization, incorporate situational factors, and integrate other elements (e.g., change management or other issues not addressed in-depth in a particular models) to develop customized visualizations for a specific context. This section shows how using a systems thinking method to examine data governance approaches can set the stage for developing flexible graphical representations that support adaptive data governance. The following section continues this discussion to show how the AT-EASE elements provide a structure to create systemic models for data governance that can integrate information from various sources.

Recent data governance approaches recognize the need for systemic or holistic approaches that consider the complex interconnections between different elements in implementing data governance. Broadly, systems thinking can be seen as a language (Goodman, 1991) that allow us to create simple, yet rich, descriptions of complex, interconnected realities based on multiple perspectives (Imam, LaGoy, and Williams, 2007). Figure 7.2 uses the AT-EASE elements as building blocks for a systemic view that helps stakeholders visualize how people influence each other to learn and change. Systems thinking approaches offer a way to make mental models explicit for collective problem solving and, thus, can be a valuable tool for adaptive data governance. Systemic models show key elements, patterns, and interdependencies and help stakeholders visualize, interpret, and clarify the problem and solution approaches as they evolve over time.

The DSRP (Distinctions, Systems, Relationships, Perspectives) method is one such language that views systems thinking (Cabrera, Colosi, and Lobdell, 2007) in terms of four basic universal patterns: (1) making **D**istinctions, (2) organizing into **S**ystems, (3) forming **R**elationships, and (4) taking **P**erspectives. The DSRP method is rooted in the idea that systems thinking is a structured process of conceptualizing, and that conceptualizations are dynamically evolving as people distinguish ideas from other ideas, organize them in different ways, explore different relationships, and view them from different perspectives. This view of conceptualizations as evolving systems of concepts is better suited for adaptive data governance than a static visualization.

The discussion below introduces the use of these four patterns in thinking about existing data governance approaches as well as models in related areas, such as change management and leadership. Probing existing models using DSRP patterns sets the stage for using the DSRP language and diagramming techniques throughout the discussion of AT-EASE and change management. Using these patterns for looking at existing approaches helps clarify the differences and relationships between these models and AT-EASE.

Models of Data Governance

This section illustrates the use of DSRP patterns to evaluate existing data governance models. DMBOK (Data Management Body of Knowledge) and noninvasive data governance are compared using these patterns to clarify the use of these patterns to evaluate the extent to which AT-EASE ideas are implicitly integrated into these models. Such an analysis can serve as the starting point for integrating AT-EASE ideas and practices and current data governance approaches in a coherent way.

Making Distinctions

Making distinctions between ideas and making boundary judgments about what to include and what to exclude from the system is critical to systems thinking. The usefulness of a systemic model does not necessarily increase by including more detail, but by including elements that add value to a particular inquiry (Imam, LaGoy, and Williams, 2007). Different data governance approaches that emphasize a systemic or holistic approach may differ widely in how they define data governance, and make different choices on issues and practices included in their scope. While selecting a data governance approach, it is important to consider questions such as: What does a given model of data governance include/exclude? What are the implications of these boundary choices in practice?

While existing models may differ in many ways, the key *distinction* for this chapter involves the extent to which existing models of data governance incorporate the idea of helping people move from initial disequilibrium to greater levels of AT-EASE over time. The noninvasive data governance approach (Seiner, 2012) recognizes that data governance efforts are adversely affected by the need for above-normal work efforts and a command and control approach. The underlying idea behind noninvasive data governance practices is that data governance is already embedded in informal ways in organizations, and that formalizing and integrating these practices results in a nonthreatening approach to data governance implementation. The idea of at ease underlying noninvasive governance focuses on minimizing threat. Managers and employees are more likely to be at ease if current data governance practices are evolved gradually.

In contrast, DMBOK focuses on different areas of data management and integrating data governance and management. DMBOK materials provide detailed guidance on data governance and nine other disciplines:

- Data architecture management
- Data development
- Database operations management
- Data security management
- Reference and master data management
- Data warehousing and business intelligence management
- Document and content management
- Meta data management
- Data quality management

The DMBOK also includes seven environmental variables:

- Goals and principles
- Organization and culture

- Activities
- Deliverables
- Roles and responsibilities
- Practices and techniques
- Technology

However, the notion of at ease is not explicitly addressed and change management is mentioned briefly as one element of one of the environmental variables (organizational culture).

Organizing into Systems

Organizing elements into a system of parts and wholes is central to systems thinking and helps visualize the system as a set of interacting parts. While selecting a data governance approach, it is important to consider questions such as: How does the model organize the different parts of the model into wholes? What are the implications of such organization in practice?

Consistent with the focus on creating a nonthreatening approach, the noninvasive data governance approach is organized to emphasize the people dimension. In particular, noninvasive governance is organized to provide comprehensive guidance on roles/responsibilities and stewardship. The noninvasive data governance approach organizes roles and responsibilities into the operational, tactical, strategic, executive, and support levels. The approach provides detailed guidance on specific roles and their responsibilities at each level.

In contrast, DMBOK is organized according to different areas of data management rather than according to roles and responsibilities. DMBOK arranges the data management components in a certain way that identifies data governance as the core component at the center of the DMBOK diagram. For each data management component, the process is organized in terms of elements, such as suppliers, inputs, participants, tools, metrics, consumers, outputs. While the second part of the main DMBOK visual shows a set of seven environmental variables, issues such as change management are not highlighted in the model's organization.

Forming Relationships

Relationships are at the heart of systems thinking. While selecting a data governance approach, it is important to consider questions such as: What interdependencies does the model emphasize? What are the implications of focusing on these interdependencies in practice?

Given the emphasis on roles and responsibilities, noninvasive governance focuses on interactions between different roles in realizing data governance. The noninvasive data governance model focuses on stewardship. Hence, it emphasizes relationships between different stakeholders. As discussed in the next section, these relationships and interactions can be organized in a consistent way using the AT-EASE diagram in order to better visualize the systemic interconnections in noninvasive governance.

In contrast, the relationship between data governance and the other components is central to the DMBOK model. Data governance refers to the system of authority, control, and shared decision making that guides and supports other data management functions. While the DMBOK organization may not focus on change management, the organization of elements and interdependencies in DMBOK can be leveraged in implementing change management practices. For example, responsibilities and process for planning and monitoring change can be developed as part of data governance and utilized while implementing any data management area.

Taking Perspectives

A final element emphasized by systemic approaches is consideration of multiple perspectives. Leaders must consider questions such as: How do stakeholder perspectives about different model components vary? How can these diverse perspectives be integrated in practice?

We can view any model through multiple lenses. For example, we can view DMBOK through the AT-EASE lens. This perspective shifts the thinking to questions such as: How can we implement DMBOK in a way that helps employees be more at ease with the change? How can we create a holding environment and maintain tension in the zone of productive disequilibrium to ensure that people engage, but are not overwhelmed?

Similarly, we can view noninvasive governance through an AT-EASE lens and pose questions such as: How do noninvasive governance practices help in creating a holding environment for introducing and sustaining data governance?

While noninvasive governance does not include the term *holding environment* explicitly, the focus on making change nonthreatening can help create a holding environment where people feel safe and comfortable with data governance. Initial experiences of this nature can help prepare people for more challenging experiences.

In summary, the noninvasive data governance and DMBOK approaches have different mental models that incorporate the notion of at ease to different degrees, and, hence, recommend different kinds of practices. Both of these models offer valuable insights. No single model may be structured in a way that meets the needs of an organization at all times. Rather than evaluating models to identify the best one, an organization's model of data governance can be seen as a dynamic construction that draws upon diverse sources and integrates them in a way that meets the organization's needs. The following section uses DSRP diagramming techniques to develop such representations.

CONSTRUCTING AND USING AT-EASE MODELS

The AT-EASE model can be adapted to different situations, by incorporating elements from models such as DMBOK and the non-invasive data governance model, to create a systemic model that links learning and problem-solving for specific contexts. In terms of DSRP elements, *distinguishing* between elements included and excluded in different data governance models is the first step in selecting appropriate elements for constructing an AT-EASE model for a particular environment. The selected elements must then be organized into *systems* that facilitate visualization and interpretation of the key *relationships* and interdependencies in the system. The selected elements then can be considered from different *perspectives* over time to support adaptive data governance.

Constructing an AT-EASE Model: Noninvasive Data Governance

This section shows how the AT-EASE model can be applied to the noninvasive governance approach. This example was selected because of its focus on implementing data governance in an incremental and nonthreatening way. The DSRP diagram in Figure 7.3 shows an AT-EASE model for noninvasive data governance. The following conventions are used in preparing these diagrams consistently:

- *Make Distinctions:* Choose the stakeholders (e.g., operational data stewards and data steward coordinators) to be included in a particular

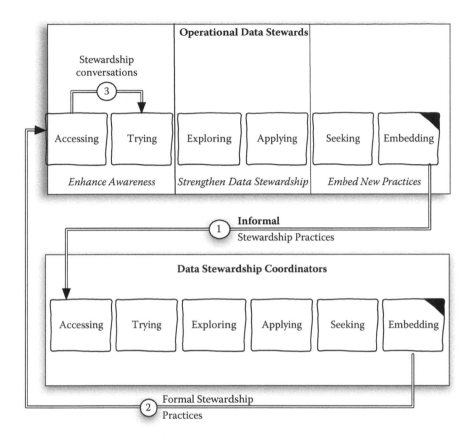

FIGURE 7.3
AT-EASE and noninvasive data governance™.

diagram. Draw the six AT-EASE components of the learning process for each of these stakeholders. The noninvasive data governance approach organizes roles and responsibilities into the operational, tactical, strategic, executive, and support levels. At each level, the approach identifies several stakeholders with specific roles and responsibilities for data governance. High-level AT-EASE diagrams can be drawn to show the general flow of learning from **A**ccessing to **E**mbedding for each of the five different levels. Alternatively, AT-EASE diagrams can identify specific stakeholders at one or two levels. For example, Figure 7.2 *distinguishes* two key stakeholders (operational data stewards and data steward coordinators). Each of the six AT-EASE components are shown using a rectangle. While each of these components is distinct, solid triangles are used at the upper right-hand corner of some rectangles to draw attention to important distinctions in a context. As shown in Figure 7.3, the distinction between the two rectangles for the embedding components is key to the noninvasive approach since the ideas and practices already embedded in the organization represent the starting point for the approach.

- *Organize into Systems:* Based on the stakeholders selected, the AT-EASE elements can be organized in different ways. Figure 7.2 organizes the six AT-EASE components for data stewards and data steward coordinators into a system. The AT-EASE components for data stewards have been grouped into three categories: (1) enhance awareness of data stewardship practices, (2) strengthen stewardship practices, and (3) embed enhanced data governance practices.

- *Document relationships:* The model emphasizes interdependencies between the AT-EASE components for each individual as well as the *relationships* between the AT-EASE elements of different stakeholders. Figure 7.3 also shows key *relationships* for invasive data governance. The noninvasive governance approach uses what is currently embedded within the organization as the starting point. The focus of this approach is on identifying the informal data governance mechanisms already existing within the organization and using these mechanisms as the foundation of a more formal data governance approach. The noninvasive data governance approach thus focuses on identifying operational data stewards who already have some level of responsibility over the data they define, produce, and use as part of their daily routine (link 1 in Figure 7.3). These operational stewards are identified and recognized, and their role is formalized in order to improve communications, coordination, and cooperation among stewards (link 2 in Figure 7.3). While current informal data stewardship practices serve as the starting point, these practices may not be effective or efficient. Once operational data stewards are identified, data awareness programs can be set up to help these stewards learn how to manage the data in a way that ensures compliance, security, privacy, and other governance objectives. Data stewards are provided the knowledge, tools, and practices to enhance their data management (link 3 in Figure 7.3).

- Finally, any AT-EASE model can be viewed from different perspectives. For example, we can look at the interactions between the operational data stewards and data steward coordinators from the perspective of the Data Governance Council. While noninvasive governance frames at ease in terms of being nonthreatening rather than in terms of orchestrating conflict, the idea of productive zone of disequilibrium and holding environments provides useful insights into this approach. From the perspective of the Data Governance Council, recognizing data stewards and creating communication channels between steward coordinators, operational coordinators, and other stakeholders is part of the process of creating a holding environment for data governance. The specification of a range of roles and the responsibilities of each role in detail under noninvasive governance can provide the structure to create a strong holding environment. In other words, identification of stewards supports the creation of a holding environment that enhances access and supports individuals' efforts to work collaboratively. In terms of the AT-EASE components, the holding environment is about making the change accessible to employees.

Constructing an AT-EASE Diagram: Adaptive Data Governance

The six key practices identified for adaptive leadership include: getting on the balcony, identify adaptive challenges, regulate distress, maintain disciplined attention, give work back to people, and protect voices of leadership from below. Figure 7.2 visualizes these practices in term of the AT-EASE components.

Make Distinctions

Figure 7.4 distinguishes change leaders and employees and underscores the idea that the leader also progresses through the six AT-EASE steps. The adaptive leadership model recognizes the fact that leaders and employees learn as they meet adaptive challenges.

Organize into Systems

As seen from Figure 7.4, the six adaptive components can be organized into two groups. The first two practices relate to the leader's own learning and problem solving. The second practice of identifying adaptive challenges corresponds to "Trying" under AT-EASE. The broad range of information accessed by the leader is narrowed down to frame adaptive challenges. The next three practices (regulate distress, maintain disciplined attention, and give work back to people) represent steps that leaders take to facilitate

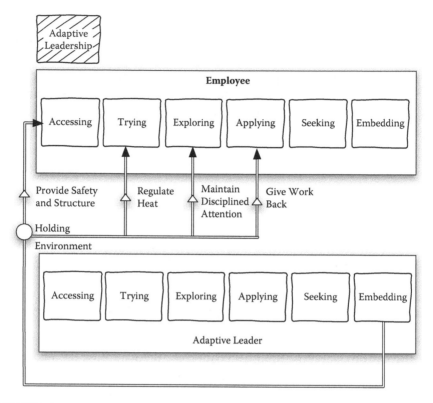

FIGURE 7.4
AT-EASE and adaptive leadership.

learning and problem solving by others. Viewing these practices in terms through the AT-EASE lens, some of these practices may be more significant at different stages of learning/problem solving.

Document Relationships

Three key relationships are shown in Figure 7.4 to clarify the evolution of the holding environment created by leaders over time. The first link between Embedding on the leader side and Accessing on the employee side represents the holding environment that provides a safe and structured environment for employees to begin exploring data governance. The practice of regulating distress is shown as a link from the leader to Trying for the targets of change.

The process of maintaining disciplined attention may be most significant in the exploration step. Leaders have to help employees maintain their attention on the issues, choose and commit to a particular course of action, and help people acquire the knowledge and skills required to implement the chosen course of action.

The practice of giving work back to people corresponds to the Accessing component of the AT-EASE model. Once employees know what needs to be done and how, greater responsibility can be transferred to them. These components reflect the increasing ownership assumed by the stakeholders in addressing the challenge.

SUMMARY AND IMPLICATIONS FOR PRACTICE

This chapter discussed the AT-EASE approach to managing change associated with data governance. The notion of "getting to at ease" was developed as a way to frame an individual's journey from initial awareness to increasing initiative and ownership of data governance practices. The process of getting to at ease is broken down into the six AT-EASE steps that represent progressively greater levels of at ease as individuals learn about and implement data governance.

We explored the use of systems thinking and the DSRP diagramming technique to support dynamic visualization of AT-EASE elements in a given context. As illustrated by the examples, such dynamic visualizations can be used to integrate technical guidance on data governance; adaptive elements, such as change management and learning; situational factors, such as history of data governance in an organization. The intention behind the AT-EASE model is not to provide a linear list of best practices or a universal checklist. Rather, the core ideas and principles can be used to construct systemic models to help translate AT-EASE concepts into practice.

The AT-EASE models can be used at different levels of analysis. The AT-EASE model can be used to describe the progression of learning for one individual. The model also can be used to show how individuals influence each other during the process of change. The examples in this chapter focused on leaders and employees. Other possible influences also can be captured in a similar way. For example, because the AT-EASE model is rooted in guided participation, it can be used to analyze training support activities that help employees acquire specific knowledge and skills.

The construction and use of an AT-EASE model itself can be viewed through the AT-EASE lens. These models are dynamic and expected to evolve with time. Further, individuals need time to progress from initial awareness of the AT-EASE approach and associated systems thinking tools and practices to a point where such ideas and techniques are routinely embedded in organizational practice. However, AT-EASE is a general model of learning that is independent of specific data governance issues being implemented at a given time. Investing in a learning foundation can support all subsequent data governance efforts. Further, the model is intuitive and easy to use, thus making it more feasible to integrate it routinely in organizational practice.

The discussion and examples highlighted some key relationships that are central to the AT-EASE model. However, many other possible relationships can be considered. As an example, the link between trying and seeking is an important relationship that is significant for adaptive leadership. If leaders are committed to fostering employee ownership, it is important to create a holding environment that frames the issues and invites people into dialog. It is possible for leaders to narrow down the choices and do the problem setting themselves and focus on realizing early wins. Such implementations can be successful, but may not result in employees wanting to engage in data governance and taking greater responsibility. In other words, strengthening "AT" creates "EASE."

This chapter also illustrated how elements from other approaches can be deeply embedded in constructing the AT-EASE model. The vocabulary of adaptive leadership including ideas such as adaptive challenges, productive zone of disequilibrium, holding environment, regulating distress, and maintaining disciplined attention, was integrated throughout the chapter. Thus AT-EASE offers a flexible structure to integrate a variety of ideas into a coherent model that can be shared and discussed with diverse stakeholders. Other models of change management may provide useful ideas as well that can be integrated into the AT-EASE model.

REFERENCES

Ambler, S. 2012. Agile/Lean data governance best practices. Online at: http://www.agiledata. org/essays/dataGovernance.html

Cabrera, D., L. Colosi, and C. Lobdell. 2007. Systems thinking. *Evaluation and Program Planning* 31: 299–310

Ciborra, C. 2004. Encountering information systems as a phenomenon. In *The social study of information and communication technology: Innovation, actors, and contexts,* eds. C. Avgerou, C. Ciborra, and F. Land (pp. 17–37). Oxford and New York: Oxford University Press.

Corcoran, C. K. 2009. People and organizational cultural issues in data governance. https://www.msu.edu/~corcora1/proposals/corcoranck_confppt.pdf

Evans, P. 2012. What big data means for the future of self-service business intelligence. *Information Management*. Online at: http://www.information-management.com/newsletters/big-data-BI-self-service-Peter-Evans-10022611-1.html

Goodman, M. 1991. Systems thinking as a language. *Systems Thinker* 2 (3): 1–2. Online at: http://www.appliedsystemsthinking.com/supporting_documents/IntroLanguage.pdf

Harris, J. 2011. Retrograde organizational motion. *The Data Roundtable*. Online at: http://www.dataroundtable.com/?p=6926

Heifetz, R., A. Grashow, and M. Linsky. 2009a. *The theory behind the practice: A brief introduction to the adaptive leadership framework*. Cambridge, MA: Harvard Business Press. Online at: https://www.cu.edu/articles/upload/theory_behind_practice.pdf

Heifetz R., A. Grashow, and M. Linsky. 2009b. Orchestrate conflict: Leading adaptive change by surfacing and managing conflict. Excerpted from the authors' *The practice of adaptive leadership: Tools and tactics for changing your organization and the world*. Boston: Harvard Business Press.

Hiatt, J. M. 2006. *ADKAR: A model for change in business, government and our community: How to implement successful change in our personal lives and professional careers.* Loveland, CO: Prosci Learning Center Publications.

Imam, I., A. LaGoy, and B. Williams. 2007. Introduction. In *Systems concepts in evaluation: An expert anthology American evaluation association*. Point Reyes, CA: EdgePress on Inverness.

Immordino-Yang, M. H., and A. Damasio. 2007. We feel, therefore we learn: The relevance of affective and social neuroscience to education. *Mind, Brain, and Education* 1 (1): 3–10.

Kahn, W. A. 1990. Psychological conditions of personal engagement and disengagement at work. *Academy of Management Journal* 33 (4): 692–724.

Kotter, J. P. 1996. Leading Change. Harvard Business Press: Boston, MA.

McAfee, A. 2003. When too much IT is a dangerous thing. *Sloan Management Review* (Winter): 83–89.

Moseley, M. 2008. DAMA-DMBOK functional framework, ver 3.02. DAMA International. Online at: http://www.dama.org/files/public/DAMA-DMBOK_Functional_Framework_v3_02_20080910.pdf

Porges, S. W. 2004. Neuroception: A subconscious system for detecting threats and safety. *Zero to Three* 24 (5): 19–24.

Rock, D. 2009. *Your brain at work: Strategies for overcoming distraction, regaining focus, and working smarter all day long*, 1st ed. New York: Harper Business.

Schore, A. 2009. The paradigm shift: The right brain and the relational unconscious. Invited plenary address to the American Psychological Association 2009 Convention, August, Toronto, Canada.

Schell, S. 2012. Data security and privacy: Can it be institutionalized and internalized. Online at: http://www.isaca.org/Education/Upcoming-Events/Documents/2012-NACACS-Presentations/314-nac2012.pdf

Seiner, R. S. 2012. Real world data governance: Non-invasive data governance—The practical approach. Monthly Webinar Series, Dataversity. Online at: http://www.slideshare.net/Dataversity/seiner-dataversity-real-world-data-governance-webinar-3-noninvasive-data-governance-20120315-final-ii

8

Case Study: State Level Governance of Health Information Exchange

Christopher B. Sullivan

CONTENTS

INTRODUCTION

One of the major revolutions taking place in healthcare in the United States is the move from paper to electronic records in physicians' offices and hospitals across the country. This is a transformation that is more than just adopting the use of a computer and electronic health record software to replace the paper prescription pad and handwritten notes. It is a fundamental change from inaccessible, office-bound paper documents to electronic records in a database that can be queried, summarized, and used to track patient care. The electronic record increases accessibility to a patient's health information by office staff and physicians, benefitting administrative efficiency. Having the data in electronic format means that it can be sent electronically to another physician any time a patient is referred or transferred for care, bypassing the paper-based facsimile machine for the electronic exchange of records. This ability to exchange records electronically is the key to the transformation of patient care.

Implementing an electronic health record software system comes with associated expenses that include financial capitalization, technical training, and practice down time while the system is installed and learned. Adoption has been slow among American physicians because of these costs, but it is taking place inexorably due to government incentives and market pressures. Once the physician's office is fully electronic, then the potential to connect to a health information exchange becomes possible. Health information exchanges have been emerging over the past decade as the principal means to provide for the bidirectional transfer of health records between physicians. The step up to a health information exchange, though, brings the physician out of his or her office into a community of physicians who can now access the same records for the coordination of patient care.

VALUES OF HEALTH INFORMATION EXCHANGE (HIE) GOVERNANCE

Moving from a single point of care to coordinated points of care requires managing multiple partners and often divergent perspectives, all of whom are connected through the electronic exchange of health information. Thus, the development of the health information exchange (HIE) brings with it the need to create an effective form of governance to manage the community of healthcare participants who are connected within the exchange network. These participants may have diverse or competing interests, dissimilar needs for data, unique requirements for the practice of medicine, and different technical capabilities. To make this all work at a community level, a governance group needs to be created, preferably a trusted body of members from the healthcare community who can address competing interests and craft a consensus for the rules of exchange among participants in the HIE. The consensus-building and leadership values that a trusted, neutral group of people can bring to the governance of health information exchange are essential for its success.

The following discussion looks at the important issues in developing a governing organization for health information exchange and addresses the value a governing board brings to the exchange of health data. All health information exchanges entail data access, data sharing, and the authorizations required to share protected health information among physicians.

The exchange of medical records brings with it potential liabilities that must be addressed and controls must be put in place to limit who has access to the records. This role is best undertaken by a governance body that has the ability to bring a diverse group of healthcare stakeholders to the table and to create trust relationships among them. Herein lies the value of good governance. The governance organization must function as a neutral body to convene stakeholders, to work out the rules for data-sharing activities, to establish business sustainability, and to hold all participants accountable for their responsibilities for sharing health information. Only through this deliberative method of building trust, agreement, and accountability for sharing data will a healthcare community lower its barriers to exchanging health records.

CASE STUDY: STATE-LEVEL GOVERNANCE OF HEALTH INFORMATION EXCHANGE

The steady development of community-based HIE was disrupted in 2009 when the passage of the American Recovery and Reinvestment Act (ARRA) (http://www.gpo.gov/fdsys/pkg/BILLS-111hr1enr/pdf/BILLS-111hr1enr.pdf. p. 116) altered the health information technology landscape in the United States. The law specifically targeted building a national HIE infrastructure to support the creation of a Nationwide Health Information Network. The Office of the National Coordinator for Health Information Technology was authorized to develop a broad set of strategies to drive the adoption of electronic health records systems, create interoperability among them, and foster the exchange of medical records electronically. Funds were allocated for paying incentives to doctors to adopt electronic health records and to make them interoperable through the construction of state-level health information exchange infrastructures.

A significant feature of the American Recovery and Reinvestment Act created state-designated entities that would become the recipients of federal funding for health information exchange and would act as the de facto governing boards of the new state-level infrastructure. With the passage of this act, all 50 states and seven territories of the United States were pulled into facing the realities of constructing an HIE infrastructure and dealing with the issues of the governing of health information exchanges.

Placing governance responsibilities on the state-designated entities made them responsible for convening stakeholders statewide, crafting consensus among them, and developing statewide policies for data sharing. Their challenge was to implement the lessons learned from a decade of health information exchange governance attempts at the local level.

The following discussion moves from consideration of the major values of governance for community HIE to the challenges of implementing state-level governance organizations. The creation of the state-designated entities and the efforts of state governments to craft the right balance between public and private sector control through an appropriate governance structure are examined. The case study considers how the important governance principles that were developed at the community level are translated into the national and state approaches to governance following the passage of the American Recovery and Reinvestment Act.

BACKGROUND TO THE DEVELOPMENT OF STATE-LEVEL HEALTH INFORMATION EXCHANGE

Technical Background to Health Information Exchange

Health information exchange (HIE) is a telecommunication-based solution that enables medical record sharing among physicians, hospitals, clinics, and other provider organizations. HIE is often used as both a verb and a noun. As a verb, it refers to the electronic exchange of health information among providers and across healthcare organizations. As a noun it refers to an organization that facilitates the exchange of health information. The HIE (as a noun) integrates records from a wide variety of healthcare sources and presents them in a longitudinal, integrated view for the treating physician. The value of HIE lies in the coordination of patient care among physicians, hospitals, and other healthcare facilities. It allows access to records from participants, such as laboratories, pharmacy benefit networks, radiology or digital imaging facilities, health plans, and electronic health record systems, and ensures the secure and timely delivery of records for patient transitions of care.

State-level HIEs are being built across the country to leverage the implementation of electronic health record (EHR) systems in hospitals, clinics, and physicians' offices, and connect them to HIE networks to access patient records from other healthcare participants. Federally funded state-designated entities have been created to govern and promote health information exchange and work with the federally funded regional extension centers authorized to help implement EHRs in physicians' offices. Often these are the same organization.

Patient Lookup Model of Health Information Exchange

The HIE is based on a communication network model that facilitates the movement of electronic data among nodes on the network. What is generally considered the health information exchange model can be referred to as the *patient lookup* model. When a clinician enters a patient's identifying information into the HIE portal, it connects to a medical record repository and uses database software to search out all available electronic medical records from the data sources on the network (Just and Durkin, 2008). The records thus aggregated are then displayed on the computer screen for a physician to select. Because the records form a longitudinal record on the patient from disparate sources, a physician can obtain a broader view of the patient's medical history than might be available from paper records. Records can include demographics, discharge notes, continuity of care records, problem lists, medications, lab results, encounter histories, and so on. The availability of records is dependent on the number and type of participants who join the HIE as data sources and on the data sharing rules embedded in HIE participation agreements (Kolkman, 2011; HIE Guide Work Group, 2009).

A representative use case of the patient lookup model can be seen in the emergency room where a patient comes in without records. The ability to send a record request to the community HIE allows the emergency room physician to find vital information on the patient, potentially reducing duplicate tests and providing more informed care and treatment. This use case is shown in Figure 8.1, in which an emergency room physician can draw on data resources in the hospital and from the community HIE.

The technical infrastructure of the HIE is more complicated than the simple description of the patient lookup model. There are both hardware and software requirements that allow a physician to submit a request for a patient's records, accurately identify that patient, and match him/her to a correct set of medical records within several seconds before delivering a listing of them. A typical HIE query starts from an online portal that

Health Information Exchange Emergency Room Use Case

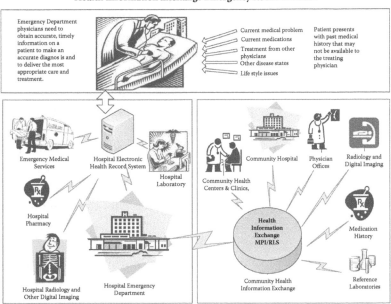

FIGURE 8.1
Emergency room health information exchange (HIE) use case.

is an entry point for a query, or it can be embedded in the physician's EHR, which is connected to the HIE over an HL7 interface and across an encrypted, secure network connection, typically using the CONNECT standard (Health Level Seven, 2004; Office of the National Coordinator for Health IT, 2010). The cost of creating interfaces between HIEs and data sources has been a significant constraint on their rapid development.

Queries are generally submitted one at a time and the patient identifiers are matched to demographic information contained in a Master Patient Index (MPI), which is a registry for patient identification. Accurate patient identification is essential in a functioning MPI and a software standard, such as the Patient Identity Cross Reference and Patient Discovery Query (PIX/PDQ) Manager, is often employed to locate the correct patient (Dimitropoulos, 2009; IHE International, 2010). Once the patient is identified, the HIE then accesses the Record Locator Service (RLS) that holds a listing of patient records from disparate data sources. Again, a software standard, such as the Cross-Enterprise Document Sharing (XDS) application from Integrating the Healthcare Enterprise (IHE), is used to locate and access records from any of the data sources participating in the HIE (Majurski, 2011; Ruggeri and Peytchev, 2011).

The records returned to the clinician also reflect numerous standards. A patient summary may be packaged in the Continuity of Care Document (CCD) (Healthcare IT Standards Panel, 2009); a digital x-ray or other image may need to be viewed with a Digital Imaging and Communications in Medicine (DICOM) viewer (Mustra, Delac, and Grigic, 2008; IHE International, Inc., 2011a; 2011b; 2011c). These and other similar technical standards are essential factors in the interoperability of electronic health record systems. Without technical standards such as these, each proprietary software system would require its own separate interface to connect to the network. One of the important duties of an HIE governance organization is to specify the technical standards under which all participants operate.

Another example of the need for standards applies to common nomenclature. For example, the naming conventions for laboratory results are typically unique to the lab, and are not consistent even between the largest reference laboratory companies, LabCorp (Burlington, NC) and Quest (Madison, NJ), for the same lab test. For an EHR to receive a set of laboratory results and save them as structured data requires that they be translated into a standardized format. The benchmark developed to normalize the laboratory results is the Logical Indicators, Indicators, Numbers, and Codes (LOINC) standard. LOINC bases its identification of lab results using six attributes:

- The component or analyte that is measured
- The property observed
- The timing of the measurement
- The type of sample
- The scale of measurement
- The method of measurement

The use of these six identifiers allows a lab result to be fully described and distinguished from any other lab result. Without this step of standardization, laboratory results from different reference laboratories could not be compared for patient care management (McDonald et al., 2010).

The use and deployment of these technical standards ultimately falls under the purview of the HIE governing organization that must ensure the interoperability of EHRs and the community HIE, and must be implemented by the HIE technical vendor. Equally complex for the HIE governing organization are the social, legal, and political constraints developed to maintain the privacy and security of each patient's protected health information and to manage the rights and responsibilities of participants in the record exchange.

Secure Messaging for Health Information Exchange

A second approach to health information exchange is secure messaging, in which a physician can use an encrypted email application to send medical records securely to another physician for treatment purposes. Most EHR systems offer secure messaging, but often cannot exchange records with EHRs from a different vendor.

In 2010, the Office of the National Coordinator for Health IT (ONC) funded the development of a secure messaging platform, the Nationwide Health Information Network Direct Secure Messaging (NwHIN Direct) application (http://wiki.directproject.org/). The intent of ONC was to develop a policy framework and a set of standards that would enable a simple and scalable service over the Internet for the secure exchange of records between doctors (Office of the National Coordinator for Health IT, 2011c). NwHIN Direct is a secure, encrypted email program that allows providers to send and receive email messages and attachments containing a patient's clinical data. Its implementation is generally overseen by the state-designated entity and state HIE governance entity. The secure email service does not require providers to use an EHR or purchase special software. If a physician meets the registration requirements and has an Internet connection, he or she can use NwHIN Direct. Providers participating in the Medicare or Medicaid EHR Incentive Program can use NwHIN Direct as a means to qualify for Meaningful Use by exchanging electronic data that can be saved in an EHR (Office of the National Coordinator for Health IT, 2011a).

NwHIN Direct connects healthcare providers through Simple Mail Transfer Protocol (SMTP), but takes this one step farther by employing the Secure/Multipurpose Internet Mail Extension (S/MIME) standard, using public key encryption for secure email communication (Office of the National Coordinator for Health IT, 2011a). Because it is built on Internet-based email standards, there is no need for a central network authority and NwHIN Direct is scalable to include anyone in a provider's professional network.

NwHIN Direct uses the X.509 digital certificate standard that identifies the user as a trusted participant in the exchange and allows him/her to securely transmit and receive protected health information. The certificate guarantees that users will abide by a set of rules that create a circle of trust (Housley et al., 1999; Giles, 2012). Users connect through a Health Information Service Provider (HISP) that maintains the certificate authority for each participant. The HISP also maintains a Provider Directory to allow providers to locate the NwHIN Direct address of any other physician participating in the email network.

Both of these approaches are covered under the governance oversight of the state-level HIEs, but the patient lookup model is generally the center of governance attention and drives decisions on data sharing and patient authorization requirements. The secure messaging model is often equated with the direct physician-to-physician communication of a fax used for treatment purposes (Health IT Policy Committee, 2010a), while health information exchange is associated with the need for patient consent and enhanced security to maintain the privacy and confidentiality of patient records.

VALUES OF GOVERNANCE IN HEALTH INFORMATION EXCHANGE

Following the passage of the American Recovery and Reinvestment Act in 2009, a nationwide project was initiated to build an HIE infrastructure that would support the exchange or records for the coordination of care all across the United States. One of the key actions of ARRA for building this nationwide network was to require each state government to establish a "state-designated entity." These organizations would be responsible for managing the funding for state-level HIEs provided in the act and for engaging resources within the state to actually construct the HIE infrastructure. With this action, the federal government passed the role of HIE governance to the states. Following ARRA, ONC launched the HIE Cooperative Agreement Program for state-level HIEs and governance of HIEs by the state-designated entities became an important state issue. Governance of local HIEs is manageable, because many of the healthcare stakeholders are familiar with each other. At the state level, governance takes on greater complexity in part because the diversity of stakeholders can increase substantially, especially in large states, and the effort to foster collaboration and data sharing increases exponentially.

The Value of HIE Governance
in Convening Healthcare Stakeholders

The eHealth Initiative, one of the premier associations voicing support for health information exchange efforts, publishes an online HIE Toolkit that provides organizational, legal, technical, and business advice and resources for HIEs (http://www.ehealthinitiative.org/hie-toolkit.html). In its opening section on governance, the HIE Toolkit presents the basic value proposition that "governance is the foundation of a health information exchange initiative (HIE). It is the first step, and the most important, in the process of forming and implementing an HIE" (eHealth Initiative, 2011a).

The type of governance structure that is established, the mission and value orientation of the governing entity, its legal status, and even its funding strategies are determined by the participation of its stakeholders and their needs and resources. Thus, while governance, in general, is a key factor for HIE, the form and structure through which healthcare stakeholders are brought together for collaborative decision making is critical, and creates the foundation for sustainability of operation. Community buy-in and participation are a major value that good governance brings to the successful exchange of health information among providers.

The State Level HIE Consensus Project, sponsored by the Foundation of Research and Education of the American Health Information Management Association (AHIMA), proposed that the governance role "consists of neutral convening and a range of explicit coordination activities that facilitate data sharing and HIE policies and practices among statewide participants" (State Level Health Information Exchange Consensus Project, 2008). This simple sentence is fraught with implications about what it means to be neutral and which body has the authority to convene stakeholders, let alone undertake coordinating the level of activity that will result in policy creation and health information exchange.

The value of governance of HIE is seen by its embodying a number of traits that must be combined successfully. The governing body "is generally responsible for setting strategy, securing funding, and exercising oversight over the operational work of the HIO [health information organization]" (Alfreds, 2009, p.15). Again, it is reiterated that the state-level HIE must function as a neutral coordinating body, convening stakeholders, and working with the potentially divergent interests of healthcare competitors to mitigate potential conflicts between them (State Level HIE Consensus Project, 2009; Bakalar, 2008). According to the National Governor's

Association, the HIE governing body should be made up of a balance of healthcare stakeholders who work together to set strategy for the operational and business activities of the HIE (Alfreds, 2009). From these examples, it is evident that one of the key values that a governing body offers to an HIE is its ability to bring competing interests to the table to work out agreements for the exchange of healthcare information to enable the coordination of care among doctors and patients.

The Value of HIE Governance for Data Sharing

The development of an HIE directly impacts issues of data sharing and trust among healthcare providers. These are sensitive issues, covering control of the data, data stewardship, trustworthiness, and accountability. A major value that the governing entity brings to stakeholders is as the neutral, trusted convening entity that can work with competing interests to build trust, ensure accountability, and clarify agreements about how different healthcare stakeholders can exchange data.

The National Committee on Vital and Health Statistics (NCVHS) argued that maintaining accountability for proper data stewardship was an important value of governance of HIE (National Committee on Vital and Health Statistics, 2010). Health data stewardship refers to an organization's ability to guarantee that personal health information is used appropriately. "The purpose of stewardship is to realize the greatest possible benefit from the effective and appropriate use of data while minimizing the risk of harm" (Kanaan and Carr, 2009, p. 2). Responsible data stewardship strengthens trust that an organization will be held accountable for the proper use of an individual's health information.

The HIE governing organization thus plays a critical role in maintaining rules of stewardship while developing the data-sharing agreements that contractually bind participants in the exchange of health information and set the foundation for healthcare stakeholders to work together. It also is responsible for holding participants accountable to the rules and to their roles in the data exchange (State Level HIE Consensus Project, 2008). How the HIE governance organization is created, who is brought to the table, and how it functions to create consensus around sharing clinical records are critical to the development of a state-level HIE (Alfreds, 2008).

Another role of the governing entity in establishing data-sharing agreements is to maintain a balance between the trust requirements of the healthcare community and its patients and the requirements of state and federal law. Data stewardship and the control of medical records are written into state and federal laws that specify the requirements of record storage, record protection, and the limits of record sharing. Federal laws, such as the Health Insurance Portability and Accountability Act (HIPAA), Family Educational Rights and Privacy Act (FERPA), and the Public Health Services Act contain strict guidelines for maintaining the security and privacy of records and provide for penalties in the case of a breach that releases records improperly. HIPAA limits the transfer and use of patient records for treatment, payment, and operations only. HIPAA allows physicians to exchange medical records with another physician for treatment purposes, but also allows patients the right to "opt out" of sharing their records. While HIPAA was enacted to facilitate the exchange of medical records, healthcare providers sometimes misinterpret its intent and use it to limit access to their records.

Most states also have statutes that protect specific classes of records, such as mental health notes, HIV information, and drug abuse treatment, requiring physicians to obtain patient authorization before transferring them to another physician. While both state and federal laws set constraints on the exchange of a patient's medical records, state laws prevail when these laws are more strict than HIPAA. Some state laws require the patient to actively "opt in" by authorizing the transfer of records over a health information exchange, while other states endorse the "opt out" approach.

These two issues of opt in versus opt out of record exchange form a major challenge for the governance of health information exchange and for setting exchange policies (Goldstein and Rein, 2010). To make things more complex, some states have addressed the issue through statute, others through administrative rules, and others through the subscription agreements for joining the health information exchange. The lack of consistency of medical record laws from state to state is a challenge to governance of health information exchange and one factor in the variance of governance models across the states (Pritts et al., 2009).

Value of HIE Governance in Bridging Public and Private Sectors

The HIE governance organization, be it the state-designated entity or some other organization, plays a critical and valuable role in bridging the interests of the state with those of private sector healthcare providers. Each state in the HIE Cooperative Agreement Program is taking its own approach to establishing the HIE governance model to oversee health information exchange. There are many similarities and many differences. In some states, the state-level HIE governance organization was created by statute before ARRA and became the state-designated entity. In other states, the state-designated entity was created by executive order, while in others, by appointment of the governor. In all cases, a primary role of the state-designated entity is to manage the HIE Cooperative Agreement with the ONC (Covich et al., 2011).

The locus of control for the HIE governance organization differs by state as well. In some states, the HIE governance organization is controlled by the state government through a state agency that directly oversees the development of the state-level HIE or manages another technical or administrative organization that takes responsibility for the HIE. In other states, the HIE governing organization is an independent, not-for-profit organization that takes on the responsibility of developing the state-level HIE for the state-designated entity. The form of governance structures thus adapts to the unique requirements of each state, though many states are moving from the state-driven direct governance to a not-for-profit governing body.

In each case, the HIE governance organization plays a unique and valuable role as the mediator between state interests and the private healthcare sector. It "serves as a neutral and skilled resource for convening diverse statewide stakeholders and leading and coordinating consensus-based efforts to develop and implement a statewide road map for interoperability" (Dierker, 2008). To succeed in this role, the HIE governing organization has to address and facilitate agreement on numerous issues surrounding the exchange of medical records both for public health and for private providers. It has to represent the interests of both the state government and private enterprise. Finally, the HIE governing organization has to become the vehicle by which competing public and private interests are coordinated and combined.

Determinants of Value for Governance of Health Information Exchange

The Markle Foundation (New York City), as part of its Connecting for Health initiative, argues that governance is dynamic, embodying a number of decision-making and policy-making stages, and that each stage may have different participants of institution engaged in the process. Markle proposes three main value components of governance for health information sharing: (1) clear goals and objectives; (2) processes for the development, coordination, oversight and enforcement of policies, standards, and services; and (3) a clear set of policies, standards, and services. The HIE governing body must ensure participation, representation, accountability, transparency, and effectiveness at each stage of HIE development to enable the secure and trusted exchange of healthcare information (Markle Foundation, 2012). The state-designated entities or the HIE governing organizations must be able to engage their communities of interest, coordinate policies and standards, engage in business development, and hold participants accountable for their use of health data.

The characteristic values of the HIE governance organization can be summarized into the following characteristics:

- Authority
- Leadership
- Neutral Convener
- Coordinate Policy Development and Strategic Planning
- Business Operations
- Accountability
- Transparency

Authority

The HIE governing body must be granted the authority to engage with stakeholders as a convening and coordinating body. Under the ONC HIE Cooperative Agreements, each state government nominated a state-designated entity, either a state agency or a not-for-profit Health Information Organization. With this designation, the authority to convene healthcare stakeholders was established as well as start-up funding from ONC. However, it is up to each state-designated entity to craft its governance model and determine the extent to which it puts together public–private partnerships. Some state legislators have crafted state laws designating the state-level HIE, others have relied on executive orders or on the current HIE environment to delegate authority for state-level HIE. Every state is unique.

Leadership

The state-level HIE governing body will be expected to take the lead in decisions that define expectations for the HIE, grant power to participants, and verify their performance. It must take the lead in aligning HIE policies and practices with the legislative and regulatory environment, then develop consistent and cohesive policies to manage the processes and decision rights for participants in the state-level HIE.

Neutral Convener

The HIE governing organization must serve as a bridge between stakeholders at the local, regional, state, and national level. The role of the convening is to create a trusted entity by facilitating professional and consumer input. It must make local Regional Health Information Organizations (RHIOs) or hospital Integrated Delivery Networks (IDNs) part of the state-level HIE, as well as bringing in consumer advocate groups as part of the system to balance the healthcare rights and needs of all residents. The HIE governing organization must engage communities and build trust relationships at the local, regional, and state level, realizing that regional and statewide governance is as important as local governance. It has to understand healthcare stakeholder needs at all levels and meet those needs through public policy. Healthcare stakeholders in the community must be brought to recognize and to buy into what is being done by state-level HIEs.

Coordinate Policy Development and Strategic Planning

The state-level HIE must deliver the processes and organizational capacity to support HIE serving all healthcare stakeholders. The statewide entity can drive public good by enabling the development of local as well as state-level HIEs. Its role is to develop policy and implementation guides to ensure that local, regional, and state-level operators of HIEs act in coordinated fashion, and it serves as a means for consensus on the adoption of HIE standards. Private and public actors must work together to achieve the goals of the HIE based on a realization that everyone is better off negotiating around differences and collaborating toward progress.

Business Operations

The HIE governance organization will have to address business models for the state-level HIE and to plan a strategy for sustainability. It will have to deal with technical operations and determine what it takes to build, operate, and maintain the HIE, even if the HIE operations are undertaken by a technical vendor that is contracted to the HIE governing organization. In this situation, the HIE governing organization must distinguish between the coordination of effort and actual HIE operations. Nonetheless, it will have to estimate the costs and resources needed to maintain the HIE, determine financing approaches to support HIE functions, and develop and payment policies. Without clear business leadership, the state-level HIE may not become sustainable.

Accountability

In order to maintain confidence in the state-level HIE, the HIE governing organization must hold network participants accountable for their actions, or inactions. There must be clear rules that lay out acceptable and proper uses of individual health information and the responsibilities of data stewardship. If the HIE is to build trust in its operations, it must be vigilant in the potential for health information to be misused or for health records to be improperly accessed. The state-level HIE must maintain the highest technical, operational and physical security to maintain the confidentiality of the healthcare records it holds and exchanges. As such, to protect itself and the data it holds in trust, the HIE must create and enforce penalties against the potential for unauthorized access, misuse, or disclosure of that data.

Transparency

In order to gain the trust of its participants and its stakeholders, the HIE governing organization has to operate under the principle of governance with transparency and openness. It needs to rely on the professional trust of its members and its customers in order to succeed in its governance activities. The HIE governing organization needs to develop policies that make its meetings and decisions open to the public, and should accept input from all interested parties.

CASE STUDY: DEVELOPMENT OF HIE GOVERNANCE THROUGH FEDERAL INITIATIVES

With the determinants of value for HIE governance established, it is instructive to turn to the case study of emerging state-level governing organizations for HIE. Few of these HIE governance organizations existed at the state level prior to the American Recovery and Reinvestment Act of 2009, and the state-designated entities are only three years old at this point. Their having to work through the principals of HIE governance to launch state-level networks becomes an interesting case study in how well the values of governance underlie their efforts.

A starting point for HIE began with the establishment of the Community Health Information Networks (CHIN) in the early 1990s. Their goal was to facilitate the exchange of health data among all members of the healthcare system, including providers, payers, managed care companies, clinical laboratories, pharmacies, and others. The CHINs were an exciting concept, but due to technical and financial constraints, most CHINs were not successful (Soper, 2001). However, the CHINs did set the stage for the resurgence in health information exchange 10 years later.

In 2001, the National Committee on Vital and Health Statistics proposed the development of the National Health Information Infrastructure (NHII) to facilitate the exchange of medical records for the coordination of care. The study compared multiple healthcare settings and focused on an infrastructure that facilitated information sharing and "health-oriented interactions" more so than just technical data systems (National Committee on Vital and Health Statistics, 2001). The study finished by recommending the creation of a permanent office in U.S. Department of Health and Human Services (HHS) to oversee the creation of the NHII.

In 2004, President George W. Bush announced the creation of the Office of the National Coordinator for Health Information Technology (ONC) and the secretary of HHS appointed Dr. David J. Brailer as the first national coordinator. ONC was to become the major federal conduit for funding health information technology projects, but the first set of demonstration projects to promote health information exchange and engage with community HIE governance efforts came from the HHS Agency for Healthcare Research and Quality (AHRQ).

AHRQ Health Information Exchange Grants

In 2004 and 2005, AHRQ initiated a set of research grants to promote health information exchange under its Health Information Technology (Health IT) Portfolio (Agency for Healthcare Research and Quality, 2006). The intent of the grants was to support health information exchange projects that would use telecommunication and information technology to provide clinical information to physicians at the point of care.

TABLE 8.1

AHRQ State and Regional Demonstrations in Health Information Technology Awardees

State	Contracting Institution	Governing Organization	Description of Project
Colorado	University of Colorado Health Sciences Center	Colorado Regional Health Information Organization	Develop a statewide HIE for physician access to clinical records
Delaware	Delaware Health Information Network	Delaware Health Information Network	Develop a statewide health information exchange for physician access to clinical records
Indiana	Indiana University School of Medicine	Indiana Network for Patient Care	Develop HIE and implement a statewide public health surveillance network to share emergency department data
Rhode Island	State of Rhode Island, Department of Health	Rhode Island Quality Institute	Develop a Master Patient Index to facilitate interoperability and sharing patient data
Tennessee	Vanderbilt University Medical Center	Mid-South e-Health Alliance	Implement a regional data sharing and interoperability services in three counties
Utah	Utah Health Information Network	Utah Health Information Network	Expand current statewide network for the electronic exchange of patient administrative and clinical data

The demonstration projects were funded to develop and evaluate patient indexing systems, facilitate interoperability among healthcare providers for the coordination of care, and explore strategies to create sustainable health information exchange. One goal of the projects was to generate data that would show improvements in the quality and effectiveness of care related to the exchange of medical records (Agency for Healthcare Research and Quality, 2004).

Between 2004 and 2005, AHRQ made awards to a number of institutions including universities, regional health information organizations, and health information networks and state agencies in six states, as shown in Table 8.1.

The lessons learned from these projects indicated that the technical development of the health information exchange was actually the least challenging part of their operations. Of more import was the ability to manage the project and apply strategic business planning, and, most importantly, to enable strong governance to ensure healthcare stakeholder engagement in the project and maintain responsiveness to the needs of the community. Appropriate governance of projects with this scope is the most valuable means to ensure the success of clinical data sharing. The grant recipients all noted that the sense of engagement and ownership of the health information exchange process in a community fostered trust in the health information organization and establishing trust is essential to successfully implement HIE (Yi et al., 2011).

It was of great benefit for the recipients to identify business partners who would participate in the exchange of data and involve them in program decisions. This helped foster a sense of ownership in the HIE and to invest them in the success of the project. The recipient HIOs found that reaching out to patient advocacy groups and other healthcare stakeholders and allowing them to voice their concerns about privacy policies or the data to be exchanged helped create community trust and fostered participation. It is interesting to note that the HIOs funded by AHRQ are now among the leaders of HIE in the nation (Yi et al., 2011).

ONC Nationwide Health Information Network Awards

NHIN Prototype Architecture Project, 2005–2007

In 2005, ONC announced a program to demonstrate the Nationwide Health Information Network (NHIN) architecture for the exchange of patient records. The demonstration projects were expected to validate the "network of network" concept of the NHIN by connecting communities and healthcare organizations without the need for a centralized infrastructure. The project was intended to demonstrate the HIE architectures that could be used to provide interoperability among healthcare participants, and make a show of functionality based on a set of use cases that included the exchange of laboratory results, electronic data from EHRs, interoperability with personal health record (PHR) software, and biosurveillance. In addition, the recipients were to demonstrate how their system would maintain the confidentiality and security of all data.

Four major IT companies received awards for this project, each of whom engaged with a number of healthcare providers in different parts of the country. These companies are shown in Table 8.2.

TABLE 8.2

NHIN 1 Prototype Architecture Awardees

States	Contracting Institution	Participating Organizations
West Virginia	Accenture	West Virginia Medical Institute
Kentucky		Eastern Kentucky Regional Health Community
Tennessee		CareSpark
North Carolina	IBM	North Carolina Healthcare Information and
New York		Communications Alliance (NCHICA)
		North Carolina Division of Public Health
		Taconic Health Information Network Community (THINC)
		New York State Dept. of Health
Indiana	CSC	Indiana Health Information Exchange
Massachusetts		MA-SHARE
California		Mendocino HRE
Colorado	Northrup Grumman	Quality Health Network
California		Santa Cruz RHIO
Ohio		University Hospitals Health System

The technical demonstration of interoperability was the focus of this project, so governance was the responsibility of the healthcare facilities in each of the consortia. Each of the technical solutions demonstrated interoperability with EHRs and PHRs, showed that different technical architectures could support the same decentralized HIE solution, and that the NwHIN could use standardized interfaces to support interoperability. The project did not offer any new knowledge on governance of HIE (Gartner, 2007).

NHIN Trial Implementations Project, 2007–2009

In 2007, ONC commissioned a second phase of the NHIN project, the "NHIN Trial Implementations," that sought to engage a group of nine of healthcare organizations in a trial implementation of the NHIN "network of networks" (Kuperman et al., 2010). The participants were required to demonstrate technical expertise in health information exchange by deploying specific use cases developed by ONC. They also were expected to actively engage their communities in a governance structure that had already developed trust relationships among healthcare stakeholders. A major requirement was for each participant to be an "HIE that demonstrates an open

TABLE 8.3

NHIN 2 Trial Implementation Awardees

States	Participating Organizations
Virginia	MedVirginia
Tennessee	CareSpark
Delaware	Delaware Health Information Network
Indiana	Indiana University
California	Long Beach Network for Health
New Mexico	Lovelace Clinic Foundation
	New Mexico Health Information Collaborative
New York	New York eHealth Collaborative
North Carolina	North Carolina Healthcare Information and Communications Alliance
West Virginia	West Virginia Health Information Network

and participatory governance process supporting state, regional, or non-geographic health information exchange with involvement from a broad and representative range of healthcare-related organizations" (Office of the National Coordinator for Health IT, 2007, pp. 22–23).

The NHIN Trial Implementation Project pushed the need for governance much more so than the prototype project. Participants were expected to ensure transparency in all meetings, ensure open selections for governing board members, and provide for conflict of interest requirements for all members. Participants had to provide full descriptions of their governance processes and had to demonstrate the extent to which they have achieved the trust and buy-in of their members.

The technical requirements for the implementations extended the use cases of the first prototype project and added core services that formed the basis of technical operations. The use cases formed a critical foundation for the exchange of records because they provided the context in which record exchange would take place. Each participant had to deploy at least one use case in its health information exchange project, as shown in Table 8.3.

As a group, each of the participants continued to demonstrate ongoing leadership in health information exchange and in their governance of the data sharing. One of the important outcomes of the NHIN Trial Implementation was the creation of a workgroup among the trial participants who developed the first draft of the NHIN Data Use and Reciprocal Support Agreement (DURSA). "The DURSA is a legal agreement created to promote and establish trust among the Participants. It codifies a common set of trust expectations into an enforceable legal framework, and eliminates the need for point-to-point agreements" (DURSA Task Group, 2011, p. i). The DURSA was created to be a comprehensive agreement that multiple participants could sign for the purpose of engaging in health information exchange using mutually agreed upon national standards for data sharing.

By using a set of common standards, the DURSA creates a framework of trust among its participants and establishes a level playing field of responsibilities, obligations, and expectations for each participant. It also ensures that all parties to the agreement will follow the same set of rules and guidelines to protect the security of their respective health information networks and the privacy and confidentiality of the protected health information that is exchanged. The DURSA is a "living document" that has been updated several times since its first publication in 2009. As a document developed solely for the purpose of addressing the requirements of health information exchange, the DURSA creates the baseline for any state to use, or to take as a starting point to develop a similar data-sharing agreement among its HIE stakeholders (Gravely, 2011).

American Recovery and Reinvestment Act of 2009: Leveraging State-Level HIE Governance

In 2009, the U.S. Congress enacted the American Recovery and Reinvestment Act of 2009 (ARRA) as the centerpiece of its stimulus package. Embedded in ARRA was the Health Information Technology for Economic and Clinical Health Act, or HITECH, which contained fundamentally transformative language addressing the adoption and implementation of health information technology. The HITECH Act established ONC as a permanent office in the Department of Health and Human Services (HHS), headed by the coordinator for Health Information Technology. HITECH empowered ONC to carry out a broad set of strategies to facilitate the adoption of electronic health records systems and "to support regional or subnational efforts toward health information exchange" (American Recovery and Reinvestment Act, 2009, p. 65).

Health Information Exchange Technical Infrastructure

In the HITECH Act, the secretary of HHS was directed to invest in the technical infrastructure necessary to "support the nationwide electronic exchange and use of health information in a secure, private, and accurate manner, including connecting health information exchanges." ONC was expected to promote the development of an infrastructure that would support telemedicine, interoperability among clinical data repositories, and public health reporting (American Recovery and Reinvestment Act, 2009, pp. 132–133).

The actual construction of the state-level HIE infrastructure was made the responsibility of state governments, through a state-designated entity (American Recovery and Reinvestment Act, 2009). This mandate placed the responsibility of governing the HIE on the state itself, whether through a state agency or through a not-for-profit organization. These requirements set the stage for the creation of new HIE governance bodies in each state and territory.

The HITECH Act specified a number of programs to promote, build, implement, and support health information technologies in all forms; tightened privacy and security measures under HIPAA; and required HIE organizations to sign Business Associate Agreements to enhance the security of health information being exchanged. The HITECH Act was not a specific about governance of these programs, but stipulated that the "national coordinator shall establish a governance mechanism for the nationwide health information network" (American Recovery and Reinvestment Act, 2009, p. 119).

Governance of the Nationwide Health Information Network

The HITECH Act established two new committees under ONC to provide quasigovernance activities of the Nationwide Health Information Network, though their function is to provide recommendations rather than oversight to ONC. The HIT Policy Committee was created to develop a policy framework for the development of the health IT infrastructure, and develop standards and specifications for building the infrastructure for secure health information exchange. The mission of the HIT Policy Committee also included developing policy standards for the security of health information exchange, public health biosurveillance, and telehealth monitoring technologies. The HIT Policy Committee was expected to offer a balanced representation to all sectors of the healthcare system and serve as a forum for stakeholder input, which is its major governance function.

The second committee created was the HIT Standards Committee. Its job was to recommend technical standards and specifications for health IT and specifically for the exchange of healthcare records to overcome the major technical barriers to interoperability among health IT systems. The HIT Standards Committee was expected to represent all healthcare sectors, including providers, health plans technology vendors, researchers and experts in privacy and security, and to serve as a forum for health IT stakeholders to provide input to ONC on the development of technical standards for HIEs. The HITECH Act outlined the need for governance through inclusivity and stakeholder buy-in from each committee, but provided no powers to either committee to actually govern the development of HIE at the national level. This was left to ONC as a federal agency (American Recovery and Reinvestment Act, 2009).

In 2010, the HIT Policy Committee formed a governance workgroup to consider the requirements of governance for the newly renamed NwHIN. The governance workgroup issued a draft recommendation on its governance roles and responsibilities at the end of the year. The workgroup recommended nine principles of governance for the NwHIN (Health IT Policy Committee, 2010b):

1. Transparency and openness: Governance approach should maximize openness and engage the public and data-sharing participants.
2. Inclusive participation and adequate representation: Demonstrate preference for including diverse stakeholders and encourage robust participation.
3. Effectiveness and efficiency: Functionality of HIE governance should have a goal of maximizing efficiency and effectiveness.
4. Accountability: Stakeholders must be held accountable and responsible to the national agenda, which should be reflected in governance mechanisms.
5. Federated governance and devolution: Governance structure should allow multiple entities to take ownership of decisions closest to them and with the greatest stake in resolution. The federal government should take the lead in areas essential to maintaining public trust in its meeting NwHIN goals.
6. Clarity of mission and consistency of actions: The rights, responsibilities and obligations of all stakeholders should be clearly documented and decision making should be consistent.
7. Fairness and due process: Governance processes should include due process and responsiveness to stakeholders and governance decisions should be fair for participants.

8. Promote and support innovation: Governance should create conditions for innovation and should minimize administrative burdens so as not to inhibit innovation.
9. Evaluation, learning, and continuous improvement: Evaluation of governance should be appropriate and fair based on clear performance guidelines.

These recommendations were developed following an open comment period in which the governance workgroup solicited comments on a number of topics. The comment topics included governance experiences from people who had implemented HIEs, especially how they established authority and executed the governance process. Comments on experiences with governance models in other domains were solicited as well, with comparisons of public–private relationships and the appropriate control of data sharing. The issue of establishing trust through governance was of major interest, and comments were requested on how to establish trust among multiple stakeholders, how the privacy and security of patient data was established, and how effective participation was established. The two last areas of interest were accountability and interoperability, and comments were sought based on the experiences of existing HIEs (Lumpkin, 2010). The results of this feedback, and the recommendations proposed by the governance workgroup, were implemented in an RFI that ONC published in May, 2012, soliciting guidance on how to establish a "voluntary framework for entities that facilitate electronic exchange" for purposes of validating them as a trusted entity (Federal Register, 2012, p. 285550).

Federal Health Information Technology Strategic Plan

The HITECH Act directed ONC to update the Federal Health IT Strategic Plan that it had published a year earlier in 2008. ONC was required to address specific objectives and metrics with respect to implementing HIE, such as strategies for incorporating privacy and security protections for HIE, educating the public about health IT, and developing strategies to ensure quality health outcomes from the use of health IT for the coordination of care. ONC was also to establish a framework to coordinate the recommendations and policies that stemmed from the HIT Policy and Standards Committees (American Recovery and Reinvestment Act, 2009).

The Federal Health IT Strategic Plan, published in 2008, addressed the governance of HIEs as an integral part of its strategy by inserting a governance objective in each of its strategic goals. At that time, the ONC strategic plan argued that "planning, consensus building, priority setting, and consistent approaches to implementing policies can best be achieved through appropriate structures and mechanisms for collaborative governance" (Office of the National Coordinator for Health IT, 2008, p. 4). In the view of the 2008 ONC strategic plan, proper governance of HIE should include individuals and organizations who are healthcare stakeholders cutting across both public and private sectors.

In 2011, ONC published its second Strategic Plan, as required by the HITECH Act. In this new plan, there is little discussion of HIE governance, except by way of reference. ONC states that it will "establish a governance mechanism through rulemaking that seeks to include accountability and oversight of nationwide information exchange" (Office of the National Coordinator for Health IT, 2011b, p. 18). The governance mechanism proposed by ONC was published as a Request for Information (RFI) in 2012 and was based, in part, on the recommendations of the governance workgroup of the HIT Policy Committee (HIT Policy Committee, 2010b). The approach taken by ONC in the RFI proposed the "creation of a voluntary program under which entities that facilitate electronic health information exchange could be validated with respect to their conformance to certain ONC-established 'conditions for trusted exchange (CTEs)'" (Federal Register, 2012, p. 28544). Under these governance guidelines, the ONC was offering a validation or credentialing mechanism for HIEs to promote trust rather than an approach that promotes engaged stakeholder collaboration and input. This approach was a step back from the consensus-building priority of governance in its previous strategic plan in 2008, and the evidently "hands on" approach of the HIT Policy Committee recommendations. In September 2012, the ONC pulled back from the governance plan established in the RFI in favor of leading through action and guidance rather than direct regulation (Office of the National Coordinator for Health IT, 2010).

Policy Drivers for Healthcare Transformation Using Health Information Technology

The HITECH Act represented a fundamental change in the way political drivers were pushing electronic health record systems and health information exchange into the healthcare arena. Multiple federal agencies were engaged in promoting, funding, and influencing a shift in the way healthcare records were recorded, stored, obtained, and exchanged. The technical infrastructure received a considerable amount of incentive funds to moving it in the direction of a national healthcare infrastructure for HIE. However, the change was mostly technically oriented. There was little guidance for how the complex and expensive HIE systems would be overseen and governed in their development.

Subsequently, ONC included governance expectations in its HIE Cooperative Agreements awards, but left the actual governance of the state-level HIEs open to the states. It was up to the states and territories to determine what governance mechanism would work best for them and what approach would provide the appropriate balance of leadership and consensus to create and maintain the technical infrastructure. This is where the value of governance lies, in its ongoing collaborative efforts to manage the important issues of health record exchange and among treating physicians and the consent of patients for that exchange.

Development of State-Level Health Information Exchange Governance Models

The development of community and state-level HIEs between 2004 and 2011 had occurred at an accelerated pace across the period and provided models of HIE governance for the state-designated entities created under ARRA. In addition to the state agencies, universities, and health information organizations spurred by the AHRQ and ONC funding programs, other organizations also were emerging as viable HIE entities. Not all were successful, and many struggled to find a sustainable business model. The one thing in common to all of the nascent HIEs was the concerted attempt to develop a governance model that worked to create buy-in, develop collaborative partnerships among healthcare competitors, and facilitate the acceptance of data sharing among healthcare providers.

In 2004, eHealth Initiative circulated its first HIE survey to evaluate the health information exchange environment across the country. These surveys have continued every year since (eHealth Initiative, 2005; 2006; 2007; 2008; 2009; 2010; 2011b). eHealth Initiative created an evaluation framework of six stages that identified at which stage an HIE had reached in their survey. The first four stages were increasingly functional, but only in Stage Five was the HIE fully operational, transmitting data, and sustainable. In the final stage, the HIE had moved beyond its initial sphere of operations to include a broader set of stakeholders (eHealth Initiative,

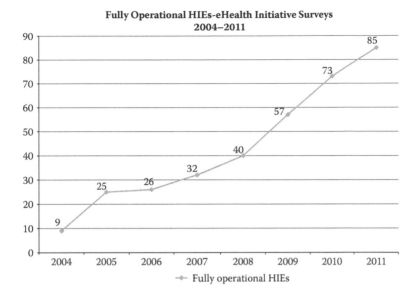

FIGURE 8.2
eHealth Initiative survey of fully operational HIEs, 2004–2011.

2005). The data from the eHealth Initiative surveys on the number of fully operational HIEs in Stages Five and Six is shown in Figure 8.2. Each of these HIEs had to demonstrate success in their governance models for bringing community stakeholders to the table and for developing the rules of data sharing among them. These governance models would become the basis for furthering the exchange of health information under the new requirements of the HITECH Act.

Development of Governance among State-Level Health Information Exchanges

Following the passage of ARRA and the HITECH Act in 2009 and the opportunity for obtaining funds for the development of health information exchange infrastructure, states and territories were faced with the task of creating governance structures for their state-level HIEs. In states with existing RHIOs or Health Information Networks, the fundamentals of governance were present in the state. For other states, planning for HIE governance began with the launch of the ONC State Health Information Exchange Cooperative Agreement Program in 2009, which was intended to kick-start the planning and construction of HIE infrastructure in each state and territory.

The purpose of the HIE Cooperative Agreement Program was to "facilitate and expand the secure, electronic movement and use of health information among organizations according to nationally recognized standards" (Office of the National Coordinator for Health IT, 2009, p. 7). Awards were to be made to the state-designated entities as specified in the HITECH Act. These could be a state agency, a not-for-profit, or another organization as determined by the state's governor. The program's intent was to develop a state-level HIE infrastructure based on statewide policies, governance, and business operations models.

With the publication of the Funding Opportunity Announcement, states started on the path of planning and building state-level HIEs. The program proposal required each state-designated entity to specify its plan for implementing state-level HIE along five dimensions: (1) governance, (2) finance, (3) technical infrastructure, (4) business and technical operations, and (5) legal/policy (Office of the National Coordinator for Health IT, 2009). Each of these dimensions represented one major variable in the total strategy to develop state-level HIE. ONC left it up to each state to determine the HIE governance and technical model that it would follow; carrying out the plan would be accomplished through a negotiated, cooperative relationship between the state and ONC.

Under the State HIE Cooperative Agreement Program, the state-designated entity was responsible for creating a governance model for the state-level HIE. Governance was defined by ONC in terms of convening health stakeholders from both public and private sectors, creating trust relationships among them, and achieving consensus for the best way to create the state-level HIE, as listed below (Office of the National Coordinator for Health IT, 2009):

- Base the governance approach on stakeholder buy-in, trust, and collaboration
- Establish goals and objectives for the HIE, based on the consensus of healthcare stakeholders and develop performance measures to track progress
- Coordinate HIE efforts with Medicaid and public health
- Develop a plan to ensure oversight of the HIE and to enforce accountability among participants
- Maintain the flexibility required to adapt to future HIE governance requirements from ONC

The actual governance model adopted by each state was determined by the authority vested in the state-designated entity by the governor, or by the legislature in states with statutory mandates. The governance model reflected the types of public–private policy approaches adopted by the state and the strategy for implementing the technical HIE architecture. Given the flexibility open to state-designated entities for designing state-level governance models, each state still faced four basic tasks for establishing that governance: (1) creating trust and stakeholder buy-in, (2) coordinating HIE strategic planning, (3) figuring out resources and sustainability, and (4) establishing accountability requirements (State Level HIE Consensus Project, 2009).

To address the requirement to establish state-level governance bodies, each of the states took an approach that was unique to its needs, though there are many similarities. In many states, the locus of control for state-level HIE governance was an important issue—whether to establish it in a state agency or in an independent not-for-profit. For example, in 2005 the state of Vermont had authorized a not-for-profit, Vermont Information Technology Leaders (VITL), to develop and lead the state-level HIE. Following ARRA, the Vermont legislature changed the governance control to the Office of Vermont Health Access, leaving VITL to manage the technical side of the state-level HIE (Vermont Agency of Human Services, 2010). This approach of locating control of the HIE in the government and managing it through a not-for-profit is common in many states. However, there is also a pattern emerging to transfer control and governance out of the state government into a not-for-profit.

The approach taken to construct the state-level HIE infrastructure differs depending on the designation of the lead HIE organization in each state and on the model chosen by the state government to manage and govern the development of HIE. The governance model, sometimes guided by state statute, determines who brings stakeholders to the table and how trust is built around their activities. Because the state-designated entities are authorized by the state government, each is dedicated to serving the policy interests of the government by serving the interests of stakeholders across the state to achieve the public good and to ensure the privacy and confidentiality of health information.

Because the state-designated entity is positioned between the state government and the private healthcare sector, it requires a neutral, reliable leadership that can develop the trust of all stakeholders. According to a survey of state-level HIEs, "even in states where government currently plays a key sponsorship role for early HIE efforts, it is most valuable for a state-level HIE entity to be a structure that engages, but sits outside of, state government" (State Level HIE Consensus Project, 2008). In this model, then, the role of the independent not-for-profit organization as the HIE governing entity brings value to governance by virtue of its independence and ability to represent all stakeholders.

HIE policy research identified several models of HIE governance that had emerged prior to the ONC HIE Cooperative Agreement Program, but were very influential in creating the governance models that have emerged among the state-designated entities (Alfreds, 2009; Deloitte Center for Health Solutions, 2006). The basic models for government-based HIE include:

- A government-led model, in which the state government runs the HIE directly and maintains immediate oversight of its use and governance.
- A public utility model, in which the government maintains a strong oversight and regulatory role, but the HIE is provided through a contract with a technical HIE vendor.
- A private sector led model, in which the state government plays only an advisory and stakeholder role in governance. The HIE entities are generally not-for-profit organizations that maintain a governance relationship with the state.
- A private collaborative HIE model, often formed as a physician/payor collaboration, or as a private Independent data network among healthcare facilities or provider groups.

Each of these organizational and governance models displays a different locus of control, different approaches to convening stakeholders, establishing trust for public–private HIE collaboration and, most importantly, financing of the HIE operations. The government-led and public utility models reflect their source of government authority through the control they establish over the governing boards for HIE policy, for HIE operations, and for oversight of the HIE. The private models reflect both government advisement and completely independent governance approaches. Under the HIE Cooperative Agreement Program, state-designated entities would follow on the first three models, but would have to work with and include any HIEs working under the fourth model. For the governance to work in any of these models, the state-designated entity has to reflect each participating organization's interests and must provide incentives for stakeholders to join the HIE, regardless of the locus of control. This is its important role as the neutral convener. It must also provide a mechanism for conflict resolution among competing interests because often there are disagreements over who should sit on the governing boards of the developing HIEs, and this can hinder the formation of a functional governance model (West and Friedman, 2012).

A second approach for portraying approaches to state-level HIE comes from a report on emerging state HIE models published by ONC. In the report, it classifies state approaches to HIE in four ways: (1) the Elevator, (2) the Capacity Builder, (3) the Orchestrator, and (4) the Public Utility (Office of the National Coordinator for Health IT, 2010). Each of these models categorizes the levels of direct involvement that the state-designated entity takes in governance and development of the state-level HIE, but ONC focuses mainly on the technical aspects of the HIE rollout. For example, the Elevator model focuses on establishing interoperability among healthcare providers, while, at the other end of the spectrum, the Public Utility model offers centralized HIE services across the state. The issues of governance are not discussed in detail in the report, but are included in the summary table of the report. Nonetheless, it seems obvious that the requirements of HIE governance will change depending on the level of state control and technical implementation that is followed.

Another approach to categorizing governance models taken by an eHealth Initiative and Thomson Reuters research team outlined the issues raised by the variation in state HIE infrastructure approaches and offered a taxonomy of different state-level HIE models: a centralized model, a decentralized model, and a hybrid model. In their white paper, the authors argue that the governance functions for each model contain both advantages and disadvantages for statewide HIE development (Covich et al., 2011).

Centralized Model

The state-designated entity establishes the state-level HIE either directly or through a public–private partnership with a not-for-profit to provide core HIE services from a central technical platform for the entire state. Independent RHIOs, hospital-based IDNs, public health entities, and other exchanges can connect to the centralized HIE. The governance advantages of this model are that governance oversight is for a single technical solution that can manage access, accountability, and sustainability from a centralized position. The downside is that there are greater liability issues for the state and the need to maintain consensus across a diverse set of healthcare communities.

Decentralized Model

The state-designated entity acts as a facilitator for the HIE, convening meetings of stakeholders, building trust as a neutral body, and developing HIE policy for the public good. In this model, the state-designated entity does not provide core HIE services, but coordinates local HIE infrastructure. Nonetheless, it has the responsibility to ensure that the state-level HIE is operational. The benefit of this model is that it leverages the community basis of existing HIEs, but both governance and technical challenges increase. The governance organization has to maintain trust and buy-in from multiple stakeholder organizations, and must craft consistent public policy from potentially divergent perspectives.

Hybrid Model

The state-designated entity facilitates the development of statewide HIE and also provides HIE services as one of several HIE entities. The state-designated entity is still responsible for the construction of the state-level HIE, so must remain positively engaged in governance activities. The governance advantages of this HIE model are that it can still leverage existing community HIEs, and minimize its liability issues, while still driving unified public policy for the HIE. The governance challenge is again technical in that it must oversee the interoperability of multiple HIEs and manage input from diverse communities across the state.

Variations of Value from Governance of State-Level HIE

In each of the state-level HIEs discussed, there is evidence of state legislatures and state-designated entities working to engage in meaningful governance activities to carry out the requirements of the HITECH Act and the HIE Cooperative Agreement Program. In some states, the governance functions are working well; in others, they are slowly being organized. When the various technical approaches to implementing the state-level HIE are multiplied by the different challenges of HIE governance models, the complexity and difficulty of deriving one best practice for governing data sharing becomes evident.

The variants of organizational authority and control, the methods of convening diverse stakeholders and working toward consensus and trust, and developing public policies for participation, accountability, and responsibility in the HIE network all demonstrate that appropriate governance must be thought through carefully. In addition to these common governance values, the type of HIE infrastructure that is implemented, the technical requirements that differ between centralized and decentralized models, and the level of technical coordination determined by the choice of HIE infrastructure all place pressure on the requirements of appropriate governance. The unique determinants of each state-designated entity mirror the needs of its unique communities, and the ability to draw stakeholders together and encourage competitors to compete on everything else except sharing the data is a challenge that must be addressed straight on to ensure the successful implementation of a state-level HIE.

CONCLUSIONS

The institution of governance oversight is critical for establishing successful health information exchange among a diverse set of healthcare providers. There are many concerns and issues about data sharing that create barriers to the effective exchange of health information. It takes a strong, neutral group of concerned people to bring the different healthcare stakeholders to the table to work through their differences to create some common ground for sharing the healthcare records for which they are data stewards. This role as the Neutral Convener is a key value for governance of the HIE because it must establish the trust among all participants and must display a preference only for maintaining an equal playing field for all. A related value for the governance body in its neutral convening role is transparency of actions, in which all meetings, discussions, and decisions are accomplished in the open. This value is essential to the formation of trust and for maintaining its credibility in the healthcare community.

There are other values that the HIE governance brings to the table. The HIE governing body must have Authority vested in it, either by the community of healthcare stakeholders or, as in the case of the state-designated entities, by the state government. This is essential for its credibility and representation of all participants. With that responsibility comes the task of Leadership in articulating a vision of health information exchange that enables the sharing of healthcare data while addressing the concerns and issues of all stakeholders. One of the major requirements of the HIE governance body in its leadership role is Policy Development by which it negotiates consensus on the rules and expectations of implementing data sharing through an HIE. It then must express stakeholder agreements as a set of clear guidelines and policies that all participants are willing to follow and hold them accountable to the rules that are established. The governance value of Accountability is essential for maintaining the credibility and trust of HIE operations.

Finally, the HIE governing organization has to address the operational and business side of the HIE. For this responsibility, it must apply the value of Strategic Planning to look to the future and determine how to bring in more participants in data-sharing activities, engage their needs, and work to develop policies and rules that benefit all participants. In addition to planning for the expansion of its membership, the governing body must apply skill in determining the appropriate Business Operations that will move it forward technically. It has to ensure that the HIE infrastructure maximizes its potential and the needs of participants and can maintain a sustainable revenue stream. These last two value function of the governance organization speak to its ability to build a business entity that can continue to operate and provide its members with a reliable technical infrastructure for the ongoing exchange of health information.

With the passing of ARRA and creation of state-level state-designated entities, the knowledge and lessons learned from developing local HIEs did not necessarily translate to the state-designated entity. The first issue to be dealt with was the locus of power and authority for the state-designated entity, whether within the state or with a state-level not-for-profit. Some states had already worked through this decision, like Rhode Island and Delaware, in part due to prior work on HIEs with AHRQ and ONC funding. Most states had to work through this problem for the first time, which was a challenge. Also, whereas local HIE governance could deal principally with a known set of healthcare stakeholders, the state-designated entity had to bring stakeholders together from disparate parts of the healthcare system, such as physicians, hospitals, payers, health departments, and consumers. Some stakeholders do not have the same goals or objectives in endorsing health information exchange, so these minor conflicts add to the difficulties of the governing body in negotiating consensus and achieving a coordination of effort among participants (eHealth Initiative, 2012a).

There are other problems facing the state-designated entities. They have the common problems of a day-to-day governing board participation, but also have to deal with issues such as a lack of technical knowledge of HIE among board members as well as competing interests, if not conflicts of interests, among board members (eHealth Initiative, 2012a). In addition, government control of the state-level HIE does not necessarily engender trust in participants, although it can. However, the pattern in many states is to migrate the control of the state-level HIE from a government agency to an independent not-for-profit. This could indicate the difficulty of establishing a functioning HIE with state resources, or it could indicate a general perspective on the appropriate locus of control. The approach that state governments and the state-designated entity have taken to building out the HIE infrastructure, whether a centralized or decentralized or hybrid model, raises governance issues unique to that model. It is still too soon to determine which is most successful.

Yet, the requirements of good HIE governance do not go away, and the state-designated entities are the generally responsible organizations, many mandated by state statute, to get the job done. The success of the federal initiative to create a national HIE infrastructure will be determined by the steady efforts of the state-designated entities as they engage in the HIE governance of their state-level HIEs and apply the lessons learned from their community-based counterparts.

REFERENCES

Adams, L. (president and CEO of Rhode Island Quality Institute). 2012. Personal communication. April 30.

Agency for Healthcare Research and Quality. 2004. AHRQ State and Regional Demonstrations in Health Information Technology. Online at: http://archive.ahrq.gov/fund/contarchive/rfp040015.htm

Agency for Healthcare Research and Quality. 2006. AHRQ Health Information Technology Programs: Update 2005-06. Online at: http://www.ahrq.gov/research/hitfact.htm

Albritton, P. (executive director, Colorado Regional Health Information). 2012. Personal communication, April 4.

Alfreds, S. T. 2008. Examination of public oversight, accountability, and financing of a sustainable electronic health information exchange industry. Web presentation to the National Conference of State Legislators, September 10. Online at: http://www.ncsl.org/print/health/forum/accountability.pdf

Alfreds, S. T. 2009. Report to the State Alliance for e-Health: Public governance models for a sustainable health information exchange industry. Shrewsbury, MA: University of Massachusetts Medical School Center for Health Policy and Research, National Opinion Research Center, National Governors Association Center for Best Practices. Online at: http://www.nga.org/files/live/sites/NGA/files/pdf/0902EHEALTHHIEREPORT.PDF

American Recovery and Reinvestment Act. 2009. Online at www.gpo.gov/fdsys/pkg/BILLS-111hr1enr/pdf/ (p. 116).

Anderson, H. (executive director, North Carolina Healthcare Information & Communications Alliance, Inc.). 2012. Personal communication, May 29.

Bakalar, R. 2008. Establishing governance: Focus on sustainability and community inclusion. Best Practices for Community Health Information Exchange. New Haven, CT: Center for Community Health Leadership. Online at: http://www.allscriptscenter.com/NR/rdonlyres/6B8E9E8A-93BD-467D-A3BB-52B0E4DC6107/0/CCHL_BPG.pdf

Barnes, K. (HIT coordinator, Commonwealth of Virginia). 2012. Personal communication, April 5.

Blair, H. (deputy commissioner and HIT coordinator, Department of Vermont Health Access). 2012. Personal communication, April 24.

Block, R. (HIT coordinator, New York State Department of Health). 2012. Personal communication, April 12.

Covich, J., D. R. Jones, G. Morris, and M. Bates. 2011. Governance models for health information exchange. eHealth Initiative and Thomson Reuters. Online at: http://healthcare.thomsonreuters.com/hie/assets/Governance_Models WP.pdf

Deloitte Center for Health Solutions. 2006. Health information exchange (HIE) business models: The path to sustainable financial success produced by the Deloitte Center for Health Solutions (Chicago). Online at: http://www.providersedge.com/ehdocs/ehr_articles/Health_Info_Exchange_Business_Models.pdf

Dierker, L. 2008. State-level efforts in health information exchange. Working Paper, American Health Information Management Association. Online at: http://library.ahima.org/xpedio/groups/public/documents/ahima/bok1_038086.hcsp?dDocName=bok1_038086

Dierker, L. (senior program director, National Academy for State Health Policy). 2012. Personal communication, May 30.

Dimitropoulos, L. L. 2009. RTI International. Perspectives on patient matching: Approaches, findings, and challenges. Online at: http://healthit.hhs.gov/portal/server.pt/gateway/PTARGS_0_11673_911437_0_0_18/PatientMatchingWhite_Paper_Final.pdf

DURSA Task Group. 2011. Data Use and Reciprocal Support Agreement (DURSA). Version date: May 3, 2011. Online at: http://healthit.hhs.gov/portal/server.pt/gateway/PTARGS_0_16869_956178_0_0_18/Restatement_I_of_the_DURSA_5.3.11_FINAL-forPARTSIGN.pdf

eHealth Initiative. 2005. Emerging trends and issues in health information exchange. Selected findings from eHealth Initiative's Second Annual Survey of State, Regional and Community-Based Health Information Exchange Initiatives and Organizations, 2005, Washington, D.C.

eHealth Initiative. 2006. Improving the quality of healthcare through health information exchange, September 25, Washington, D.C.

eHealth Initiative. 2007. eHealth Initiative's fourth annual survey of health information exchange at the state and local levels overview of 2007 findings, December 19, Washington, D.C.

eHealth Initiative. 2008. eHealth Initiative's fifth annual survey of health information exchange at the state and local levels overview of 2008 findings, September 11, Washington, D.C.

eHealth Initiative. 2009. Migrating toward meaningful use: The state of health information exchange eHealth Initiative's sixth annual survey. A report based on the results of the eHealth Initiative's 2009 sixth annual survey of health information exchange, Washington, D.C.

eHealth Initiative. 2011a. Report on health information exchange: The changing landscape. based on results from eHealth Initiative's eighth annual survey of health information exchange, Washington, D.C.

eHealth Initiative. 2011b. Setting up a governance structure. Online at: http://www.ehealth-initiative.org/setting-up-a-governance-structure.html

eHealth Initiative. 2012a. HIE toolkit. Governance challenges. Online at: http://www.ehealthinitiative.org/setting-up-a-governance-structure/governance-challenges.html

eHealth Initiative. 2012b. HIE toolkit. State run HIE. Online at: http://www.ehealthinitiative.org/setting-up-a-governance-structure/types-of-legal-entities/state-run-hie.html

Federal Register, vol. 77, no. 94. Tuesday, May 15, 2012.

Fox, H. (administrator of the Office of Health Information Exchange, Florida Agency for Healthcare Administration). 2012. Personal communication, April 2.

Gartner, Inc. 2007. Summary of the NHIN prototype architecture contracts: A report for the Office of the National Coordinator for Health IT, Washington, D.C., May 31. Online at: http://healthit.hhs.gov/portal/server.pt/gateway/PTARGS_0_10731_848093_0_0_18/summary_report_on_nhin_Prototype_architectures.pdf

Giles, B. 2012. Introduction to digital certificates, Part 3: X509v3. Online at: http://invariant-properties.com/2012/05/29/introduction-to-digital-certificates-part-3-x509v3/

Goldstein, M. M., and A. L. Rein. 2010. Consumer consent options for electronic health information exchange: Policy considerations and analysis. Online at: http://.hhs.gov/portal/server.pt/gateway/PTARGS_0_10741_911154_0_0_18/ChoiceModelFinal.pdf

Gravely, S. 2011. Restatement I of the data use and reciprocal support agreement: DURSA briefing on recent amendments. Nationwide Health Information Network Exchange, May 19. Online at: http://assess4ed.net/sites/default/files/nhin303special-briefingslidesnwhin.pdf

Health IT Policy Committee. 2010a. A Public advisory body on health information technology to the national coordinator for Health IT. Recommendation letter to Dr. David Blumenthal, MPP Chair, HIT Policy Committee, August 19. Online at: http://healthit.hhs.gov/portal/server.pt/document/947492/tigerteamrecommendation-letter8-17 2 pdf

Health IT Policy Committee. 2010b. Nationwide Health Information Network Governance Workgroup: Revised draft recommendations on nationwide health information network governance roles and responsibilities, December 1, v8. Online at: http://healthit.hhs.gov/portal/server.pt/gateway/PTARGS_0_11673_949146_0_0_18/draftrecs-govwg-120210.ppt

Health Level Seven, Inc. 2004. HL7 EHR system functional model: A major development towards consensus on electronic health record system functionality. Online at: http://www.hl7.org/documentcenter/public_temp_A7BC6625-1C23-BA170C299757440ACEB8/wg/ehr/EHR-SWhitePaper.pdf

Healthcare IT Standards Panel. 2009. HITSP summary documents using HL7 continuity of care document (CCD) component. HITSP/C32, v 2.5. Online at: http://exchange-specifications.wikispaces.com/file/view/HITSP_V2.5_2009_C32_-_Summary_Documents_Using_CCD.pdf

Housley, R., W. Ford, W. Polk, and D. Solo. 1999. Network working group. The Internet X.509 public key infrastructure certificate and CRL profile. Online at: http://www.ietf.org/rfc/rfc2459.txt

HIE Guide Work Group. 2009. A HIMSS guide to participating in a health information exchange, November. Online at: http://www.himss.org/content/files/HIE/HIE_GuideWhitePaper.pdf

IHE International, Inc. 2010. Patient identifier cross-reference HL7 V3 PIXV3 and patient demographic query HL7 V3 PDQV3 trial implementation, August 10. Online at: http://www.ihe.net/Technical_Framework/index.cfm

IHE International, Inc. 2011a. Integrating the healthcare enterprise. IHE radiology technical framework, vol. 1 IHE RAD TF-1 integration profiles. Revision 10.0, final text, February 18. Online at: http://www.ihe.net/Technical_Framework/upload/IHE_RAD_TF_Rev10-0_Vol1_2011-02-18.pdf

IHE International, Inc. 2011b. Integrating the healthcare enterprise. IHE radiology technical framework, vol. 2 IHE RAD TF-2, transactions. Revision 10.0, final text, February 18. Online at: http://www.ihe.net/Technical_Framework/upload/IHE_RAD_TF_Rev10-0_Vol2_2011-02-18.pdf

IHE International, Inc. 2011c. Integrating the healthcare enterprise. IHE radiology technical framework, vol. 3. IHE RAD TF-3, transactions. Revision 10.0, final text, February 18. Online at: http://www.ihe.net/Technical_Framework/upload/IHE_RAD_TF_Rev10-0_Vol3_2011-02-18.pdf

Just, B. H., and S. Durkin. 2008. Clinical data exchange models: Matching HIE goals with IT foundations. *Journal of AHIMA*, February, 79: 2.

Kanaan, S. B., and J. M. Carr. 2009. *Health data stewardship: What, why, who, how—An NCVHS primer*. U.S. Department of Health and Human Services, NCVHS, Washington, D.C., September, p. 2. Online at: http://www.ncvhs.hhs.gov/090930lt.pdf

Kolkman, L. 2011. *The health information exchange formation guide*. Chicago: Health Information Management Systems Society.

Kolkman, L. (president, Mosaica Partners). 2012. Personal communication, May 30.

Kuperman, G., J. Blair, R. Franck, S. Devaraj, and A. Low. 2010. Developing data content specifications for the Nationwide Health Information network trial implementations. *Journal of the American Medical Informatics Association*, January 171: 6–12.

Lumpkin, J. 2010. HIT policy committee's governance workgroup seeks comments, September 15. Online at: http://healthit.hhs.gov/blog/faca/index.php/2010/09/15/hit-policy-committee%E2%80%99s-governance-workgroup-seeks-comments/

Majurski, B. 2011. Cross-enterprise document sharing XDS. IHE IT infrastructure webinar series. Online at: http://www.ihe.net/Participation/upload/iti6_ihewkshp07_xds_majurski.pdf

Markle Foundation. 2012. Connecting for health common framework for private and secure health information. Exchange policies in practice. governance of health information sharing efforts: Achieving trust and interoperability with meaningful consumer participation. Online at: http://www.markle.org/sites/default/files/Governance%20softlaunch.pdf

McDonald C., S. Huff, K. Mercer, J. A. Hernandez, and D. J. Vreeman. 2010. Logical observation identifiers names and codes LOINC® users' guide. Regenstrief Institute, Inc., Indianapolis. Online at: www.loinc.org/downloads/files/LOINCManual.pdf (accessed September 4, 2010).

Moon, G. (director of Statewide Policy, New York eHealth Collaborative Inc.). 2012. Personal communication, March 28.

Mustra, M., K. Delac, and M. Grgic. 2008. Overview of the DICOM Standard. Paper presented at the 50th International Symposium ELMAR-2008, September 10–12, Zadar, Croatia. Online at: http://www.vcl.fer.hr/papers_pdf/Overview%20of%20the%20DICOM%20Standard.pdf

National Committee on Vital and Health Statistics. 2001. *Information for health: A strategy for building the National Health Information infrastructure. Report and recommendations.* National Committee on Vital and Health Statistics, Washington, D.C., November 15. Online at: http://www.ncvhs.hhs.gov/nhiilayo.pdf

National Committee on Vital and Health Statistics. 2010. Toward enhanced information capacities for health—An NCVHS concept paper. Washington, D.C.: HHS/NCVHS, June, p. 9. Online at: http://www.ncvhs.hhs.gov/100526concept.pdf

Nationwide Health Information. 2012. Network direct secure messaging (NwHIN) application. Online at: http://wiki.directproject.org

Office of the National Coordinator for Health Information Technology. 2007. Nationwide Health Information Network trial implementation, RFP No. 07EASRT070057. Online at: https://www.fbo.gov/index?s = opportunity&mode = form&id = d16029 b4beec031ffb518f6c2be6657c&tab = core&_cview = 1

Office of the National Coordinator for Health Information Technology. 2008. The ONC: Coordinated federal health IT strategic plan: 2008–2012, June 3. Online at: http://healthit.hhs.gov/portal/server.pt/gateway/PTARGS_0_10731_848083_0_0_18/HITStrategicPlan508.pdf

Office of the National Coordinator for Health Information Technology. 2009. American Recovery and Reinvestment Act of 2009, Title XIII—Health Information Technology, Subtitle B—Incentives for the use of Health Information Technology, section 3013, State grants to promote health information technology. Online at: http://healthit.hhs.gov/portal/server.pt?open = 512&objID = 1336&mode = 2&cached = true

Office of the National Coordinator for Health Information Technology. 2010. Nationwide Health Information Network (NHIN) exchange architecture overview. Online at: http://healthit.hhs.gov/portal/server.pt/gateway/PTARGS_0_11113_911643_0_0_18/NHIN_Architecture_Overview_Draft_20100421.pdf

Office of the National Coordinator for Health Information Technology. 2011a. Anatomy of direct session, April 12. Online at: http://wiki.directproject.org/file/view/Session+3_Direct+Boot+Camp_Anatomy+of+Direct_Final2.ppt

Office of the National Coordinator for Health Information Technology. 2011b. Federal Health Information Technology strategic plan, 2011–2015. Online at: http://healthit.hhs.gov/strategicplan

Office of the National Coordinator for Health Information Technology. 2011c. Statewide rollout of the direct project. A case study approach to understand five states' respective rollout plans and unique uses of the direct project. Online at: http://health.utah.gov/phi/getfile.php?id = 327

Office of the National Coordinator for Health IT. 2012. ONC's proposed strategy on governance for the Nationwide Health Information Network following public comments on RFI. Presentation to the HIT Policy Committee Meeting, September 6, 2012. Online at http://www.healthit.gov/sites/default/files/hitpc_briefing_090512.pdf

O'Mara, L. G. (HIT coordinator, Nevada Department of Health & Human Services.) 2012. Personal communication, March 22.

Pritts, J., S. Lewis, R. Jacobson, K. Lucia, and K. Kayne. 2009. Privacy and security solutions for interoperable health information exchange report on state law requirements for patient permission to disclose health information. Online at: http://www.healthit.hhs.gov/portal/server.pt/gateway/PTARGS_0_10741_910326_0_0_18/DisclosureReport.pdf

Root, J. (president and CEO, Utah Health Information Network (UHIN)). 2012. Personal communication, May 23.

Ruggeri, R., and V. Peytchev. 2011. Cross-enterprise document sharing-b XDS.bb. IHE IT infrastructure webinar series. Online at: http://www.ihe.net/Participation/upload/iti9_ihewkshp07_xds.pdf

Soper, P. 2001. Realizing the potential of community health information networks for improved quality and efficiency through the continuum of care: A case study of the HRSA community access program and the Nebraska panhandle partnership for health and human services,WHP023A, December. Online at: http://www.stchome.com/media/white_papers/WHP023A.pdf

Stark, S. (Rhode Island Quality Institute). 2012. Personal communication, April 30.

State Level Health Information Exchange Consensus Project. 2008. State-level health information exchange: Roles in ensuring governance and advancing interoperability, final report, Part I, March 10. Chicago: Foundation of Research and Education of the American Health Information Management Association. Online at: http://library.ahima.org/xpedio/groups/public/documents/ahima/bok1_040348.pdf

State Level HIE Consensus Project. 2009. Advancing effective state-level approaches to interoperability in the new federal context realizing state-level HIE value and sustainability, May 15. Chicago: Foundation of Research and Education of the American Health Information Management Association. Online at: http://library.ahima.org/xpedio/groups/public/documents/ahima/bok1_045664.pdf

Turner, C. (Florida Center for Health Information and Policy Analysis, Florida Agency for Healthcare Administration). 2012. Personal communication, April 2.

Vermont State Agency of Human Services. 2010. Vermont Health Information Technology Plan. Department of Health Access, Division of Healthcare Reform. Online at: http://hcr.vermont.gov/sites/hcr/files/Vermont_HIT_Plan_4_6__10-26-10__0.pdf

Ward, S. (HIT coordinator, Florida Agency for Healthcare Administration). 2012. Personal communication, April 2.

West, D. M., and A. Friedman. 2012. Health Information Exchanges and megachange. Brookings Institute, Washington, D.C. Online at: http://www.brookings.edu/research/papers/2012/02/08-health-info-exchange-friedman-west

Whitlinger, D. (executive director, New York eHealth Collaborative Inc.). 2012. Personal communication, March 28.

Yi, R. H., A. Samarth, C. Dearfield, J. Wong, A. Gluck, P. Vazquez, and A. Bhardwaj. 2011. Final report: Synthesis of lessons learned in the first 5 years of state and regional demonstration health information exchange projects, AHRQ Publication No. 11-0050-EF. Washington, D.C.: Agency for Healthcare Research and Quality, U.S. Department of Health and Human Services. Online at: http://healthit.ahrq.gov/portal/server.pt/document/954515/synthesis_of_lessons_learned_pdf (pp. 11–13).

9

Bridging the Gap between Business and IT: An Information Governance Perspective in the Banking Industry[*]

Fernando A. Faria and Gladys E. Simpson

CONTENTS

INTRODUCTION

Discussed in this chapter will be information governance (IG) and how an information governance framework (IGF) can be helpful in bridging the gap between business and IT by clarifying the factors that must be

---

[*] Based on Information governance in the Banking Industry, by Fernando de Abreu Faria, Antonio Carlos, Gastaud Macada, Antonio Carlos, and Kuldeep Kumar. 46th Annual Hawaii International Conference on Systems Sciences. 2013. IEEE.

considered by organizations in order to successfully implement an IG strategy. The practical relevance of the factors considered on the proposed IGF is illustrated in the context of the banking industry experience. To understand the current situation of IG inside banks and the possibilities of an IGF, 16 executives of 13 banks in Brazil, Hong Kong, and the United States were interviewed.

THE GAP BETWEEN BUSINESS AND IT

The widespread use of rapidly evolving information technology (IT) for business process improvement has completely transformed the banking industry to its core in the past 60 years. Since the era of punch card machines in the 1950s, followed by the introduction of mainframes in the 1960s, banks have tried to improve their overall system performance, cut labor costs, and speed up the business processes in a competitive environment.

Indeed, IT has opened new markets, products, services, and delivery channels for the banking industry. Furthermore, IT transforms not only products and processes, but even the nature of competition itself, and it does this in three different ways: (1) by creating a lever with which to achieve competitive advantage, (2) by generating completely new business, and (3) by changing the structure of the industry (Beccalli, 2007). For example, in recent years, the banking industry has experienced significant improvements in their ability to enable their customer timely access to their services and information through ATMs, online, and mobile applications. The relationship between banks and customers has changed drastically as a consequence of these improvements. Furthermore, the widespread use of Internet banking and phone banking has permitted banks to offer a variety of new products and services to customers.

The result of this stunning evolution is that IT is pushing and changing business in established organizational structures everywhere. The trend is likely to continue, as organizations around the globe continue to invest heavily in IT. According to Gartner's estimates for 2012 (IDG, 2012), IT spending will reach US$3.8 trillion, which represents an increase of 3.7% compared to 2011 figures. For comparison, if considering only the banking industry, the global spending expectation was US$363.8 billion in 2011 (CELENT, 2011).

However, despite the technology investments, keeping up with the fast-paced business process changes triggered by them inside organizations is not so simple. There are many challenges involved, given the long-standing gap between business and IT, which makes it difficult to align IT investments and efforts with business strategy.

This gap is a result of years of disconnected strategies from IT and business areas inside organizations. Despite the efforts to deal with this problem through the formulation of IT strategic plans, promoting executive meetings, increasing the CIO's (chief information officer) presence on the boards, and use of IT governance frameworks, the problem persists. It is not an easy task to align what sometimes represents different interests even inside the same company. Harmonizing IT strategies with business strategies, making decisions about what is necessary for business and IT, executing plans within time and budget, and balancing IT investments among interested areas are some of the difficulties for the alignment.

This gap arises in great part due to the communication barriers that exist between IT and non-IT people in organizations. People from IT tend to have a technical background and use a language unfamiliar to business people. For example, thinking about some commonly used IT acronyms, such as C#, C++, .NET, Java, VB, XML, SQL, DB2, ADABAS, ODBC, BPM, ECM, ERP, CRM, SOA, VPN, PKI, OLAP, among many others, is possible to state that people from IT know the meaning of these awkward words, but we cannot say the same about people from the business side. The terminology used in IT is so vast that it is very difficult, even for the experienced CIO, to know about all of the terms. On the other hand, depending on the business area, it is quite possible to have similar issues with specific technical jargon used by business professionals that are unknown to IT people. Another source of conflict that contributes to the gap between IT and business comes from the need to balance IT investments among the company areas following business demands. How to decide what is the priority for the company's success or determining if it is better to invest in IT to support what exists, or to invest in business growth, can create internal tensions within a company.

To reduce the gap between business and IT, it is essential that technical and nontechnical people share a common knowledge base and learn to collaborate effectively in spite of their differences.

When this doesn't occur, organizations end up focusing mostly on data capture, production, and storage while devoting little attention to the use of information and deriving value from it. In other words, the focus is not on the "information" but on the "technology" part of IT. Deriving value from information requires closing the gap and having an effective interplay of the business and IT areas.

One of the contributing factors to the gap between business and IT is the lack of a framework to clarify how the different roles within the organization become a part of information governance. Such a framework can identify critical elements that must be explicitly considered by business and IT in key decision-making processes and communications. Furthermore, the framework must consider information as an asset that has some special characteristics, very different from usual goods (Kooper, Maes, and Lindgreen, 2011):

- It is both an end product and an input into the creation of other goods.
- It is expensive to produce and cheap to reproduce.
- Its value is subjective.
- Its context should be considered when consumed.

This chapter presents some initial results of a doctoral research on Information Governance, conducted by one of the authors in the highly dynamic and information-intensive banking industry. Information, undoubtedly, is recognized as the most important resource in the banking business. To make the scope of the work broader and applicable to a global set of banking practices, the study considered banks in Brazil, Hong Kong, and the United States.

The following sections show an alternative way to reduce the gap between business and IT by using an information governance perspective to restore "information" to its real and relevant position inside the organizations.

AN INTRODUCTION TO INFORMATION GOVERNANCE IN THE BANKING INDUSTRY

Tom Davenport (1998) made the following observation over a decade ago: "Our fascination with technology has made us forget the main purpose of the information: to inform." Even nowadays it seems clear that the field of IT is still being dominated by the T (Technology). The annual expenditure on IT, globally, was nearly $4 trillion dollars in 2012 (IDG, 2012) and half of it goes explicitly to the digital infrastructure of organizations.

Not surprisingly, in the "information age," organizations have more data to cope with than ever before. However, the abundance of information can have both positive and negative impact on organizations. While good use of information represents an opportunity to gain competitive advantage, overabundance of information increases the risk to running the business.

Information is being created and is multiplying with an amazing speed, due to the facilities offered by IT tools. In 2005, mankind created 150 exabytes (a billion gigabytes) of data, and, in 2010, the number was estimated to be 1,200 exabytes (The Economist, 2010). People in organizations are beginning to realize that they are overloaded with information.

At the same time, Internet and other technological innovations have increased the speed with which business operations are conducted. For instance, according to statistics from Internet World Stats (2012), the number of users on the Internet grew from 361 million people in December 2000 to 2.267 billion in December 2011. The business world is moving at a much faster pace. Consequently, managers and their teams are increasingly under pressure to meet tighter deadlines and make quicker decisions. Because of this, they need reliable information delivered to them with greater speed.

While most information management initiatives have had a tendency to focus on the technology aspect of IT, companies are starting to realize that the full value of information depends in large part on the policies and procedures that govern and control their use, access, analysis, retention, and protection. Another important aspect is that, in a world controlled by a sense of objectivity and technological artifacts, it is common to find the misconception that information is a product of technology. However, information is essentially the result of subjective interpretation of objective facts (Beijer, 2009). Information belongs to business areas and, therefore, they should be accountable for it.

Contemporary organizations face a new situation; they have a context with both rising volume and complexity of the data, and the challenge is not to lose their ability to generate value from them. The explosion of available data, structured and nonstructured, is real and is a big threat to modern corporations. Under the IT perspective, they need to evaluate if their current database management systems and information systems are prepared to run on this new reality in order to handle the exponential increase in the amount of information. Under the business perspective, they need to learn how to govern information to optimize their value.

Defining Information Governance (IG)

Information governance (IG) is an emerging concept in the field of governance (Van Grembergen and Haes, 2009) and it is part of the response to the inadequacy of IT governance with respect to the increasing importance of information in modern organizations (Kooper, Maes, and Lindgreen, 2009). The concept of information governance was introduced by Donaldson and Walker (2004) as a framework to support the work at the National Health Society on security and confidentiality arrangements to be applied at multiple levels in electronic information services. Some definitions of information governance are presented below.

Soares (2011) states that "information governance is the formulation of policy to optimize, secure, and leverage information as an enterprise asset by aligning the objectives of multiple functions."

Kooper, Maes, and Lindgreen (2011) state that information governance "involves establishing an environment of opportunities, rules, and decision-making rights for the valuation, creation, collection, analysis, distribution, storage, use, and control of information."

For Gartner, "*Information governance* is the specification of decision rights and an accountability framework to encourage desirable behavior in the valuation, creation, storage, use, archival, and deletion of information. It includes the processes, roles, standards, and metrics that ensure the effective and efficient use of information in enabling an organization to achieve its goals."

Organizations need IG to be able to respond to those basic, but sometimes awkward, questions: What information do we have? For what do we need this information? Who is responsible for this information? Who can use this information? or For how long do we have to keep this information? If a bank is able to respond to these questions for all its information, it is probably working over some IG factors, or in other words, it is already on the way of IG. If not, it is time to start an IG program as soon as possible. For example, a very common situation in banks is when no one wants the responsibility for deleting outdated IT content. Who pulls the trigger? Knowing its information catalog is basic for every organization, and there is no doubt that information belongs in the business areas.

Dealing with structured data is usual, but unstructured content like email, images, social media data, and others is critical in many business areas and it should be mandatory to implement an IG program. Managers of different business sectors can perceive easily the hurdles faced by organizations when there is a lack of standards, policies, and procedures related to information. An IG program can help organizations in many ways, including:

- Mitigating the risk of information misuse
- Deciding about what information must be kept
- Disposing of information in order to reduce the cost and complexity of IT processes
- Reducing the volume of information for e-discovery
- Taking control of email and all other types of unstructured data
- Responding to new regulations and technologies

Banking and IT

The core of the business practice of banking has not changed; a bank still acts as an intermediary between people who have money to invest and people who want to borrow money. However, the way banking operations are carried out has changed drastically in the past three decades. Technological developments have had and will continue to have a major impact on the delivery of banking services. Banks no longer need hundreds or thousands of physical branches to provide their services. The relationship between banks and their customers can now be based entirely on electronic and automatic processes. The goal of IT in banking is to support these business processes.

Furthermore, banks also have undergone major transformations due to financial and legal reasons. For example, the crisis of 2008, triggered by the collapse of the U.S. subprime mortgage market and the reversal of the housing boom in other industrialized economies, caused the fall of world stock markets and the collapse of large financial institutions, which resulted in the rise of government's rescue packages to bail out their financial systems (Global Issues, 2010).

The crisis provoked a wave of litigations that required banks to reveal large amounts of information. Consequently, banks were forced to put their houses in order and rethink their processes for managing information. The ability to handle information effectively inside a company depends on a variety of factors, including executive involvement and a business culture that supports collective ownership of information.

Besides showing the current relevance of information governance for banks, interesting statements from executives of 13 banks in 3 countries were recorded concerning the usefulness of an information governance framework (IGF), and on the composition of that framework. The IGF covers a set of very helpful elements to bridge the gap between business and IT.

THE BRIDGE: IGF AND ITS POSSIBILITIES

Having greater clarity of the scope entailed in information governance, including the wide range of business and technology responsibilities involved, can help reduce the gap between IT and business.

An IGF that spans both technical and business aspects of the organization with adequate balance can facilitate the two-way exchange of ideas and promote close alignment of interests between business and IT people in organizations. In other words, the IGF proposed here encompasses factors from a broader range of domains and, most important, without a technology bias. Strategically created, enterprise-wide frameworks that define how information is controlled, accessed, and used are arguably the most critical elements in a successful information governance program.

However, there is no one-size-fits-all IGF solution. Which factors contained in the IGF will be considered by an organization and which will not will depend on a group of elements, such as level of maturity, its own characteristics, and its decisions regarding the desired improvements. Nevertheless, an IGF can help to reduce the gap between business and IT by:

- Providing a shared perspective for business and IT areas on IG (the use of common framework).
- Dealing with information as an organizational resource that belongs to business areas and the quality of which is derived from good governance practices.
- Having a common understanding of the different factors involved in IG can guide and even regulate the communication flows between business and IT and improve alignment.

- Allocation of decision rights and responsibilities that consider all relevant aspects of IG. IGF shows a more complete picture that encompasses business aspects that are usually overlooked in favor of greater focus on technological aspects.

IGF Dimensions and Factors

The proposed IGF consists of dimensions and factors. Dimensions are the first level of the framework and are a grouping of a set of interconnected factors. Factors are the second level of the framework and they identify the issues that should be addressed by a company to implement an IG strategy. Factors are implemented by policies, practices, and actions.

The first step in assembling the IGF is identifying and defining the dimensions of the framework. Three dimensions are identified: people, policies, and technology. Figure 9.1 shows the IG subject according our vision.

The sides of the triangle bordering both the triangles of policies and people can be considered as the enablers of an IG program. Policies and technology provides the tools that support the program, and the conjunction between people and technology set the context for information governance. In Figure 9.1, is possible to look at IG from different perspectives. First, IG is implemented by policies that are defined and applied by people

FIGURE 9.1
IG under different angles.

with the support of technology. Second, IG always involves three elements: enablers, tools, and context.

The second step in developing the IGF is the factor definition. The following 20 factors were identified for the IGF and are listed here in alphabetical order:

- Accessibility
- Accountability
- Communication
- Compliance
- Consumerization
- Context
- Culture
- Ethics
- Formal structure
- Mobility
- Monitoring
- Privacy
- Quality
- Retention
- Security
- Sharing
- Standardization
- Systems
- Transparency
- Value

All of these factors have come from theoretical elements (agency theory, resource-based view of the firm, dynamic capabilities) and each one was associated with one of the three dimensions; by proceeding this way, the IGF was formatted. The IGF derived from this process is summarized in Figure 9.2.

The first of the three IGF dimensions, People, includes factors such as context, culture, and ethics. The second dimension, Policies, represents the central part of the model, and has the following factors: accessibility, accountability, communication, compliance, formal structure, monitoring, privacy, quality, retention, security, sharing, standardization, transparency, and value. The third and final dimension is Technology, which

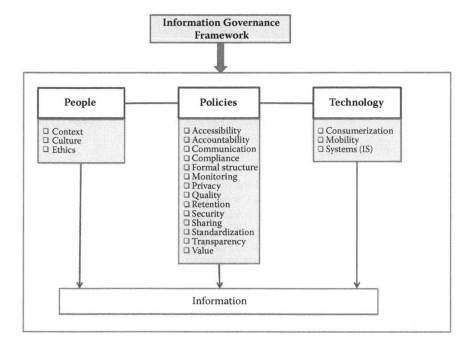

FIGURE 9.2

Information governance framework (IGF). (From: Faria, Macada, and Kumar. 2013. Paper presented at the proceedings of the 46th Annual Hawaii International Conference on System Sciences, January 7–10, Maui, HI. IEEE Computer Society Press. With permission.)

is composed of three factors: consumerization, mobility, and systems. Table 9.1 presents some additional descriptions for all IGF dimensions and factors.

LESSONS AND EXAMPLES ON IG FROM THE BANKING INDUSTRY

The Context and the Case Studies

This chapter considers three sets of banks in three different countries: Brazil, the United States, and China (or, more specifically, in Hong Kong, a Special Administrative Region (SAR) of People's Republic of China). Sixteen interviews with executives of 13 different banks in three countries were conducted. The strategy provided a broader vision of current IG practices in banks. The executives in the study include global CIOs,

TABLE 9.1

IGF Dimensions and Factors Description

People: *Refers to people within the organization and the people who relate to it*

FACTOR	DESCRIPTION	REFERENCE
Context	Context is an element of the information environment, which incorporates all the factors affecting how an organization deals with information.	Davenport and Prusak (1998)
Culture	Organization culture is thought to shape values and norms, is learned and transmitted between individuals and teams through social learning, role modeling, and observation, and, as a result, assists organization members in dealing with external pressures that threaten organizational survival and/or internal integration.	Kondra and Hurst (2009)
Ethics	When we talk about morality and ethics within government, public, and private sector organizations, we are referring to the behavior and collective outcome of actions taken by the managers and staff.	McManus (2004b)

Technology: *Refers to the set of technological mechanisms or artifacts that support the IG strategy*

FACTOR	DESCRIPTION	REFERENCE
Consumerization	The term *consumerization* first gained popularity in 2001 when it was used by Douglas Neal and John Taylor as a description for how information technology innovation was emerging in consumer-based technology, with the expectation it would eventually migrate into the enterprise.	Clevenger (2011)
Mobility	Mobile ICT provides workers the means to access and utilize work-critical data and information wherever and whenever they need it. However, these benefits represent only the tip of the iceberg. Enterprise mobility solutions have the potential to fundamentally transform organizations, supply chains, and markets.	Basole (2008)
Systems (IS)	The combination of hardware, software, data, and communication formed the core of information systems. As each of these dimensions developed and integrated, the concept, design, and capability of information systems underwent massive changes.	Mukherji (2002)

TABLE 9.1 *(Continued)*

IGF Dimensions and Factors Description

Policies and Practices: *Refers to the set of IG policies and practices adopted by the organization*

FACTOR	DESCRIPTION	REFERENCE
Accessibility	It means that information is able to be found and presented to the person who needs it, when he or she need it, as well as in the appropriate form.	Martin, Dmitriev, and Akeroyd (2010)
Accountability	Accountability is the linkage of two components: the ability to know what an actor is doing and the ability to make that actor do something else.	Schedler (1999); Hale (2008)
Communication	Refers to transferability (signs) and the mechanisms for transfer across individuals, across space, and across time.	Grant (1996)
Compliance	Compliance is the duty to comply and enforce internal and external regulations imposed on the institution's activities.	ABBI (2009)
Formal Structure	Governance bodies to create strategies, policies, and procedures surrounding the distribution of information inside and outside the firm.	The Economist (2008)
Monitoring	Monitoring is done to increase the amount of information available to shareholders and can alleviate agency problems when insider ownership is low.	Anderson, Melanson, and Maly (2007); Becher and Frye (2011)
Privacy	Claim of individuals, groups, or institutions to determine for themselves, when, how, and to what extent information about them is communicated to others.	Westin (1967)
Quality	Information quality can be defined as information that is fit for use by information consumers.	Huang, Lee, and Wang (1999); Eppler (2003)
Retention	Formal or consistently observed procedure for ensuring that records are kept for legal or statutory compliance, or for judging the potentially historical importance of records.	Bailey (2011)
Security	The aim of information security is to assess the level of risk to the information and take appropriate measures to protect the security and confidentiality of the information without compromising the need for the information to remain accessible to authorized users.	McManus (2004a)

Continued

TABLE 9.1 *(Continued)*

IGF Dimensions and Factors Description

FACTOR	DESCRIPTION	REFERENCE
Sharing	Sharing is the free exchange of nonsensitive and sensitive information. Sharing occurs between individuals in teams, across functional boundaries, and across organizational boundaries (i.e., with customers, suppliers, and partners).	Marchand, Kettinger, and Rollins (2000)
Standardization	Metadata or data about data is information DNA. Consistency here will pay dividends and make compliance and auditing less painful. By standardizing foundational components, you become more agile.	Samuelson (2010)
Transparency	An institution is transparent if it makes its behavior and motives readily knowable to interested parties. A *transparency mechanism* is a policy that makes an institution more transparent.	Marchand, Kettinger, and Rollins (2000)
Value	The value of information is subjective, because it may be more useful in satisfying the wants of one person than another, or of no use to one person and of use to another.	Kooper, Maes, and Lindgreen (2009)

Source: Faria, Macada, and Kumar. 2013. Paper presented at the Proceedings of the 46th Annual Hawaii International Conference on System Sciences, January 7–10, Maui, HI. IEEE Computer Society Press. With permission.

IT directors, and managing directors. For confidentiality reasons their names and banks are not given.

The choice of the three countries was made because their importance in local, regional, or global markets. Brazil, one of the BRICS (Brazil, Russia, India, Chine, and South Africa) countries, is an important center in Latin America. Hong Kong is a major financial center in Asia and also is, at the same time, highly integrated with banks in the United Kingdom and Europe. Finally, the United States is the preeminent global power, and its banking system is included in the study for its presence and influence in the international markets. Three big Europeans banks are included in the selected sample, and among the 13 banks there are 4 included in the list of the 10 bigger banks in the world, published by The Banker (http://www.thebanker.com/information) in 2011.

The data were collected through interviews with the high executives of the banks. The script for the interviews is based on the proposed IGF. The instrument is a semistructured questionnaire composed basically

TABLE 9.2

List of Case Studies

	Bank		
Case Study	City of Interview	Country of Origin	Number of Employees
1	Brasília	Brazil	120,000
2	Brasília	Brazil	86,000
3	São Paulo	Brazil	8,200
4	Hong Kong	China	310,000
5	Hong Kong	Japan	26,000
6	Hong Kong	China	13,000
7	Hong Kong	France	157,000
8	Hong Kong	Germany	102,000
9	New York, Fort Lauderdale, São Paulo	United States	230,000
10	New York	United States	48,000
11	New York	United Kingdom	288,000
12	New York	United States	62,000
13	New York	United States	240,000

Source: Faria, Macada, and Kumar. 2013. Paper presented at the Proceedings of the 46th Annual Hawaii International Conference on System Sciences, January 7–10, Maui, HI. IEEE Computer Society Press. With permission.

by questions about each IGF factor. Some additional questions like those related to topics such as dynamism of the banking industry or the relevance of IG subject, complete the document.

The interviews were carried out between October 2011 and March 2012 in the cities of Brasília, São Paulo, New York, Fort Lauderdale, and Hong Kong. All interviews were recorded with the express consent of the interviewees, and their contents transcribed and analyzed by authors using NVivo software. Sixteen major executives of banks were interviewed: five in Brazil, five in Hong Kong, and six in the United States. All interviewees are male and occupy high positions in their organizations. The case studies are summarized in Table 9.2.

Each bank had at least two basic methods adopted in the research: an interview with a major executive and analysis of documents captured in the organization Web site. In some banks the researcher had access to internal documents, and, for others, articles in journals and trade magazines were selected.

To complete the scope, a special conversation was conducted in Hong Kong to discuss the IG subject with a senior consultant of CBRC (China Banking Regulatory Commission). CBRC is the agency that regulates the banking sector in China. The interview's main purpose with the CBRC consultant was to investigate the vision of Chinese regulation on IG practices. Additionally, it was possible to understand the different stages of governance between the Hong Kong and mainland China banking systems.

IG Relevance

Many banks are currently engaged in attempts, for example, to achieve KYC (know your customer). This is only additional evidence from all the interviewed executives that banking is basically "information." Indeed, information is highlighted as a very sensitive subject presently in banks. To illustrate the importance of information governance, there is the statement of a senior advisor from China: "Reliable information is the real asset for banks. It helps bankers to make good decisions. Reliable information comes from governance."

When asked whether they believe that information governance is an important issue for banks, the bank executives from the three countries offered different and interesting answers. One Brazilian executive stated, "Yes. At the moment, within the IT area, we are creating a specific structure to deal with information management and information governance. That initiative is linked to an auditing project." Another Brazilian executive was more emphatic: "I'd say that what was once desirable will become essential. Those who do not have good IG will be out the market. And, I also think at some point in the future, it will be criteria for obtaining a license to operate or not."

A bank executive in Hong Kong provided a very comprehensive answer: "Yes. Without proper governance, one can use information for improper activities, which may damage a firm's reputation, revenue, credibility, and may be subject to regulatory and legal litigations." In a similar way, another Chinese executive said, "Yes. With better use of information, a bank can be more efficient, reduce risks, and improve services. All [of] these combined will lead to higher returns for shareholders and create greater employee engagement."

A particularly interesting response was given by an executive in the United States: "Yes. My central thesis is that information governance is increasingly important, massively important in the megadata world. If we don't get these policies right, we'll have unnecessary duplication, unnecessary linkage, unnecessary complexity." From an experienced executive, the answer was "yes, because, fundamentally, our product is information. We provide liquidity, we provide risk transference, we provide ideas, and we provide services as well, I guess, but underlying all of that is information."

Despite all the positive answers regarding the demand of information governance in banks, there is an outstanding observation made by an IT bank executive in Hong Kong: "If banks recognize information as 'the asset,' the absence of information policies or information governance shows that something is wrong." There seems to be a paradox here because while almost all banks recognize information as "the asset," the vast majority still does not have specific policies and processes that directly address the subject.

Implementing IG through an IGF

The bank executives were asked whether they think that an information governance framework would help banks in their activities. One executive from a large bank in Brazil gave the following short answer: "I think so. It's very convergent with our discussions and what we are trying to do." The answer from another Brazilian banker was: "I think if you had discussed it before, since the technological renewal, from the times of technological evolution, if you had had this guidance … I think you would go in one direction without losing focus."

In Hong Kong, an executive said, "The IGF can raise the awareness of senior management regarding the need for banks to a process by which they can allocate resources to manage their information. An IGF can make implementing IG in banks easier." Another executive agrees with the framework, but sees the subject of IG as being part of the risk management area: "I totally agree. We're going in this direction, but we don't recognize it as an IGF. We're working with risk management."

In the United States, one executive was very concerned with the costs and risks: "The rate of consumption is outpacing the reduction in the unit cost of storage. The legal process is extraordinary expensive and if you know exactly what information needs to be stored and for how long, the cost can be cut." This bank is discovering how to save money by implementing an IG program. Another very frank answer was given by an American executive: "I think it can help to simplify and reduce costs and increase security. However, I think the hurdles to effective IG are very high, because it is a strategic decision, taken by top management, and not a tactical one." This is a very important aspect; it is clear that implementing IG is not an easy task.

The importance of IGF was demonstrated by the use of the words *cost, risk*, and *performance*. In the words of one banker: "I think it helps you manage risk, I think it helps you manage costs, I think it helps you manage the service levels that you provide." For another, "With no proper governance framework, information might be used for improper activities, which may damage the firm's reputation, revenue, credibility, and the firm may be subject to regulatory and legal litigation." Complementing the responses above, there is a notable remark from a senior advisor in China: "An information governance framework can help banks ensure data quality, speed up time to market in product creation and innovation, simplify data architecture, and reduce costs and risks."

Perceptions of the Proposed IGF

Listening to the executives' responses to the question of what factors should be considered by banks in an information governance framework was very important. The IGF shown in Figure 9.2 was presented to and discussed with bank executives. Specific questions were put to the executives in an attempt to validate the dimensions and factors in the IGF. Thirteen case studies were completed and included triangulation processes involving at least two different sources of data, interviews, and documents obtained from the banks' Web sites.

Several important points can be drawn from the preliminary results of the research. Firstly, without exception, the factors accessibility, accountability, compliance, ethics, privacy, and security are strongly present among the banks when the topic is an IGF. Secondly, the factors consumerization, mobility, and standardization are causing additional concerns and leading the banks to make efforts in relation to those factors, as would be expected considering the recent technological changes in telecommunications around the world.

In general, the executives agreed with the IGF factors presented. When questioned about other factors not included in the framework, cost and usability were remembered by a few executives. One executive did not agree with the inclusion of the factor value in the IGF; in his opinion, this is the desired result or outcome rather than a factor. Another executive disagreed with the inclusion of the factor culture. An interesting comment came from an executive in Brazil who suggested grouping some factors together as an alternative to eliminating them, considering the extended scope of the IGF. There were also some references to the difficulties involved in implementing such an IG framework in banks, most of which are concerned with the need to prioritize the results. Others pointed out that IG is included in IT governance.

A particularly noteworthy finding is that amongst the banks included in the study, a U.S. bank is currently implementing an IG program. They found that they can save time and also a lot of money by implementing such a program. It is interesting to note that, in this case, the project was assigned to the global CIO. The project's objectives are to reduce costs and mitigate legal risks.

Lastly, it is interesting to note that while the majority of the banks included in this study has some policies or practices that address the factors contained in the proposed IGF, information is not usually their focal point. Moreover, in general, such policies and practices tend to be disconnected from each other.

CONCLUDING REMARKS

This final section starts with setting a new definition for IG. Information governance refers to the establishment of policies through formal structures that define rules, procedures, and decision-making rights regarding information management, in order to mitigate regulatory and operational risk, reduce costs, and optimize the performance of the organization.

Some of the executives interviewed in this study agreed that there is a tendency for the *T* (Technology) in *IT* to predominate in the IT field. In recent years, organizations of all sizes have become fascinated by the resources created by information technology. This is easy to understand when one looks at the global figures for IT. According to Gartner, global spending on IT in 2012 will reach US$3.8 trillion (IDG, 2012), a large part of which will be used to acquire new products and infrastructures. As mentioned before, to reduce the gap between business and IT is necessary to change the present technology bias from the enterprises' investments in IT. An IGF can help organizations review their investments priorities by refocusing them on the subject of information. In 2003, Nicholas Carr published "IT Doesn't Matter," which caused a huge stir in the IT industry. Indeed, mainly since the advent of Internet, the evolution in software production, the spread of networks, and the rise of the consumerization phenomenon, there is a common perception that technology is available everywhere. The differential lies with information use. That is a clear sign of what is happening in the business world today—information is being elevated to its former prominence, a privileged position that was over-taken for a while by the glamour of IT. In other words, the "I" matters. That does not mean the "T" is not important; on the contrary, it is vital to support the information processes inside organizations.

The comments made by the bank executives during interviews on differ-ent continents, such as:

> "Information is one of our key assets in the firm,"
> "With better use of bank information, we can be more efficient, reduce risks, and improve services,"
> "The bank is nothing but information,"
> "Our product is information"

could certainly lead one to conclude that information is a priority. However, in the real world this does not seem to be the case. Cortada (2011) argues that corporations rarely have a comprehensive approach to the manage-ment of its most used and most important asset: information. The initial findings of this work with banks indicate that he is absolutely right.

The results show that, in general, banks have already begun to imple-ment some of the listed IGF factors in some way, although predominantly in unstructured forms that do not directly address information. That is a paradox because, while they all recognize information as the key "asset" in banking, the vast majority still has not introduced specific and integrated IG policies and processes.

The IGF validation process was carried out among 16 top executives from 13 banks in 3 countries, none of whom said the IGF was invalid or not applicable. Some still see IG as part of IT governance and here there is a point of discordance. When dealing with all the aspects of information, using IT governance frameworks is inappropriate because they contain a clear technology bias. Furthermore, things are changing and, in many of the participating banks, the present researcher was able to identify an awareness of an uncomfortable situation and the need to move toward IG.

An important aspect is the exponential growth in the amount of infor-mation both inside and outside these organizations. Banks are struggling to deal with the explosion of both structured and unstructured data, as suggested by this comment from an executive in New York: "As an orga-nization today, we have something like 28 petabytes of information and

TABLE 9.3

Units for Computer Data Storage

Bit (b)	Byte (B)	Kilobyte (KB)	Megabyte (MB)	Gigabyte (GB)	Terabyte (TB)	Petabyte (PB)	Exabyte (EB)	Zettabyte (ZB)
1 or 0	8 bits	1,000 bytes	1,000 KB	1,000 MB	1,000 GB	1,000 TB	1,000 PB	1,000 EB

it's growing exponentially." See Table 9.3 to understand in a simplified way the units used for computer data storage.

So, on one side, there is cost of the storage and all the processes involved with the retention and recovery of information. More importantly, on the other side is the capability of the enterprise to use information effectively, and evidently, with few exceptions, the bulk of them are not fully prepared for this. If a company is prepared, it should be able to, at least, answer the basic question proposed by Kooper, Maes, and Lindgreen (2011): "What information do we need, how do we make use of it and who is responsible for it?" Certainly, a well-implemented IGF will help banks to answer not only these basic questions, but other important questions related to the "information" resource within the organization.

Another interesting result is related to the factors consumerization and mobility. Some banks in the United States see the consumerization phenomena as an opportunity; they know it's not an easy decision, mainly for security reasons, but it is inevitable. In the words of an experienced American executive: "In my life, I've learned not only to listen to what people say, but also to watch what people do, but mainly watch where they are putting their money. So, that's a place to spend a lot of money, on this whole notion of mobility and consumerization."

Bridging the gap between business and IT in the banking industry through an IGF offers a unique and shared perspective. Such approach permits the use of a common framework across the entire enterprise. The widespread knowledge of IGF's factors and dimensions helps the enterprise in the task of aligning the interests of business and IT. The set of IGF factors covers a wide scope that can establish the use of good information governance practices, which improves the quality of information and facilitates the decision processes.

The goal for every bank is to select which factors should be considered in its IGF and work on their further development. In this way, it is possible to build an IG program addressing all relevant aspects related to the information domain in the banking business. The comments made by top bank executives leave no doubt that information governance is an increasingly important subject for the banking industry. Among the reasons given for this importance are the benefits provided, such as reduced costs, reduced exposure to legal risk, and improved performance. Therefore, developing and implementing an IGF would seem to be the natural course to take, though there is no one-size-fits-all solution. Which factors contained in the IGF presented herein will be considered of importance by an organization and which will not will depend on that organization's particular level of maturity, its own characteristics, and its decisions regarding the desired improvements.

ACKNOWLEDGMENTS

I would like to thank Professor Antonio Carlos Gastaud Maçada from Universidade Federal do Rio Grande do Sul, and Professor Kuldeep Kumar from City University of Hong Kong for their advice and suggestions. I would also like to thank Professor Neera Bhansali from Florida International University for her very helpful comments. Special thanks to all bank executives that agreed to participate in our research. Last, but not least, my thanks to CAPES Foundation—Ministry of Education of Brazil, and Universidade Banco Central do Brasil (UniBacen) for their support.

Fernando A. Faria

REFERENCES

ABBI. 2009. Função de Compliance. Online at: http://www.abbi.com.br/download/funcaodecompliance_09.pdf (accessed September 14, 2011).

Anderson, D. W., S. J. Melanson, and J. Maly. 2007. The evolution of corporate governance: Power redistribution brings boards to life. *Corporate Governance* 15 (5).

Bailey, S. 2011. Measuring the impact of records management data and discussion from the U.K. higher education sector. *Records Management Journal* 21 (1): 46–68.

Basole, R. 2008. Enterprise mobility: Researching a new paradigm. *Information Knowledge Systems Management* 7: 1–7.

Beccalli, E. 2007. *IT European bank performance*. New York: Palgrave MacMillan.

Becher, D., and M. Frye. 2011. Does regulation substitute or complement governance? *Journal of Banking & Finance* 35: 736–751.

Beijer, P. 2009. Meaningfulness in Information Governance: A new literacy is required. Primavera Working Paper. University of Amsterdam.

Carr, N., 2003. IT doesn't matter. *Harvard Business Review*. May 2003: 5–12.

CELENT. 2011. IT spending in financial services: A global perspective. Online at: http://www.celent.com/reports/it-spending-financial-servicesglobal-perspective-1 (accessed July 27, 2012).

Clevenger, N. 2011. How the iPad will change IT forever. Online at: http://www.infoworld.com/t/it-management/how-the-ipad-will-change-it-forever-166948 (accessed September 14, 2011).

Cortada, J. W. 2011. *Information and the modern corporation*. Cambridge, MA: MIT Press.

Davenport, T. H. 1998. *Ecologia da Informação: por que só a tecnologia não basta para o sucesso na era da informação*. São Paulo: Futura.

Davenport, T., and L. Prusak. 1998. *Working knowledge: How organizations manage what they know*. Boston: Harvard University Press.

Donaldson, A., and P. Walker. 2004. Information governance: A view from the NHS. *International Journal of Medical Informatics* 73: 281–284.

Eppler, M. 2006. *Managing information quality*. Berlin: Springer.

Faria, F. A., A. C. G. Macada, and K. Kumar. 2013. Information governance in the banking industry. Paper presented at the proceedings of the 46th Annual Hawaii International Conference on System Sciences, Maui, HI, January 7–10. IEEE Computer Society Press, Washington, D.C.

Global Issues. 2010. Global financial crisis. Online at: http://www.globalissues.org/article/768/global-financial-crisis (accessed July 28, 2012).

Grant, R. M. 1996. Toward a knowledge-based theory of the firm. *Strategic Management Journal* 17: 109–122.

Hale, T. 2008. Transparency, accountability, and global governance. *Global Governance* 14: 73–94.

Huang, H., Y. Lee, and R. Wang. 1999. *Quality information and knowledge*. Upper Saddle River, NJ: Prentice Hall.

IDG. 2012. Gartner lowers global IT spending forecast. Online at: http://www.itworldcanada.com/news/gartner-lowers-global-it-spending-forecast/144604#ixzz1qiim5N6p (accessed March 31, 2012).

Internet World Stats. 2012. Internet usage statistics, The Internet Big Picture. Online at: http://www.internetworldstats.com/stats.htm (accessed April 4, 2012).

Kondra, A., and D. Hurst. 2009. Institutional processes of organizational culture. *Culture and Organization* 15 (1): 39–58.

Kooper, M. N., R. Maes, and R. Lindgreen. 2009. Information governance: In search of the forgotten grail. Primavera Working Paper. University of Amsterdam.

Kooper, M. N., R. Maes, and R. Lindgreen. 2011. On the governance of information: Introducing a new concept of governance to support the management of information. *International Journal of Information Management* 31: 195–200.

Marchand, D. A., W. J. Kettinger, and J. D. Rollins. 2000. Information orientation: People, technology and the bottom line. *Sloan Management Review*. Summer 2000: 69–80.

Martin, A., D. Dmitriev, and J. Akeroyd. 2010. A resurgence of interest in information architecture. *International Journal of Information Management* 30: 6–12.

McManus, J. 2004a. Working towards an information governance strategy. *Management Services*. August 2004: 8–13.

McManus, J. 2004b. Information governance an ethical perspective. *Management Services*. December 2004: 16–17.

Mukherji, A. 2002. The evolution of information systems: Their impact on organization and structures. *Management Decision* 40 (5): 497–507.

Samuelson, K. 2010. Information governance isn't so bad after all. Online at: http://www.cioupdate.com/insights/article-php/11049_3889396_2/Information-Governance-isn't-so-bad-after-all.htm (accessed September 16, 2011).

Schedler, A. 1999. Conceptualizing accountability. In *The self-restraining state: Power and accountability in new democracies,* eds. A. Schedler, L. Diamond, and M. Plattner. London: Lynne Rienner.

Soares, S. 2011. *Selling information governance to the business: Best practices by industry and job function.* Ketchum, ID: MC Press.

The Economist. 2008. The future of enterprise information governance. Online at: http://www.emc.com/collateral/analyst-reports/economist-intell-unit-info-governence.pdf (accessed March 25, 2011).

The Economist. 2010. Data, data everywhere. A special report on managing information. Online at: http://www.economist.com/node/15557443 (accessed March 30, 2011).

Van Grembergen, W., and S. Haes. 2009. *Enterprise governance of information technology.* New York: Springer.

Westin, A. F. 1967. *Privacy and freedom.* New York: Atheneum.

Index

Milton Keynes UK
Ingram Content Group UK Ltd.
UKHW031130141024
449569UK00006B/309